THE GREAT TRAIN ROBBERY

AND MOST INFAMOUS BRITISH CRIMES

Tim Hill

PHOTOGRAPHS BY

Published by Atlantic Publishing
38 Copthorne Road
Croxley Green
Hertfordshire,
WD3 4AQ, UK

ISBN 978-1-909242-15-9

Printed and bound in the UK

Contents

SEARS CROSSING.
SIGNAL FAKED
AT RED

TO LEIGHTON
BUZZARD

TO TRING

TO LONDON

GANG'S LORRY
PARKED HERE

DRIVER FORCED TO
BRING TRAIN HERE

ESCAPE ROAD

RAILWAYMEN'S
CAPS STOLEN
FROM THIS HUT

TO CHEDDINGTON
STATION

BRIDEGO BRIDGE

WHOLESAL

TOYS

OL ESALE MERCH

EDINBURGH

HARROGATE

BRADFORD

BLACKPOOL BURNLEY
BLACKBURN HALIFAX LEEDS
PRESTON ROCHDALE HUDDERSFIELD
BOLTON BARNSLEY
LIVERPOOL OLDHAM
MANCHESTER SHEFFIELD
BUXTON
CHESTER
STOKE

LONDON

ROYAL MAIL

GPO 95

someone, somewhere
wants a letter from

Introduction

Crime fascinates us and in postwar Britain no crime has aroused greater interest than the Great Train Robbery, where the Deadly Sin of avarice was the spur in an audacious heist. It is a tale of cunning and bungling, pursuit and capture, imprisonment and escape. *The Great Train Robbery and Most Infamous British Crimes* describes every twist and turn in the plot, from the rigging of the train signals on 8 August 1963, to the discovery of the gang's hideout, where detectives found a Monopoly set covered in fingerprints, and the international manhunt that lasted almost four decades and made Slipper of the Yard as famous as the fugitives he pursued.

The Great Train Robbery and Most Infamous British Crimes also examines the lives and gruesome misdeeds of some of the most notorious criminals of the past century. There is Dr Crippen who fled with his mistress, disguised as a boy, after poisoning his wife and burying her in the cellar in a sedate north London suburb; the sensational story of acid-bath killer John Haigh, a smooth and ruthless conman who dissolved his victims' bodies in acid and then used his forgery skills to acquire their wealth;the Kray twins, rulers of the East End underworld for over a decade; Ruth Ellis, the spurned lover who served her revenge extremely hot and the Yorkshire Ripper, who was interviewed on nine separate occasions during the course of the inquiry, but coolly slipped through the net each time .

Contemporaneous reports and photographs from the *Daily Mail* archives, many reproduced for the first time, vividly recreate the impact of some of the greatest causes célèbres in legal history. It is a grimly fascinating trip along the byways of the dark side of the human psyche.

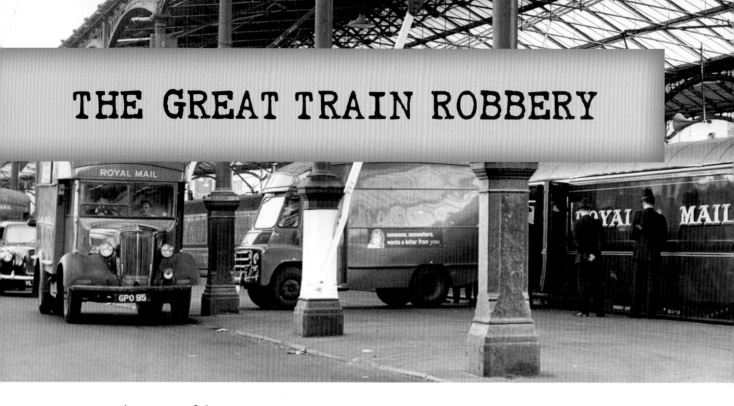

THE GREAT TRAIN ROBBERY

'Let us clear out of the way any romantic notions of daredevilry. This is nothing less than a sordid crime of violence which was inspired by vast greed.' With that trenchant remark, delivered during the 1964 trial of the Great Train Robbers, Mr Justice Edmund Davies tried to dispel the myth that theirs had been a victimless caper and that they were deserving of the folk hero status they had been accorded by large swathes of the population.

Neither the judge's remarks nor the severe sentences he handed down had much effect on the public perception of the Great Train Robbery. It became a byword for Robin Hood-style criminality, and so captured the imagination that it was still making headlines nearly fifty years after the felony took place.

Shipment of used banknotes

The thieves' target was the Glasgow to London mail train. This service had been running for well over a century, and it was said that no successful robbery had been carried out in transit during that time. A gang of London-based criminals, most of them well known to the police, aimed to change that on the night of 7-8 August 1963.

The train left Glasgow at 6.50 pm, due at Euston just before 4 o'clock the following morning. There were no passengers aboard, just some seventy Post Office employees spread throughout the carriages engaged in sorting work during the nine-hour journey. The configuration of the carriages was critical. The diesel locomotive, manned by driver Jack Mills and fireman David Whitby, was pulling a baggage wagon and eleven mail coaches. It was the first of the mail coaches in which the gang was interested, for it contained the high-value registered mail consignment, including a large shipment of used banknotes. The recent bank holiday weekend made for even richer pickings than usual. It was common knowledge that the valuable packages were transported in that section of the train, and although it was governed by extra security measures, it gave the would-be thieves an important advantage when it came to planning the robbery.

BELOW: After being stopped, the diesel engine pulling two Post Office carriages was driven a mile down the track to Bridego Bridge where the robbers' haul was loaded onto trucks that had been waiting nearby.

ABOVE: The stricken train was under tight police protection after being taken to Euston Station for further examination.

RIGHT: The gang had tampered with a signal further up the line creating a false light, forcing the driver to come to a halt.

SEARS CROSSING.
SIGNAL FAKED
AT RED

TO LEIGHTON
BUZZARD

TO TRING

TO LONDON

GANG'S LORRY
PARKED HERE

DRIVER FORCED TO
BRING TRAIN HERE

ESCAPE ROAD

RAILWAYMEN'S
CAPS STOLEN
FROM THIS HUT

TO CHEDDINGTON
STATION

BRIDEGO BRIDGE

Train halted

Just after 3.00 am the train reached Sears Crossing, near Cheddington, Buckinghamshire. Jack Mills spotted an amber light, warning him to proceed with caution, and he brought the train to a halt when he reached a red signal a little further on. What he did not realise was that the gang had rigged the lights, obscuring the green signal with a glove and using batteries to power the amber and red lamps that had prompted his reaction. Thieves had halted trains using these methods before, but the size and scale of this operation put it in a league of its own.

David Whitby left the engine compartment to use the trackside phone and try to establish the cause of the fault. Immediately he noticed that the wire had been cut, and was on his way back to inform Mills when he was overpowered by balaclava-wearing gang members. Mills himself resisted, battling with robbers on the footplate until he was clubbed with an iron bar, an assault that left him bleeding profusely from a head wound. Those who would romanticise a robbery carried out without the use of guns glossed over the vicious attack that left Jack Mills with permanent physical and psychological scars.

The engine and first two carriages were uncoupled and driven about a mile down the track to Bridego bridge. One of the gang members had been recruited for his train-driving experience, but he failed to get to grips with this particular engine and so the injured Mills was pressed into service. The 58-year-old driver was able to furnish the police with little useful information, remarking on the slickness of the military-style operation. No orders were given; the gang members knew their jobs and carried them out efficiently. Mills would be honoured for his courageous conduct and awarded 25 guineas, scant compensation for being left unable to work again. He was living in straitened circumstances when leukaemia claimed his life in 1970.

SEPTEMBER 5, 1963

'If you shout I will kill you'

At 3.02 a.m. 57-year-old driver Mills slackened speed from 80 m.p.h. to obey the fake amber signal. Slowly he approached the red. The sorters in the two locked coaches were busy with hundreds of mailbags scooped from gantries alongside the line. They were unaware, even when the train stopped, that they were ambushed and that the two leading coaches had been uncoupled. At 3.05 a.m. Driver Mills halted his diesel engine. Fireman David Whitby, 26, takes up the story: 'I got down to go to the telephone at the signal. I found the wires had been cut. I went back to tell my driver.

As I did so I saw a man between the second and third coach. It was then that one of the men carrying the flags came up to me. I said: "What's up, mate?" He walked across the line and said: "Come here." Suddenly he pushed me down the bank. Another man grabbed me, put his hand over my mouth and said: "If you shout I will kill you." I told him I would not shout. He took me back to the engine where I found they had coshed my mate. They put one handcuff on me and held the other end while they made my driver go forward to Sears Crossing. When we stopped the other handcuff was put on my mate. They made us get out of the engine and lie down by the side of the rail while they fought their way into the second coach. When they had finished unloading all the bags they put us with the G.P.O. men in the second coach. They told us to wait for half an hour and then left. The G.P.O. men had tried to stop them getting into their van but they broke in. We sat there until a guard came down the line from the ten uncoupled coaches.

ABOVE LEFT: A diagram clearly shows the stretch of line where the Glasgow-Euston mail train was held up.

ABOVE LEFT (INSET): A makeshift marker propped up beside a wheelbarrow showed gang members aboard the train the planned stopping point by the bridge.

ABOVE: Leatherslade Farm in Oakley, Buckinghamshire, was the gang's hide-out following the robbery. Police swiftly located the property after John Maris, a local herdsman, provided a tip-off after noticing strange activity around the building.

AUGUST 14, 1963

The search of Leath-erslade Farm at Oakley, Buckingham-shire - where since last Thursday the raiders had sorted and hidden their £2½ million loot - may take 3 days.

A telephone tip yesterday morning sent the Yard team, headed by Commander George Hatherill, racing to the farm - only hours after lorries and cars had been heard driving away early yesterday. And last night Mr. John Alfred Maris said he had seen lorries parked at the farm and had twice telephoned to Aylesbury police - first on Monday morning and again yesterday. Mr. Maris, a 33-year-old herdsman who lives less than a mile from Leatherslade, is the first claimant to part of the £260,000 reward. The garage was padlocked I had become suspicious about the house being sold because the property had been on the market for six months and suddenly it had changed hands overnight. I had never seen any visitors there or anybody who looked like a prospective buyer.

'Up special' attacked

At Bridego Bridge the gang launched their attack on the registered mail carriage. Under normal circumstances this had to be opened by staff on the inside in response to a coded signal from the person without. That security mechanism counted for little against an onslaught of axes and sledgehammers. The four Post Office employees made a half-hearted attempt to barricade themselves in but it merely caused a short delay to the inevitable outcome. The gang formed a human chain to transfer the booty into a waiting lorry, and the travelling post office known as the 'Up Special' was quickly relieved of 120 packages, containing £2.6 million. Mills and Whitby were bundled into the security van with the four Post Office workers and told not to move for half an hour. The lorry disappeared into the night, the operation having gone like clockwork. Or so it seemed.

It had taken some time for the occupants of the uncoupled section of the train to realise why they had ground to a halt. When the penny dropped, a guard from those rearward carriages set off up the line towards Cheddington, for there was no means of communication available to him. He met up with staff from the forward carriages, and together they managed to stop a passing train and get a ride to Cheddington, when the alarm was finally raised. It was 4.15 am when the police were alerted to the audacious robbery, the biggest cash haul in the country's history.

TOP LEFT AND MIDDLE RIGHT: Over twenty members of Scotland Yard, including forensic scientists, prepare to search the farm. Several fingerprints were found and some of the gang's phone numbers were scribbled on the walls.

RIGHT MIDDLE: Only a few days after the robbery three men left a special court in Linslade, hiding their faces under blankets. William Boal and Roger Cordrey, the first two members of the gang to be arrested, were tracked down in Bournemouth after using some of the notes from the heist in a spending spree in the town. The third man was Alfred Pilgrim who, along with his wife Mary, was charged with receiving £860.

TOP RIGHT: Children play outside the post office in Oakley. This sleepy village was suddenly the centre of attention of the national media.

RIGHT: Robert Monteith, the local farmer who employed John Maris, voices his anger to the press. Roger Cooke, Member of Parliament for Twickenham, had accused locals of not doing enough to help catch the gang, bringing cries of protest from residents.

FAR RIGHT: An upright spade was found in front of the farm. It appeared the thieves had been digging a hole to burn the empty mail bags.

> *The hideout, some twenty-five miles from the scene of the crime, was soon discovered after a local man reported suspicious movements.*

Hideout discovered

Initially, there were few leads. The handcuffs that had been used to shackle Mills and Whitby were made by a Birmingham firm that kept a record of all its sales, but soon there were more fruitful lines of enquiry. The police assumed that the gang would have holed up somewhere not too far from the scene of the crime, for they would have been fearful of being out on the public highways once the news broke. It was a correct assumption, and the hideout, some twenty-five miles from the scene of the crime, was soon discovered after a local man reported suspicious movements. Not soon enough to apprehend any of the villains, but Leatherslade Farm, situated a few miles west of Aylesbury near the village of Brill, gave up enough clues to put the law on the scent of the villains. There were discarded mailbags, banknote wrappers and three abandoned vehicles. It was clear that the perpetrators had divided the spoils and made off in less conspicuous modes of transport. Attempts to obliterate finger and palmprints were woefully inadequate. The gang had even handed a gift to the forensics team with a print-laden Monopoly board, obviously used to while away the downtime during the planning stage. It was a colossal own-goal, considering that the men had a string of convictions and were well known to the capital's constabulary. And as if that weren't enough, the phone numbers of some of the men were found scrawled on a wall, including that of architect-in-chief Bruce Reynolds.

ABOVE: Boal and Cordrey were driven away from court as officers across the country continued to search for the rest of the gang members.

RIGHT: Richard James, assistant buyer at a Chiswick garage, sold an Austin Healey sports car for £835 to a man and woman only 36 hours after the robbery. The sum was paid in cash using £5 notes. The woman gave a false name and address and the police rapidly circulated the car registration number throughout the country.

MIDDLE RIGHT AND FAR RIGHT: Rene Boal, charged with receiving £70 of the proceeds, and Mary Pilgrim, their heads protected with a police raincoat, were escorted into court. A media frenzy surrounded the accused as they were escorted to and from the court under heavy police guard.

AUGUST 9, 1963

Yard was given tape warning

How and why did the Great Train Robbery succeed? Mr. Reginald Bevins, Postmaster-General, cut short his holiday and flew to London last night to get the answers. Mr. Bevins put the haul of old banknotes and valuables at about £1 million - incredible enough. But Scotland Yard chiefs believe it reached the fantastic total of £3 million. Amazingly, the Yard had known for weeks that a mail train was to be robbed, probably "somewhere in Bucks." Yet this colossal sum travelled the length of England with no special security guard. On board the 12-coach Post Office mail train from Glasgow to Euston, apart from the driver and his mate, were some 70 unarmed sorters, working non-stop. All this and every other possible detail about the train, its load, the ambush spot and escape routes, were known to the man with the Midas touch who planned the raid.

First arrests

On Thursday 15 August, just a week after the robbery had taken place, the first arrests were made. Fingerprint evidence wasn't needed to nail Roger Cordrey and William Boal, who sealed their fate by going on a spending spree in Bournemouth. They splashed out wads of cash on a rented flat, three vehicles and a lock-up garage. The elderly widow with the garage to let became suspicious and contacted the police, who arrested Cordrey and Boal after a struggle. Some of the notes used to purchase the vehicles were identified as coming from the mail robbery, and a search of the flat, the garage and the cars revealed suitcases stuffed with money, £141,000 in total.

The reaction of the two men was typical of all the miscreants, and a further example of near-comical ineptitude. Under caution, Boal said: 'I am silly to get involved in this. I should have known better', which rather undermined his subsequent denial of any participation in the robbery. His amended story was that Cordrey owed him money and he tagged along on the Bournemouth trip in the hope of being repaid. Cordrey told him the cases contained glass, which he said he had no reason to disbelieve. As for Cordrey, he admitted that the money came from the robbery but denied taking part in the raid. He maintained that he was holding the money for someone he'd met at a race meeting.

> *Fingerprint evidence wasn't needed to nail Roger Cordrey and William Boal, who sealed their fate by going on a spending spree in Bournemouth.*

THIS PAGE: Gang member James White had taken refuge with his wife in a caravan in Surrey. They had purchased it in cash three days after the robbery. However, realising the police were on their trail, they hid £35,000 behind the panelling in the caravan and in the tyres, then fled from the site. Police systematically took the caravan to pieces, finally locating the cash, while the search for the couple extended to the south coast.

AUGUST 23, 1974

Banknote bonfire

Charred scraps of paper and banknotes snatched by detectives from a bonfire in a London suburban garden were being examined early today by forensic scientists aiding the train robbery hunt. News of the find was telephoned to the home of Britain's top detective, Commander George Hatherill of Scotland Yard.

He ordered the clues gained from the back-garden South London bonfire - still smouldering when detectives found it - to be circulated to police throughout Britain. A Flying Squad team went to the house, a semi-detached home in a side street. They raked over the bonfire and tipped out pieces of charred notes and half-burned documents.

As this discovery was made police all over Britain were stepping up the hunt for two men the Yard wish to interview in connection with the £2,600,000 raid. Scotland Yard gave their names and issued photographs. One is a 6ft. 1in. cleft-chin Cockney, Bruce Richard Reynolds, 41. The other is James E. White, 43, with a Royal Artillery crest tattooed on his right forearm. Both live in London.

A third man named by the Yard, bookmaker Charles Frederick Wilson, 31, of Crescent Lane, Clapham, was charged at Aylesbury, Buckinghamshire, last night with being concerned in the train robbery. He will appear in court at Linslade this morning. Wilson was taken from his home to Cannon Row police station at lunchtime yesterday. His wife, Patricia, and three children stayed at home.

New hunt for 'Buster' Edwards and the Black Rose

Look around you this morning. You may see the couple pictured above. They are Ronald Edwards, 32, and his wife June Rose, 31, known as "Black Rose," whom Scotland Yard detectives investigating the Great Train Robbery would like to interview. The Yard believes the couple may be "not very far from London," with their daughter, Nicolette, two. Their hair may be dyed, but you could still recognise them. Edwards is one of five men police have said they would like to see since the raid at Cheddington, Buckinghamshire, on August 8. There is a substantial reward for information leading to the conviction of the train raiders. The mail robbery hearing will continue at Aylesbury today. Nine people are accused of conspiring to rob the Glasgow-London travelling Post Office and another six are accused of receiving part of the loot. Train trial opens today.

Arrest no. 9

Another man was arrested last night and charged with taking part in the Great Train Robbery. He is Ronald Arthur Biggs, 34-year-old carpenter, of Alpine Road, Redhill Surrey. Police swooped on his small, detached house and turned out cupboards and drawers in the kitchen. Biggs was out, but his wife, Charmian, and sons Nicholas, three, and Christopher, five months, were at home. The detectives waited until he returned. He is the ninth person to be arrested by train raid police, and the fourth to be accused of taking part in the robbery. The other five are accused of receiving.

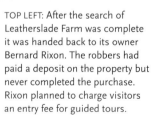

TOP LEFT: After the search of Leatherslade Farm was complete it was handed back to its owner Bernard Rixon. The robbers had paid a deposit on the property but never completed the purchase. Rixon planned to charge visitors an entry fee for guided tours.

MIDDLE LEFT: The search also followed a lead to a house in Oxford where a landlady had rented out two rooms to two men the day after the raid. They had paid from a thick wad of £5 notes. Police believed that the house was used as another base from which to share out the proceeds.

BOTTOM LEFT: The search for the gang was soon extended to Ireland when three men and a woman were seen in Dun Laoghaire freely spending money from a bag filled with £5 notes. After renting a flat for two months in advance, they spent six days there and then disappeared. Clem Furlong (pictured) had hired his car to them for £20.

ABOVE MIDDLE: Mrs Betty Last, a resident of Bournemouth, had witnessed the arrest of Boal and Cordrey outside her house. The police found £100,000 in their cars.

ABOVE AND ABOVE (INSET): Two weeks after the raid police were following further leads and the search for the gang members was extended. Charles Wilson was arrested at his home in Clapham while descriptions of Bruce Reynolds and James White were widely circulated. Reynolds, a motor and antique dealer, had been living in a second-floor flat in Battersea.

Nerve centre purchase

Back at Leatherslade Farm, the owner Bernard Rixon told how he had entered into negotiations to sell the property, a tale that would lead three more men into the dock. Brian Field, managing clerk for the London firm of solicitors acting for the proposed sale, had inspected the premises on behalf of the prospective purchaser, accompanied by another man, Leonard Field. The two men weren't related, other than being part of the team assembled to rob the mail train. After the viewing, a ten per cent deposit on the £5,550 purchase price was paid. The Rixons moved out on 29 July, but the balance was never paid, the transaction remaining uncompleted. Brian Field's boss, solicitor John Wheater, was also arrested and charged. The Rixons were soon making plans to turn Leatherslade Farm into a tourist attraction, charging visitors 2/6 for the privilege of seeing the Great Train Robbery's nerve centre.

Twelve apprehended

On 16 August a motorcyclist who pulled in by a wood near Dorking chanced upon four suitcases containing £100,000. In one of the cases there was a hotel receipt for an establishment in Hindelang, Germany, made out to Herr and Frau Field and dated February of that year. Brian Field's fingerprints were found on the case. Five days later, 31-year-old bookmaker Charles Wilson was in custody. His fingerprints had been among those found at the farm, yet he bullishly told police: 'I do not see how you can make it stick without the poppy (the loot) and you won't find that.' He was both right and wrong: the vast majority of the stolen money was never recovered, but that didn't help him to escape conviction.

One by one the robbers fell into police hands, invariably protesting their innocence despite the wealth of evidence stacked against them. By the time the trial opened at Aylesbury Assizes on 20 January 1964, twelve men had been apprehended and came to court facing a range of charges. The others in the dock were Ronald Biggs, James Hussey, Roy James, Thomas Wisbey, Douglas Gordon Goody and Robert Welch. All pleaded Not Guilty, except for Cordrey, who admitted to the charge of conspiring to stop the train – he was the signals expert – and receiving stolen money. His plea of Not Guilty to the robbery charge was accepted by the prosecution.

TOP LEFT: Police had also managed to trace Reynolds and White to the Grafton Hotel in Bedford. Two men matching their description stayed for one night but had checked out before the police arrived.

TOP LEFT (INSET): The shop window of Bruce Reynold's antique business.

TOP RIGHT: Douglas Goody was arrested at the Grand Hotel in Leicester two weeks after the raid. He lived with his mother in Putney, where his fiancée Pat Cooper ran a hairdressing business for him.

ABOVE: James White was finally arrested at Littlestone-on-Sea in Kent, nearly three years later. Using the alias Bob Lane, he had lived in the flat with his wife Sheree and their baby, mixing freely with locals who were totally unaware that he was a wanted man.

ABOVE LEFT: John Daly's house in Sutton, Surrey. He and his wife had bought the house before the heist and filled the property with expensive furniture and gadgets. It appeared that no one had lived there since the robbery had taken place.

LEFT: In December 1963 John Daly was brought in for questioning after being arrested at a flat in Eaton Square, Belgravia, where he and his wife Barbara had been staying with a 'Mrs Grant'. His wife was heavily pregnant with their second child at the time of his capture.

METROPOLITAN POLICE

On the 8th August, 1963, the Glasgow to Euston mail train was robbed of about two and a half million pounds.

Substantial rewards will be paid to persons giving such information as will lead to the apprehension and conviction of the persons responsible.

The assistance of the public is sought to trace the whereabouts of the after described persons:

RONALD EDWARDS alias RONALD CHRISTOPHER EDWARDS, also known as "BUSTER," aged 32, florist/club owner, 5ft. 8in., stocky build, complexion fresh, hair dark brown, eyes brown, London accent, scar left of nose and right forearm.

JUNE ROSE EDWARDS, née ROTHERY, aged 30, 5ft. 3in., hair black. May be accompanied by daughter NICOLETTE, aged about 3 years.

BARBARA MARIA DALY, née ALLAN, aged 22, 5ft. 1in., hair brown. May be pregnant and accompanied by daughter LORRAINE PATRICIA, aged 1 year. **JOHN THOMAS DALY**, aged 31, born at New Ross, Eire, antique dealer, 5ft. 11in., complexion fresh, hair dark brown (wavy), eyes blue, scar right of forehead.

BRUCE RICHARD REYNOLDS, alias RAYMOND ETTRIDGE and GEORGE RACHEL, aged 31, born London, motor and antique dealer, 6ft. 1in., complexion fresh, hair light brown, eyes grey (may be wearing horn-rimmed or rimless spectacles), slight cleft in chin, scar left eyelid, cheek and right forearm.

FRANCIS REYNOLDS, aged about 24, 5ft. 4in., slim build, hair brown.

ROY JOHN JAMES, aged 27, born London, silversmith, 5ft. 6in., medium to slim build, complexion fresh, hair light brown, eyes hazel. Is a racing car driver.

JAMES EDWARD WHITE, alias JAMES BRYAN and JAMES EDWARD WHITEFOOT (uses many aliases), aged 43, born Paddington, London, café proprietor, 5ft. 10in., slim build, complexion sallow, hair and eyes brown, may wear moustache. Royal Artillery crest tattooed right forearm.

SHEREE WHITE, aged 30 to 35, 5ft. 9in., complexion light coffee-coloured, hair dark brown. May have 4 months old baby and be accompanied by white miniature poodle dog called "GHI".

Persons having information are asked to telephone WHItehall 1212 or the nearest Police Station.

Final share-out

The Great Train Robbery gang was split up last night - to serve jail terms totalling 307 years. Immediately after Mr. Justice Edmund Davies passed the sentences, the 12 men in the dock were paired off. Each pair was carefully chosen to keep the most dangerous thugs apart. Then manacled and under heavy escort, they were taken to top security jails throughout Britain. They took with them the secret of where more than £2 million of the train-raid cash still is. The total stolen: £2,517,975. Recovered so far: Nearly £260,000 And they left behind their families, including 15 sons and daughters aged 15 months to 21 years.

Seven of them were jailed for 30 years - the longest sentences of the century apart from the 62 years imposed on Russian spy George Blake. Two faced 25 years, one 24, another 20, and one three years. One by one they were brought into the dock of the assize court at Aylesbury to face the judge. His voice betrayed the tremendous strain he was under as he took just 28 minutes to impose the 307 years jail. Mr. Justice Edmund Davies said in 1948 when he was Recorder of Swansea: "Stealing from railway vans is becoming a favourite national pastime. I intend to embark with others trying to crush it." The 30-year sentences reflect his hatred of violence and his determination to strip crime of any glamour.

'Stealing from railway vans is becoming a favourite national pastime. I intend to embark with others trying to crush it.'

TOP LEFT: The wanted poster put out by the Metropolitan Police in their attempt to apprehend the gang members.

FAR LEFT: Ronnie Biggs was soon brought in for questioning after his fingerprints were found in the farm.

LEFT: At the trial held in October, John Furnivall gave evidence against Cordrey who had purchased a Rover car from him the day after the raid.

LEFT: Janet McIntyre, the receptionist from the Grand Hotel in Leicester, was called to confirm that Douglas Goody had stayed there on August 22. At this stage 18 people were accused of crimes relating to the robbery.

ABOVE: A year after the robbery several people were able to claim rewards that were offered for information about the crime. John Ahern and Esa Hargrave were given £10,000 to share after finding £100,000 in the woods near Dorking, Surrey.

THE GREAT TRAIN ROBBERY

'A diabolical crime'

The all-male jury returned guilty verdicts on all the defendants at the end of the 51-day trial. There was a brief hiatus before sentencing as a technical irregularity meant that Biggs had to be tried separately. After he, too, was convicted, Mr Justice Edmund Davies told the men their fate, creating a stir with the severity of the sentences he handed down. The fact that the accused maintained their innocence and showed no sign of remorse for their misdeeds played very badly with the judge, who was in no mood to soft-pedal with the perpetrators of 'a diabolical crime'. Moreover, he pointed out that the lack of co-operation meant that the bulk of the stolen money had not been recovered. That meant that the thieves might be able to enjoy their ill-gotten gains after serving their time, something he was determined should not be in the near future. Biggs, Hussey, James, Wisbey, Goody, Welch and Wilson all received 30 years; Brian Field and Leonard Field 25 years each; William Boal 24 years; Roger Cordrey 20 years. On appeal, Boal and Cordrey's sentences were reduced to 14 years; Brian Field and Leonard Field's terms were cut to five years.

The judge said that John Wheater's case was the saddest. It was accepted that he had no foreknowledge of the crime when he did the conveyancing work on Leatherslade Farm, but he could have volunteered information regarding the purchase that would have helped the police enquiry. He was given three years, but with full remission served 22 months. During his time behind bars he was struck off the roll of solicitors.

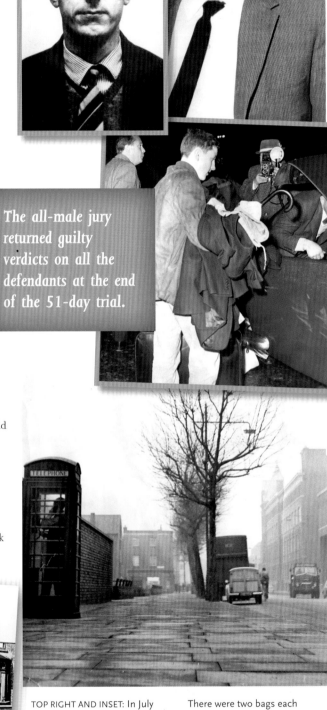

> The all-male jury returned guilty verdicts on all the defendants at the end of the 51-day trial.

TOP RIGHT AND INSET: In July 1965 Ronnie Biggs (right) and Eric Flower both escaped from Wandsworth Prison. They had been jailed for 30 years and 12 years respectively.

MIDDLE RIGHT: John Daly under tight guard after his arrest in London.

ABOVE: In December 1963, £50,000 of the robbery proceeds were found after an anonymous tip-off. It was dumped in this telephone box in Southwark.

There were two bags each weighing three-quarters of a hundredweight. The thieves had obviously decided that it was safer to abandon the money than spend it.

TOP LEFT: Tom Shepherd was another beneficiary of the train robbery rewards.

LEFT: A diagram showing some of the key locations relating to the robbery and the hunt for the perpetrators.

Fugitives

The trial took place with three gang members still at large: mastermind Bruce Reynolds, Ronald 'Buster' Edwards and Jimmy White. The number of wanted men increased to four on 12 August 1964, when Charles Wilson was sprung from Winson Green Prison in a daring raid. Wilson's liberators had acquired a set of duplicate keys to gain access to the inner doors, and they made good their escape over the 20-foot wall by means of a rope ladder. The fugitive went to ground in a small town 40 miles west of Montreal, where he took up residence with his wife and children. The long arm of the law reached him in January 1968 in the shape of Detective-Superintendent Thomas Butler, the Flying Squad officer who led the original investigation. Butler had been tasked with bringing to book the Great Train Robbers still at liberty. His workload was eased when Jimmy White and Buster Edwards turned themselves in 1966, but two names remained on his hit list. One of those was crossed off in November 1968, when Bruce Reynolds, the brains behind the operation, was tracked down to a villa overlooking Torquay harbour. Butler had been due to retire, having been granted special dispensation to be allowed to continue the hunt for Reynolds. That arrest should have closed the book, but by then another of the incarcerated crew had absconded.

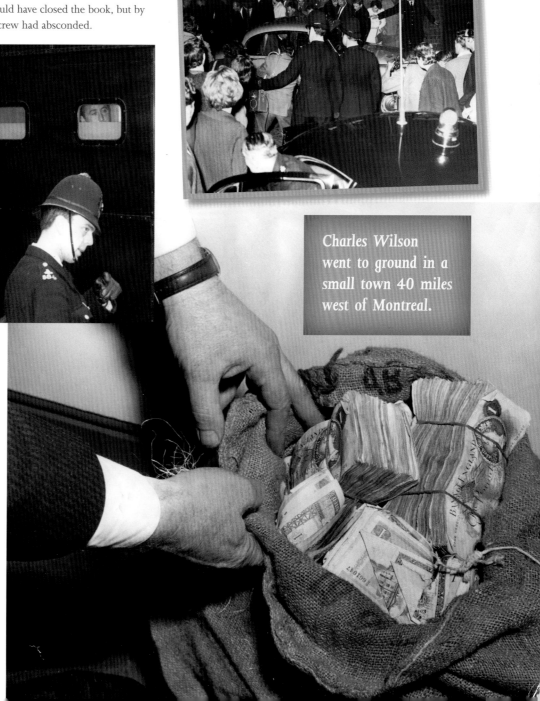

Charles Wilson went to ground in a small town 40 miles west of Montreal.

TOP RIGHT: The verdict was finally returned 253 days after the robbery was committed. In April 1964, 12 men accused of stealing £2,631,784 were given a total of 307 years' imprisonment.

ABOVE RIGHT: Crowds of onlookers continually crowded round the gang members and police during the court proceedings.

RIGHT: Police examine the banknotes found in Southwark.

ABOVE: The faces of (left to right) Thomas Wisbey, Charles Wilson and Roy James stare out of the window of the police van as they are taken away after the trial.

SEPTEMBER 20, 1966

Buster Edwards turns up broke

Ronald "Buster" Edwards, sought for three years after the Great Train Robbery, was "completely broke" when he gave himself up to police early yesterday. A senior police officer said this last night as Edwards, 35, slept in a cell at Aylesbury, Buckinghamshire. Edwards will appear in court at Linslade, ten miles away, today, on two charges concerning the robbery. He surrendered "by arrangement" to Scotland Yard Flying Squad men at a secret rendezvous in South London. The police officer said: "There had been no attempt on the part of Edwards to disguise himself. "But he had lost weight, looked much fitter and younger and his hair was a little grey. "We have been behind Edwards on a number of occasions, but he had always just gone when we arrived." It is known that Edwards attended a number of parties in South London after police began their hunt for him. Edwards's solicitor, Mr. Maurice Lesser, said last night: "I have seen Edwards and he authorised me to say that he voluntarily surrendered."

Edwards and his wife, June, 34, have a five-year old daughter, Nicolette. The surrender drama began at 1.15 a.m. yesterday, when Det. Chief-Supt. Thomas Butler, head of the Flying Squad, and Det.-Supt. Frank Williams, his second-in-command, were called by phone to Scotland Yard. They drove to an address in South London and met Edwards. An hour later the police car arrived back at Scotland Yard. At noon Edwards was driven from London with Superintendent Butler and a strong escort to Aylesbury police station. Edwards crouched in the back of the car. On the station notice board was a poster offering a substantial police reward for information about Edwards. It described him as a florist and club owner. Next to his photograph the poster showed one of his wife and a photograph of Bruce Reynolds, 31, a London motor and antique dealer. Reynolds is now the only man wanted for questioning about the robbery. He is believed to have been one of the masterminds behind the plot.

> 'We have been behind Edwards on a number of occasions, but he had always just gone when we arrived.'

TOP LEFT: Ronald 'Buster' Edwards, who lived in Southwark with his wife June and their two-year-old daughter Nicolette, was soon the subject of a police search. A gambler and boxer, he ran the 'Walk-In Club' in Lambeth Walk. Police suspected that the family were hiding on the Continent. Despite several leads, officers failed to find him but Edwards eventually gave himself up in September 1966 after the pressure of living for three years on the run.

TOP, ABOVE AND ABOVE LEFT: The following month he was taken to Linslade for a court hearing and was eventually imprisoned for 15 years for his part in the raid.

LEFT: Edwards on his way to prison after sentencing.

RIGHT: Bruce Reynolds, who masterminded the robbery, was the last member of the gang to be tracked down. Following the guilty verdict in 1968, newspapers were quick to headline his 25-year sentence.

BELOW: Reynolds had been renting a house in Torquay with his wife Frances and their six-year-old son Nicholas. They had been planning to fly to Canada the following week. Parked outside the house was the family's new Mini Cooper 'S'.

BOTTOM RIGHT: Reynolds, finally in police handcuffs after evading capture for five years.

BOTTOM: James White had originally lived at Pett Bottom Farm in Elmstead, Essex. He had also given himself up to police.

ABOVE: After appearing in court in Leicester White was driven away to begin an 18-year sentence.

THE GREAT TRAIN ROBBERY

Colourful life

Ronnie Biggs had been a minor player in the heist, yet he would become the most celebrated gang member for his dramatic escape and for successfully managing to evade recapture. Friends of Biggs came up with a simple but ingenious plan to get him out of Wandsworth Jail, and carried it out in broad daylight on 8 July 1965. A removals van was parked next to the prison's 20ft-high wall, and a rope ladder thrown over into the yard during the inmates' exercise period. Biggs shinned up the ladder and dropped through a hole cut in the vehicle's roof, followed by three uninvited inmates who seized their chance to escape. A waiting car whisked Biggs away to a colourful life on the run that would last for 36 years.

Biggs surfaced first in Australia, moving on to Rio de Janeiro in 1970 when he was threatened with exposure. He had had plastic surgery, but that didn't prevent the British press from tracking him down. Renowned Scotland Yard detective Jack Slipper was also on the case. He spent years trying to find the fugitive, and even when the quest was over he was thwarted by the lack of an extradition arrangement with Brazil. Biggs's position was made doubly secure when his girlfriend, nightclub dancer Raimunda de Castro, gave birth to son Michael. As the father of a Brazilian national Biggs was afforded even greater protection, able to enjoy the samba lifestyle unhindered. He suffered a scare in 1981 when a band of mercenary adventurers kidnapped him and took him to Barbados, hoping to claim a handsome reward. But once again the executive came to his aid, the island authorities ruling that he be allowed to return to Rio.

Free man

By 2001 Biggs's health was in decline and he returned of his own volition to the land of his birth. He spoke of his longing to stroll into a Margate pub and have a pint of bitter, but that was not an immediate prospect. With 28 years of his jail sentence still to run, Biggs would have been a centenarian were he to serve the entire stretch. That was never a serious possibility, and in the autumn of 2008, having completed one-third of his term, he was up before the parole board, hopeful that he would be released the following year. The 79-year-old Biggs had suffered a stroke, was being fed via a tube and had lost the power of speech. Those campaigning on his behalf said that he presented no threat to society, and taking into account the degree of overcrowding in British prisons it was reasonable to show compassion and grant Biggs his last wish: to be allowed to die a free man. Biggs was released in 2009.

LEFT: Ronnie Biggs. After escaping from Wandsworth Prison by using a rope ladder to climb over the prison walls, Biggs was the most successful in avoiding police capture. He underwent plastic surgery and moved to Australia, but after being recognised he left his wife and sons behind and moved on to Brazil.

ABOVE: He was spotted again in Rio de Janeiro in 1974 but by then his girlfriend Raimunda de Castro (pictured) was pregnant with his son and the Brazilian authorities refused to extradite him.

TOP: Biggs continued to live in Brazil for the next three decades with his son Michael. However, in 2001, at the age of 71, he decided to return to Britain and give himself up. He had 28 years of his sentence still to serve but was released on compassionate grounds shortly before his 80th birthday.

LEFT: Seven of the gang attended a reunion in London to mark the publication of their paperback *The Train Robbers: Their Story*. Pictured from the left are: Buster Edwards, Tommy Wisbey, Jim White, Bruce Reynolds, Roger Cordrey, Charles Wilson and Jim Hussey.

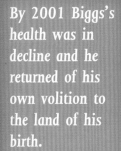

By 2001 Biggs's health was in decline and he returned of his own volition to the land of his birth.

FEBRUARY 2, 1974

Ronald Biggs arrested

The world hunt for escaped Great Train robber Ronald Biggs has ended after 3,128 days on the run. He has been detained in Rio de Janeiro, Brazil. Two Scotland Yard detectives are in Rio with him. Britain has not got an extradition treaty with Brazil, and detectives are trying to arrange for Biggs's voluntary return to serve his sentence - 30 years. Otherwise police can make a special extradition application to the Brazilian authorities.

The detectives, deputy head of the Flying Squad, Det. Chief Superintendent Jack Slipper and Det.-Sergeant Peter Jones, found Biggs in Room 909 at the £25-a-day Hotel Trocadero in Rio's Atlantic Avenue. They flew from London secretly on Wednesday after signing out in the Flying Squad duty book as being on annual leave.

Biggs was wearing only red bathing trunks when the detectives walked into his ninth-floor room. With him was a 22-year-old girl called Lucia, who burst into tears. Mr Slipper said to Biggs: 'Nice to see you again Ronnie. It's been a long time.' Despite plastic surgery to his face during his time on the run, Biggs, his grey hair slightly receding, was instantly recognisable to the detectives. Biggs told the detectives that he was planning to surrender. Apparently he was tired of looking over his shoulder for nearly nine years.

It is understood that Biggs, 41, is willing to return to London. Scotland Yard hope to have him back by the end of the weekend unless there are legal hitches.

FEBRUARY 6, 1974

Slipper of the Yard flies home without his man

Two tired and disconsolate policemen flew into Gatwick last night to tell Scotland Yard why Ronald Biggs missed the flight from Rio de Janeiro. 'Of course, we are disappointed,' said 49-year-old Det. Chief Supt. Jack Slipper. 'We went out to get Biggs and he was supposed to be coming back with us. But there it is. He's still in Rio and we're home without him.'

What foxed the Yard pair was that although Biggs at first expressed a wish to return to Britain, the Brazilian authorities had other ideas. 'I hope we may be going back for him in five or six weeks but I honestly have no idea. The position is now political and that's something I cannot talk about. I am feeling a bit fed-up. I just want to get back to some normal work.'

Biggs? 'Well, I respect him and he respects me, but we both know the score.'

TOP LEFT: Reynolds and Edwards during the book launch party.

ABOVE: Bruce Reynolds with his wife Angela and son. Reynolds died in February 2013 at the age of 81.

TOP RIGHT INSET: After his release from jail Buster Edwards ran a flower stall outside Waterloo Station. He said that all he wanted to do was 'live an ordinary life'.

RIGHT: In December 1994 Edwards died after hanging himself, allegedly in remorse. Crowds lined the streets as 12 cars followed the hearse along the funeral route from his house in Camberwell to the crematorium in Streatham.

TOP: Thirty years after the robbery several people who were involved in the hunt for gang members met under Bridego Bridge. They included the local policeman, the station porter, a reporter and two men, who as children, had been car-spotters and had provided the police with several registration numbers.

JOHN GEORGE HAIGH:
The Acid Bath Murders

Habeas Corpus has been enshrined in English law for centuries as a means of protecting the individual from unwarranted detention by the state. It is incumbent upon the state to 'produce the body' if it wishes to incarcerate a person, whereupon the accused can weigh and counter the evidence against him and due process can take place. Habeas corpus is not restricted to capital crimes, but in 1949 John George Haigh took this vital guarantor of individual freedom quite literally when he was tried for murder. He took great pains to eradicate all traces of his victim's body, then openly defied the police to secure a conviction, fully expecting the ancient writ to come to his rescue.

Expensive lifestyle

John Haigh was a conman, forger and fraudster who had killed at least five times before he was brought to book. When he was casting around for a new target early in 1949, he had every reason to believe the modus operandi that had served him so well would prove successful again. It involved murdering the chosen individual, destroying all traces of the body and using his considerable forgery skills to appropriate the deceased's worldly goods. It was a lucrative career, but Haigh had an expensive lifestyle to maintain. There was the cost of his permanent residence at a South Kensington hotel and the running of a sleek Alvis motor car, plus a weakness for gambling. By February 1949 he was running perilously short of funds. His bank account was £80 in the red and he was coming under pressure from the Onslow Court Hotel to settle arrears of £50. Salvation seemed to present itself in the shape of 69-year-old Olive Durand-Deacon, a fellow guest at the hotel and, more importantly, a wealthy widow. She would be his next victim.

TOP LEFT: Haigh, handcuffed to a police officer, smiles broadly for the cameraman as he arrives at the Horsham Court for his second hearing.

ABOVE: Crowds gather to catch a glimpse of Haigh and the witnesses as they arrive. The noise from the crowd outside the court drowned out the voice of a witness and police were sent outside to block the road if necessary.

RIGHT: Haigh's family home in Ledger Lane, Wakefield. His parents were members of the Plymouth Brethren and so the family lived within a 10ft fence that his father put up around their garden to lock out the outside world.

Business proposition

The pair were observed deep in conversation on 14 February 1949. Mrs Durand-Deacon had a proposition for the urbane John Haigh, who suavely promoted himself as a successful businessman. She had come up with the idea of manufacturing false fingernails and needed advice on how to go about bringing the idea to market. Who better to ask than a fellow guest who owned a light engineering firm in Crawley? This latter statement was stretching a point somewhat. The enterprise referred to was Hurstlea Products, and although Haigh knew the owner of the company and had at one time been invited to become a director, that offer had never come to fruition. The extent of Haigh's connection with Hurstlea Products was the use of a small workshop facility and storeroom in Leopold Road, though that didn't stop him from portraying himself in a grander light if it suited his needs.

Clock now ticking

The following day Haigh borrowed £50 from the managing director of Hurstlea Products, Edward Jones, promising to repay the principal five days later. That wouldn't be a problem, for Haigh said he was in talks with someone over the manufacture of plastic nails. Haigh used the funds to settle his hotel bill. The clock was now ticking towards 20 February, the date that the loan was due to be repaid.

> By February 1949 Haigh was running perilously short of funds. Salvation seemed to present itself in the shape of 69-year-old Olive Durand-Deacon, a wealthy widow. She would be his next victim.

TOP LEFT: By February 1949 Haigh had little money left. His bank account was £80 in the red and he was coming under pressure from the Onslow Court Hotel to settle arrears of £50.

TOP RIGHT, TOP RIGHT(INSET), ABOVE AND RIGHT: Haigh's expensive Alvis car helped to exaggerate his status but it also provided clues for the police. Following the disappearance of Olivia Durand-Deacon, Haigh is referred to in the media, as a 'friend of the missing widow'. Once police discovered his record of theft they searched his Crawley workshop and he became the prime suspect.

Police informed

Haigh arranged to take Olive Durand-Deacon to the Crawley workshop on 18 February, ostensibly to meet one of his business associates. At around 4 pm he was seen with a woman answering Mrs Durand-Deacon's description at a nearby hotel, the George, though he later claimed she failed to keep the appointment. The following morning, he played the part of the concerned friend, asking another of the Onslow Court Hotel's long-standing residents if she could shed light on Mrs Durand-Deacon's whereabouts. Constance Lane was far less enamoured with Haigh than her friend, and after finding that Olive's room had not been slept in, she felt uneasy. It went against the grain for the methodical, punctilious Mrs Durand-Deacon to go away without telling anyone at the hotel. When another twenty-four hours passed with no news, Mrs Lane resolved to inform the police. The unflappable Haigh even offered to drive her to the station, which was coolness personified considering he had already sold Mrs Durand-Deacon's watch and put her Persian lambskin coat in for cleaning.

BEACHY HEAD CAR MYSTERY

POLICE COMB DOWNS

From Our Own Correspondent

Eastbourne, Sunday morning. Following the discovery of a burnt-out car near Beachy Head last night, police were searching the Downs early to-day for the occupants.

The car, an S.S. Jaguar, was found by a holidaymaker.

So far no one has reported a missing car to the police, and there is no clue to the identity of the driver.

TOP RIGHT: Miss Kirkwood (left) and Miss Robbie, manageress and book keeper at the Onslow Court Hotel, where Olive Durand-Deacon lived for two years before her murder.

TOP LEFT, AND LEFT: A wrecked car was found at the foot of Beachy Head, Sussex, having crashed over the cliffs in June 1948. No occupants were found, but an unidentified torso was discovered near the scene three months later. A mile from the cliffs was the Birlington Gap Hotel where Dr Archibald Henderson and his wife, who Haigh later admitted to killing, had booked rooms. The couple never arrived at the hotel, the booking cancelled by letter, apparently by Dr Henderson.

ABOVE: Letters sent by Haigh from the Onslow Court Hotel to Madge Mohan.

Sinister motive suspected

A major Scotland Yard missing persons investigation was soon under way. Haigh was questioned, sticking to his story that Mrs Durand-Deacon hadn't kept their 18 February appointment. The police felt that something wasn't quite right, and when they discovered the true nature of Haigh's relationship with Hurstlea Products, it begged the question: was he a mere self-publicist who liked to exaggerate his status, or did he have a more sinister motive for wanting Olive Durand-Deacon to believe he was a successful businessman? After a third interview, Haigh complained of harassment, but the police had unearthed elements in his past that encouraged them to think it was a line of inquiry that was worth pursuing. Here was a man who had a long history as a confidence trickster, a man whose transgressions had earned him three spells behind bars.

Enfield .38 revolver found

On 26 February the police conducted a thorough search of the Leopold Street premises. Among the expected workshop paraphernalia were several items that gave cause for concern, including a gas mask, oildrums, heavy-duty gloves and an Enfield .38 revolver that had recently been fired. There was also a dry-cleaning ticket for Mrs Durand-Deacon's lambskin coat.

TOP RIGHT AND TOP MIDDLE: Barbara Stephens, one of Haigh's few friends.

ABOVE: Mr Stephens, father of Barbara Stephens and business partner of Haigh.

RIGHT: A police photographer emerges from the small two-storey factory used by Hurstlea Products Ltd in Crawley, where police found the remains of Olive Durand-Deacon after her body had been decomposed in acid. Haigh had told her that he was a director of the factory.

'Destroyed her with acid'

Haigh was questioned once again by the chief investigating officer Inspector Shelley Symes, and now he was forced to play what he thought was his trump card. He told Symes: 'Mrs Durand-Deacon no longer exists. She has disappeared completely and no trace of her can ever be found again. I have destroyed her with acid. You will find the sludge that remains at Leopold Road.' There was no remorse, merely a cocksure confidence that an admission of guilt was worthless if the body could not be produced. Haigh went further, describing how he slit his victim's throat and drank her

> 'She has disappeared completely and no trace of her can ever be found again. I have destroyed her with acid.'

blood before consigning her body to the acid bath. It wasn't long before such gory details reached the public domain. When the *Daily Mirror* published material deemed to be prejudicial to the case, describing Haigh as a vampire and referring to other individuals who had died by his hand, it earned the paper a £10,000 fine and its editor Silvester Bolam a three-month stay in Brixton Prison. The court frowned upon the sensational nature of the revelations aimed at increasing circulation, with no thought to the judicial process. Notwithstanding the severe penalty imposed on the national daily, it was impossible to keep the lid on the case of the 'vampire killer'.

LEFT: While detectives searched the Hurstlea factory, they repeatedly brought Haigh in for questioning. Among the items they found in the workshop that were cause for concern were a gas mask, oil drums, heavy-duty gloves and an Enfield .38 revolver that had recently been fired.

TOP RIGHT: Haigh eventually boasted to the police that no trace of Mrs Durand-Deacon would be found since he had dissolved her in acid. However, pathologist Dr Keith Simpson recovered three human gallstones, more than ten kilograms of melted body fat and a number of bone fragments. It was enough to prove the sex of the victim. It was the survival of her acrylic dentures that allowed police to trace their origin back to Mrs Durand-Deacon.

ABOVE: Chief of West Sussex CID leaving the Crawley workshop.

Carboy of sulphuric acid

The full details of the events leading up to Mrs Durand-Deacon's death on 18 February began to emerge. Police found a shopping list in Haigh's hotel room, detailing his requirements for disposing of the body. On 16 February he collected a carboy of sulphuric acid from the chemical suppliers White and Sons, and the next day obtained a 45-gallon oil-drum, making sure its interior was acid-resistant. Haigh then paid another visit to Jones, not to redeem the debt or discuss plastic fingernails but to ask him to make adjustments to the stirrup pump he'd bought. The reason was simple: the leg of the pump prevented it from being inserted into the neck of the acid container.

ABOVE LEFT: The interior of the factory in Crawley where Mrs Durand-Deacon was killed. She had mentioned to Haigh an idea that she had for artificial fingernails. He invited her down to the Crawley workshop on February 18, 1949, and once inside he shot her in the back of the head, stripped her of her valuables, including a Persian lambskin coat, and put her into the acid bath. She was reported missing two days later by her friend Constance Lane.

ABOVE RIGHT: Dr George Furfitt of Police Laboratory and H.B. Holden, Scotland Yard forensic expert.

BELOW: Scotland Yard forensic expert, H.B. Holden, searches the Crawley workshop on Leopold Road for remains of the widow.

> He drained the drum in the yard and refilled it with fresh acid to finish the job.

Body placed in acid

Haigh admitted driving Mrs Durand-Deacon to Crawley on the afternoon of 18 February, first to the George Hotel and thence to the workshop. He then shot her in the head and set about covering up the crime. He removed her lambskin coat and jewellery, took a small amount of cash and a set of keys from her handbag, then let the acid get to work. The following day, as well as playing the role of worried neighbour and selling off the first tranche of the victim's jewellery, he went to check on progress at Leopold Road. There remained some pieces of fat and bone, and the acid had had little effect on the handbag. He drained the drum in the yard and refilled it with fresh acid to finish the job. By Tuesday 22 February he thought that all traces of organic matter had been obliterated and he was in the clear. Hence his swaggering, defiant demeanour when he made his statement to the police. Eminent pathologist Dr Keith Simpson was about to prick that ill-judged hubris.

JOHN GEORGE HAIGH: The Acid Bath Murders

> Haigh had become fascinated with the idea of committing the perfect murder, and now he planned to turn theory into practice.

Body fat and bone fragments found

Simpson found bloodstains of Mrs Durand-Deacon's type, and from the sludge recovered three human gallstones. There was more than ten kilograms of melted body fat and a number of bone fragments; these proved the sex of the victim. The presence of arthritis in the joints suggested that she had been in late adulthood. But the most damning physical evidence was a set of acrylic dentures which had survived intact and could be traced back to the London dental surgeon who had fitted them for Mrs Durand-Deacon two years earlier.

Plea of insanity

The trial opened at Sussex Assizes in Lewes on 18 July 1949. Haigh entered a Not Guilty plea, which on the surface looked to be somewhat odd as chief prosecuting counsel Sir Hartley Shawcross introduced as evidence the uncontested statement detailing the murder of Olive Durand-Deacon and the attempted disposal of her body. Those facts were not in doubt; and they left the defence with just one available weapon: an insanity plea. To help his cause, defence counsel Sir David Maxwell Fyfe wanted the full details of Haigh's grisly past aired in court. Haigh was being tried only for the murder of Mrs Durand-Deacon, but he had admitted to several similar crimes. They could hardly make matters worse for the defence, and indeed could help support the contention that Haigh was insane at the time of their commission.

TOP LEFT: An early picture of Mrs McSwann with her son in 1917. They were both victims of Haigh.

FAR LEFT: The house in Grand Drive, Raynes Park, South West London, where Donald McSwann had once lived. He lived there alone for two years, his parents having moved to Pimlico.

LEFT: A fanfare outside the County Hall at Lewes as the trial of John George Haigh opens.

TOP RIGHT: Haigh is smiling as he is brought to the Horsham Police Court for the opening of the trial.

McSwann family: his first victims

Haigh's first victims had been three members of the same family, the McSwanns. He had at one time worked for William McSwann in the amusement arcade business. They lost touch when Haigh was forced to go on the run but met up again in wartime London. During one of his stints in prison Haigh had become fascinated with the idea of committing the perfect murder, and now he planned to turn theory into practice. William McSwann was lured to a basement flat in Gloucester Road, bludgeoned to death and placed in an acid bath. Haigh said he tapped the body for blood before destroying it, and after the acid had done its work he poured the remaining sludge down a manhole. He repeated the exercise with McSwann's parents, using his forgery skills to gain control of the family assets.

His next victims

When the proceeds of those crimes ran out, Haigh looked around for a new source of funds, lighting upon Dr Archibald Henderson and his glamorous wife Rosalie. Haigh met the Hendersons when he responded to an advertisement for the sale of their Ladbroke Square property. He wasn't interested in buying the house, but in cultivating the friendship of the owners. In February 1948 he took Mr Henderson to the Crawley workshop and dispatched him using his tried and trusted method. Rosalie Henderson was then summoned, told that her husband had been taken ill. She suffered the same fate and Haigh once again turned a tidy profit. He even managed to get his hands on the Hendersons' new house in Fulham by forging a deed of transfer.

> In February 1948 John Haigh took Mr Henderson to the Crawley workshop and dispatched him using his tried and trusted method.

Unsound mind?

Haigh said there were others, too, though he was hazier about the details of those crimes, apart from the fact that the victims were all impoverished. It was suggested that these belated additions to his statement were fabrications intended to balance the fact that his six known victims were all murdered for gain. It was in Haigh's – and Maxwell Fyfe's – interest to assert that some had died not for profit but as a result of the tortured childhood dreams of Christ's stigmata that Haigh claimed had haunted him. If the sole motive in those additional cases was the desire to slake his thirst for blood, then surely the perpetrator had to be of unsound mind?

ABOVE LEFT: A workman emerges from 79 Gloucester Road with a pick and a shovel. Haigh had been obsessed with committing the perfect murder and with the McSwanns he managed to put this theory into practice.

ABOVE: Mrs McSwann: her husband and her son were Haigh's first victims. After they were killed and their bodies dissolved in acid, Haigh used his forgery skills to obtain control of the family assets.

RIGHT: The entrance to the basement of 79, Gloucester Road, Kensington, where police found the remains of Mr and Mrs McSwann and their son. Haigh had once worked for William McSwann in the amusement arcade business.

Delusional and egocentric

Maxwell Fyfe called just one witness, the eminent Harley Street practitioner Dr Henry Yellowlees. The jury heard an account of Haigh's severe and austere upbringing. His parents had been religious zealots, members of the fundamentalist Christian sect the Plymouth Brethren. All forms of entertainment, even newspapers and radio, were regarded as sinful and banned from the house. John and Emily Haigh preached hellfire and damnation to their son, who was harshly dealt with for the slightest misdemeanour.

Dr Yellowlees said that Haigh was delusional and egocentric. The fact that he was forbidden from having childhood friends would have had a profound effect on his development. Yellowlees asserted: 'The disorder of mind which I submit has affected the reason of the accused is that rare but quite well known type of mental aberration which is called in psychological medicine pure paranoia'. One of the ways that the disorder manifested itself was the sufferer's belief that he was in a mystical union with a controlling external power. When Haigh had been in his mid-teens, that power had instructed him to drink his own urine, a practice he had continued ever since. All of this Dr Yellowlees had gleaned from three interviews totalling around two hours; and he was placing a medical interpretation on information exclusively supplied by Haigh himself: a practised liar whose life was in the balance.

TOP (INSET): In 1938 Dr Archibald Henderson, a Jermyn Street physician, and Mrs Rosalie Mercy Erren were married. A decade later they fell victim to Haigh's acid bath.

TOP: Dr Henderson (left) with his wife at a dinner party at a casino in Blackpool with Mr and Mrs Burlin. When the proceeds of the McSwann murders ran out, Haigh looked for a new source of funds and so he turned his attentions to the Hendersons.

ABOVE: The Dolls Hospital on Dawes Road in Fulham, owned by Henderson.

LEFT: Mr J. Davies supplied Haigh's acid and invented the rocking horse that Haigh used to lure Henderson to his death.

JULY 19, 1949

'Dreams led him to kill nine'

Sir David Maxwell Fyfe, great lawyer and interpreter of the human mind, this afternoon sought to initiate a Sussex jury of 11 normal men and one normal woman into the strange and horrifying world of fantasy in which, he contends, his client, John George Haigh, has confessed to destroying nine human lives. He told them of dreams which have haunted Haigh since childhood, dreams in which crucifixes turn into trees and drip first rain and then blood; dreams in which the Cross figures, dreams which culminate in an overmastering desire to have blood.

ABOVE: Exhibits used in the case against Haigh. Among these was the metal drum he filled with acid in order to eliminate any trace of his victims' bodies.

RIGHT: The child's motor-car invented by Haigh. This electrically driven car could do 12 miles an hour for 50 miles without the battery being re-charged and was valued at £15. This picture was taken at the Dolls Hospital, Dawes Road, Fulham, where police searched the coal cellar.

TOP RIGHT: Sergeant Patrick Heslin, Divisional Inspector Shelley Symes and Inspector Mahon, Chief Inspector of the Missing Persons Bureau, arriving at the court for Haigh's trial.

MIDDLE RIGHT: Doctor Henderson's former maid, Mrs Daisy Rowntree, is interviewed by Detective Sergeant Aspinall at the Dolls Hospital in Dawes Road.

JULY 19, 1949

'Three others'

Another statement read by Inspector Webb spoke of three others Haigh claims to have murdered. Haigh's descriptions of them were in themselves almost in the form of police "Missing Persons" circulars.

The first, he said, was: Woman, aged 35, 5ft. 9in., well built, dark hair, no hat, dark cloth coat; carrying an envelope-type of blackish handbag. In his alleged statement he said he had met her between Hammersmith Bridge and the Broadway about two months after he killed young McSwann - that is, about April 1944. He took her to the Gloucester Road flat, hit her with a cosh, and "tapped her for blood" He dissolved her body in acid. There was "next to nothing in her handbag."

He said further that in the following autumn he had murdered a man he met in the Goat public house, High Street, Kensington. The description: About 35, "same height and build as myself." (which could be interpreted as well built but shortish), brownish wavy hair; wearing dark double-breasted suit, believed blue.

'Same thing'

Haigh bought him a drink and took him to the Gloucester Road flat, where "the same thing happened... He had no jewellery and no more than a pound in money." No mention of blood in this case.

In autumn last year it had been a woman at Eastbourne. The description: Christian name Mary, surname unknown; probably Welsh. Wearing white and green summer dress, white beach shoes, carrying light-coloured handbag. They had a meal together in the old part of Hastings. He drove her to Crawley, hit her with a cosh, "tapped her for blood, put her in the tub, and left her there until the next morning." She had little property except a bottle of scent in her handbag.

Superintendent Guy Mahon said that there was no evidence in confirmation of Haigh's statement relating to the three unknown people.

At 3.40 p.m. the Attorney-General completed the case against Haigh, and Sir David Maxwell Fyfe rose to tell the jury he would ask from them the special verdict of "Guilty of the acts charged, but insane at the time they were committed." Haigh, he said, was a victim of what was known to psychological medicine as 'pure paranoia' Sir David explained: "The badge of this disorder is that the victim knows his secret life of fantasy must be lived alongside the ordinary life of the world. He is, therefore, lucid, astute, shrewd when not actually acting under the influence of his fantasy. He takes steps to avoid trouble to do the best he can for himself."

LEFT, ABOVE AND TOP: A metal drum, covered in sacking, is brought to the court in Horsham for Haigh's hearing. Haigh devloped the idea of using acid when conducting experiments with mice during a stint in prison.

Profit as the primary motive

Shawcross anticipated the insanity plea and was ready to counter. He focused on the sale of the ill-gotten goods, wanting to stress that these were cynical crimes with profit as the primary motive. Also, the fact that Haigh had already enquired about the chances of getting out of Broadmoor suggested a degree of reasoning. The elaborate planning aimed at avoiding detection, and, thus, punishment, also indicated that Haigh knew all too well what he was about. Shawcross invited Dr Yellowlees to agree that Haigh's word could not be trusted, then pointed out that the witness's assessment of the accused's state of mind had been based entirely upon utterances from that same unreliable source. The doctor was further invited to admit the possibility that a man so well practised in the arts of deceit might have fooled him. Yellowlees was forced to answer in the affirmative. Shawcross also pointed out that as the Hendersons had been murdered hours apart on the same day, wasn't it likely that the second crime was committed, not in response to some dream or inner voice but to silence Mrs Henderson? Dr Yellowlees had to concede that possibility, too. It was game, set and match to the Attorney-General.

JULY 20, 1948

'Divine course'

Haigh's "dream-ridden existence" was traceable to his mother and the strength of her belief in the effect of dreams on the future. Brought up in severe surroundings of strict Plymouth Brethren parents, he left that influence and the formative years of his adolescence were associated with Wakefield Cathedral, then very High Church. What he saw, thought, and experience there had penetrated "the cloudy recesses of his abnormal mind and personality" Thus, said Sir David, "when he came to do these dreadful deeds he thought himself to be following a divinely appointed course that had been set for him."

Sir David Maxwell Fyfe rose to tell the jury he would ask from them the special verdict of 'Guilty of the acts charged, but insane at the time they were committed.'

TOP: Sightseers crowd every vantage point in the narrow street to watch the arrival of the personalities attending Haigh's trial.

LEFT: Following a stint in prison Haigh moved into Barbara Stephen's house, which she shared with her father. Despite being 20 years his junior, Stephens was intent on becoming the next Mrs Haigh.

BELOW: Five women witnesses in the Haigh trial at Lewes Assizes drink coffee after lunch. Left to right: Mrs Hilda Kirkwood, Miss Robbie, Mrs Constance Lane, Miss Esme Fargus and Mrs Birin.

JULY 20, 1949

'To the last he smiled'

Stepping from the dock with a faint but unshaken smile, John George Haigh this afternoon joined the ranks of the most extraordinary criminals of history. All through the hot afternoon his sleek round head had rested easily against the panelled door behind him. Occasionally the door threatened to swing open and he turned round to refasten it. Otherwise he seldom changed his position. He, at least, seemed perfectly composed, and quite content to leave anxiety to the array of learned counsel.

Meanwhile the pace of the trial was rapidly accelerating. Earlier in the day the defence had produced its single witness, and the expert testimony of Dr. Yellow-lees had very soon run into somewhat heavy crossfire. For the scientific mind, with its habit of qualification, and the legal mind, with its liking for precise unqualified statements, have few common terms of reference.

Fantasy

No further witnesses were called, and from that moment the drama of the trial became the drama of three different personalities.

The solid dignity and robust realism of Sir David Maxwell Fyfe's appearances were in curious contrast as he spoke of the fantastic and mysterious character of the subject that concerned him - dreams and manias and sadistic delusions, crimes that were perhaps real, perhaps more than half imaginary. At times he reminded me of a fully armed gladiator, courageously attempting to hack his way through a world of ghosts and cobwebs.

Sir Hartley Shawcross had the easier task. Sir David now and then rose to vehemence. The Attorney-General kept his speech quiet and clear and low-tone, allowing himself now and then some telling strokes of sarcasm. But for the most part the voice he employed was that of unemphatic commonsense.

Finally came the Judge's summing up. Mr. Justice Humphreys has a delivery that many younger men might envy. He speaks quietly, almost casually, but every word is distinct, every period well-shaped. His analysis of the mass of evidence was as fascinating to observe as a piece of skilled dissection. He seemed to remove irrelevances with a flick of the fingers.

Gravely paternal towards members of the jury - 11 men and one motherly woman who bore the name Mary English and an exceedingly English-looking brown and yellow straw hat - he was merciless in his elimination of any hint of muddled thinking.

ABOVE: Mrs Constance Lane (right) and Miss Elizabeth Robbie. Lane reported Mrs Durand-Deacon missing. When her friend was not at her usual seat for dinner or breakfast the following morning, Lane knew something was amiss and reported it to the police.

LEFT AND FAR LEFT: Helen Mayo, a dental surgeon and a witness in the trial of John Haigh. She stated that she had made a set of dentures for the woman whom Haigh is alleged to have murdered. She was a crucial witness since the dentures were all that could be used to identify the remains of Olivia Durand-Deacon's body.

Fifteen minutes to reach verdict of Guilty

Presiding judge Sir Travers Humphreys passed comment on the defence's decision to call a single expert witness, when others who could have commented on Haigh's alleged mental infirmity might have been produced. The judge also made disparaging reference to Dr Yellowlees's response when asked whether the accused knew what he was doing when he murdered Olive Durand-Deacon. A psychiatrist would have to live with that person for years to form an accurate opinion, came the doctor's reply. If the jury knew what to make of that, said Humphreys, then they had greater understanding than him. The jury took just fifteen minutes to decide that there was no divine guidance at work, and no grounds for returning a verdict of Guilty but insane.

John George Haigh was hanged on 10 August 1949. Realizing that he would soon be joining the ghoulish line-up of convicted murderers at Madame Tussaud's, he even donated a suit of clothes to ensure that the waxwork effigy would look as dapper as the original.

JULY 20, 1949

Little emotion

T he jury retired, but returned to the court in 15 minutes. Their verdict was a unanimous "Guilty," but Haigh, standing in the front of the dock, a neat upright figure - hair smooth, suit unwrinkled, his hands behind his back - received it with as little emotion as though he were being fined for an incorrectly parked car. Asked by the clerk of the court if he had anything to say, he replied: "None at all" – meaning obviously "Nothing at all," the only suggestion he gave of any hidden feeling - in his rather high and cynical Kensingtonian accent.

Sentence of death was pronounced - the dreadful formula made more dreadful by the ceremony of the black cap. Haigh immediately turned to go, and as he descended the stairs one could see that he was smiling.

Grotesque and hideous series of crimes

He has left behind him a considerable question mark. In the whole history of English criminal trials I doubt if any murderer has been condemned of whom the future criminologist may decide he knows so little.

Those who had been watching him for the past two days came out into the freedom of Lewes High Street exhausted and bewildered. It was still impossible to connect that neat, commonplace figure in the dock with the grotesque and hideous series of crimes of which he had accused himself.

Impossible to find any clue to the mind that lay beneath them, or to the expression of unruffled composure with which he had heard his death sentence.

By comparison, Crippen was a sentimentalist, and Landru a boastful playboy.

> Sentence of death was pronounced – the dreadful formula made more dreadful by the ceremony of the black cap. Haigh immediately turned to go, and as he descended the stairs one could see that he was smiling.

TOP RIGHT: John George Haigh (seated at rear of car, centre) is driven away by police. Barbara Stephens (standing left with arms folded) looks on.

RIGHT AND ABOVE RIGHT: Spectators await the verdict in the Haigh trial. Some had waited all night in anticipation.

OPPOSITE TOP: Haigh is watched by crowds as he is escorted by police. He received the verdict with little emotion. When he was taken out of the courtroom and down the stairs he was seen to be smiling.

LORD LUCAN:
The Murder of Sandra Rivett

'He's murdered the nanny!' the woman cried, before collapsing and being rushed to St George's Hospital. Thus began a high-society mystery that has rumbled on unresolved for over 30 years.

Custody battle

On the night of 7 November 1974, the bloodied figure of a woman staggered into the Plumbers' Arms, a public house situated a few yards from her Belgravia home. It soon became clear that the cry for help was not just on her account. There had been another, less fortunate, victim.

The injured woman was Lady Lucan, née Veronica Duncan. She had gained her title by dint of her marriage 11 years earlier to Richard John Bingham, 7th Earl of Lucan. Lord Lucan was an Old Etonian and former Coldstream Guardsman, following in the footsteps of his father, the 6th Earl, who served as the Chief Labour Whip in the House of Lords until his death in 1964.

Lord and Lady Lucan had three children, Frances (b. 1964), George (b. 1967) and Camilla (b. 1970). By 1972 the marriage had foundered and the children became the subject of a fierce custody battle. In March 1973 Lord Lucan obtained a court order

giving him custody of the three children, but that decision was later overturned, a ruling that infuriated the earl. By the autumn of 1974, the couple had been living apart for almost two years and divorce proceedings were pending. It was a black time for Lord Lucan. He was an inveterate gambler who could win or lose thousands during an evening at the gaming tables. Friends called him 'Lucky' Lucan, but his good fortune seemed to have deserted him. He had incurred heavy financial losses, and the upkeep of two London houses following the marital breakdown represented a substantial additional burden. Many believe that on the night of 7 November 1974 Lord Lucan planned to relieve himself of at least one of the encumbrances weighing him down. In the months leading up to his disappearance Lucan reportedly told several friends that he wished to be rid of his wife.

ABOVE RIGHT: Lucan pictured in Portofino, in 1968 with Mrs Zoe Howard, wife of Greville Howard.

ABOVE LEFT: Lady Lucan pictured outside her Belgrave home. On the night of 7 November she staggered into the nearby Plumbers' Arms pub crying for help as blood poured from her head.

OPPOSITE TOP LEFT: Lord Lucan in a West End club, January, 1973.

OPPOSITE BOTTOM RIGHT: A policeman stands outside Lady Lucan's home in Lower Belgravia Street. When the police arrived at number 46 they found the body of 29-year-old nanny, Sandra Rivett.

OPPOSITE INSET: Lucan occupied a mews house in Eaton Row before moving to Elizabeth Street.

Lucan named

Police arrived at 46 Lower Belgravia Street to find copious bloodstains on the stairs leading to the basement, at the foot of which was a sack containing the body of 29-year-old Sandra Rivett, the children's nanny. She had been clubbed to death with a blunt instrument. A piece of lead pipe covered in surgical tape was recovered from the scene, later confirmed as both the murder weapon and the implement with which Lady Lucan was attacked.

Police forced their way into Lord Lucan's flat in Elizabeth Street, but he was nowhere to be found. Not until the inquest seven months later would Lady Lucan publicly name her husband as the man who attacked her, though that revelation hardly came as a shock. For within days of the incident, Detective Chief Superintendent Roy Ranson, the man heading the inquiry, said that the police weren't looking for anyone else in connection with the crime, and on Tuesday 12 November warrants for Lord Lucan's arrest were issued on charges of murder and attempted murder.

> Twenty minutes passed and the nanny failed to return, so Lady Lucan went to investigate.

At the inquest, which took place in June 1975, Lady Lucan said she was watching television upstairs with Lady Frances when Sandra Rivett went to the basement kitchen to make tea just before 9 pm. Thursday was normally Sandra's night off – a fact of which Lord Lucan was aware – but that week she had taken Wednesday evening off instead. Twenty minutes passed and the nanny failed to return, so Lady Lucan went to investigate. She reached the ground floor and called out Sandra's name, and it was then that she was attacked by her husband, whom she positively identified. He eventually broke off the assault, and, according to the countess, admitted accidentally killing the nanny. When he went to fetch a cloth to tend her injuries, Lady Lucan seized the chance to escape to the Plumbers' Arms and raise the alarm.

NOVEMBER 9, 1974

Screams

Police believe the attacker used lead piping. Moments later, Lady Lucan ran 100 yards to the Plumbers Arms to raise the alarm. She fell through the saloon bar door and screamed to head barman Derrick Whitehouse, 44: 'I've just come from a murder. Help me. 'Mr Whitehouse said yesterday: 'She was in a dreadful state. Hysterical and covered in deep cuts. We laid her on a bench and called the police 'She kept shouting "He's killed the nanny," and "My children, my children". There were about ten customers in the bar and one of them tried to quieten her.

'Within minutes of the 999 call, police smashed open the white front door of Lady Lucan's home and found Mrs Rivett's battered body wrapped in a canvas tent bag in the basement. Roadblocks were set up and teams of police began house-to-house inquiries. Other senior police went to the back of the block and knocked at the door of Lord Lucan's mews cottage in Eaton Row. When there was no reply they kicked open the yellow front door - but found that Lord Lucan had not been living there for some time.

Lord and Lady Lucan were married in the summer of 1963. Lady Lucan, then Miss Veronica Duncan, the debutante daughter of an Army major, was one of London's Society's most noted beauties.

Difficult

Lord Lucan - family motto 'Christ is my hope' - is the great-great grandson of the third earl, who led the Charge of the Light Brigade at Balaclava in the Crimean War. The Eton-educated former Coldstream Guards officer was regarded as the catch of the year. But the marriage proved a difficult one. The three children have been made wards of court. His love of baccarat and backgammon brought him into contact with leading film executives and he was screen-tested for the James Bond role won by Sean Connery.

Engaged in a violent struggle

Lord Lucan's version of events, pieced together from correspondence he entered into in the aftermath of the incident, differed markedly from that related by his wife in the coroner's court. At 11.30 pm on the night of the murder he called in on friends, the Maxwell-Scotts, who lived in Uckfield, Sussex, some 40 miles from Belgravia.

Ian Maxwell-Scott was not at home, and it was his wife Susan who received the dishevelled Lord Lucan; it was to be the last confirmed sighting of the peer. According to Mrs Maxwell-Scott, Lucan had been passing the family home when he looked through the basement window and saw a man engaged in a violent struggle with his wife. He had a key to the house and went to her aid, but slipped on a patch of blood and couldn't prevent the assailant from escaping. Lady Lucan became hysterical, accusing her husband of hiring an assassin, and fled the house while he was trying to calm her down and treat her wounds. Lucan made a telephone call to his mother relaying much the same story. He is said to have described it as a catastrophic evening of 'incredible coincidence'.

Lucan's story

Although in Lord Lucan's version of events he had no reason to reproach himself, he feared that things looked bad for him, as he indicated in a letter written to his brother-in-law William Shand-Kydd. 'The circumstantial evidence against me is strong in that V will say it was all my doing. I also will lie doggo for a bit…. V has demonstrated her hatred for me in the past and would do anything to see me accused.' The letter also expressed concerns for his children. He said he did not want to put them through the agony of seeing their father in the dock, suggesting that he had no intention of facing criminal proceedings. Some interpreted this as an indication that he planned to disappear, others that he intended to take his own life. The letter was not only a clear rebuttal of Lady Lucan's version of events but an attempt to discredit the word of an embittered spouse.

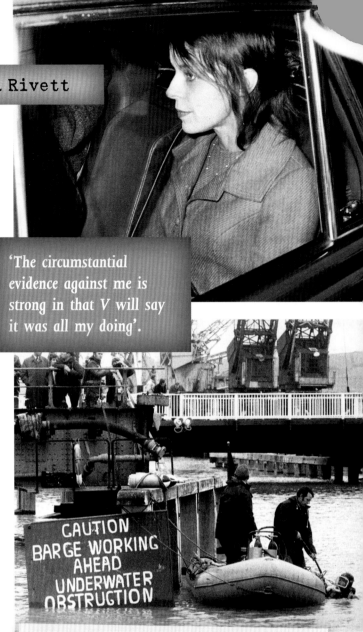

'The circumstantial evidence against me is strong in that V will say it was all my doing'.

Holiday home

Detectives were also checking every major casino from Monte Carlo to Cannes, for the earl has played in most casinos in the south and police believe his gambling instincts are so strong he could pay a visit. Lord Lucan speaks French poorly but he has an extensive knowledge of the Riviera. Some of his friends are still at their homes there, but others have returned to England. Lord Lucan could easily be staying at a vacated holiday home.

In the United States, the FBI were interviewing relatives and several business associates of Lord Lucan. The move followed the discovery of a diary which he also used as an address book. Details were immediately sent to the French police HQ in Paris and to Washington via the Interpol network.

A major point in yesterday's decision to make public the arrest warrants was that Scotland Yard wanted all of Lord Lucan's friends to know that they risk facing criminal charges for either harbouring him or aiding him while on the run. Police accept that he has dedicated friends who would take the chance. Mrs Susan Maxwell Scott, the last person to see Lord Lucan, said she was 'amazed and aghast' that arrest warrants had been issued. Mrs Maxwell Scott, who was visited by Lord Lucan at her home at Uckfield, Sussex, just two hours after Mrs Rivett was found dead, said: 'He has to be innocent.'

Car abandoned

Susan Maxwell-Scott said that Lord Lucan left at around 1.15 am on the morning of Friday 8 August. Two days later, the borrowed Ford Corsair in which he travelled to Sussex was found abandoned in Newhaven. It was stained with both type A and type B blood, matching the groups of Lady Lucan and Sandra Rivett respectively. A length of lead piping found in the boot matched the murder weapon found at the crime scene. The car's location fuelled speculation that Lord Lucan might have tried to flee the country by ferry, despite the fact that his passport was in police hands. Those who favoured the suicide theory suggested that he may not have intended to complete the crossing; perhaps he planned a watery grave.

> The feelings of hopelessness expressed in the letter gave further support to the idea that he intended to take the gentleman's way out and end it all.

Forensic evidence

The Corsair's owner was a friend of the peer's, Michael Stoop. Lucan had borrowed the vehicle as his own car, a Mercedes, had battery trouble. Stoop was also the recipient of a letter, which was read out in the coroner's court. In it Lucan referred to the missive sent to William Shand-Kydd detailing the events of 7 November, adding: '… but judging by my last effort in court no one, let alone a 67-year-old judge, would believe – and I no longer care, except that my children should be protected.' He obviously felt that a court case would go against him, as the custody battle had. The forensic evidence was certainly not in his favour. Most of the blood found in the basement was type B, Rivett's group, while the ground-floor deposits were mainly type A, Lady Lucan's group. That was consistent with the countess's story, not his. The feelings of hopelessness expressed in the letter gave further support to the idea that he intended to take the gentleman's way out and end it all.

OPPOSITE MIDDLE AND BOTTOM: Frogmen probed a hole near the swing bridge in Newhaven Harbour where bodies have been found in the past. After an hour the frogmen abandoned their hunt for Lord Lucan.

TOP LEFT: Police dog handlers search for Lord Lucan on the downs above Newhaven Harbour.

ABOVE: Lord Lucan pictured during a holiday in Spain. His version of events, that was delivered through various correspondence, differed greatly from Lady Lucan's.

ABOVE LEFT: Evidence being carried out after the hearing into Sandra Rivett's murder. The Coronor's Court committed Lord Lucan for trial at the Old Bailey but the police had yet to apprehend him.

LEFT AND OPPOSITE TOP: Lady Lucan. Lord and Lady Lucan had three children together and had been living apart from almost two years prior to the nanny's murder. During the inquest the QC acting for Lord Lucan's mother did his best to talk up Lady Lucan's alleged hatred of her husband, but the forensic evidence supported Lady Lucan's account. Lady Lucan publicly named her husband as the man who attacked her during the inquest, seven months after the incident.

JUNE 17, 1975

The night my nanny died

A sensational description by Lord Lucan's 10-year-old daughter of the night her nanny was murdered and her mother brutally attacked was read to a coroner's court yesterday. Lady Frances Bingham told of hearing a scream, then seeing her father with her mother, Lady Lucan, who was 'bleeding over her face and crying.'

Making tea

The statement said: On the Thursday evening we, that is, Mummy, George (her brother Lord Bingham, aged seven), Camilla (her sister, aged four), Sandra and I all had tea together. After tea I played one of my games in the nursery. At 7.20 I watched Top of the Pops on TV in the nursery. Mummy, Camilla, George and Sandra were downstairs watching The Six Million Dollar Man. I joined them at 8.05 and we all watched TV in Mummy's room. When the programme finished at 8.30 I went back to the nursery and played with my game. Sandra took Camilla and George upstairs and put them to bed. I had had my bath and I was wearing my pyjamas. I only stayed in the nursery about five minutes then I went downstairs again to Mummy's room at about 8.40. I asked Mummy where Sandra was and she said, 'Downstairs making tea.' After a while Mummy said that she wondered why Sandra was so long. I said I would go downstairs and see what was keeping Sandra. Mummy said No, she was going, and I said I would go with her. She said No, it was OK, she would go, and I stayed watching TV.

No light

Mummy left the room and left the door open. There was no light in the hall because the bulb doesn't work. Just after Mummy left the room I heard a scream. It sounded as though it came from a long way away. I thought that maybe the cat had scratched Mummy and she had screamed. I wasn't frightened by the scream and I stayed watching TV. At about 9.05 I ran to the door and called "Mummy." But there was no answer, so I left it. At 9.05 the news was on TV and Mummy and Daddy both walked into the room. Mummy was bleeding over her face and was crying. Mummy told me to go upstairs. Daddy didn't say anything to me and I said nothing to either of them. I only caught a glimpse of her. I don't know how much blood was on her face. As far as I can remember Daddy was wearing a pair of dark trousers and overcoat. I did not hear any conversation between Mummy and Daddy. I was on the bed when they came in the door.

Days off

I didn't see any blood on Daddy's clothes. I wondered what had happened but I didn't ask. I went upstairs and got into bed and read my book. I didn't hear anything from downstairs. After a little while - I don't know how long - I heard Daddy calling for Mummy. He was calling "Veronica, where are you?" I got up and looked down and saw Daddy coming out of the nursery. He went into the bathroom, came straight out and went downstairs.

During the last weekend I spent with Daddy, Camilla told Daddy that Sandra had boyfriends and went out with them. Daddy asked when she went out with them and Camilla said she went out with them on her days off. Then Daddy asked me when her days off were and I said Thursdays.

RIGHT: Many of Lord Lucan's belongings were auctioned off at Christie's auctioneers in order to pay off his massive gambling debts. Following his disappearance, it became apparent that Lord Lucan had accrued around £65,000 worth of debts.

> I went downstairs again to Mummy's room at about 8.40. I asked Mummy where Sandra was and she said, 'Downstairs making tea.'

Committed for trial

The court proceedings lasted four days and produced a sensational outcome. Lord Lucan was named as Sandra Rivett's murderer. It was highly unusual to name a perpetrator at a coroner's court, and indeed, legislation was passed in 1977 to outlaw such a practice. But following the jury's verdict, coroner Dr Gavin Thurston duly committed Lord Lucan for trial at the Old Bailey. First, of course, the police had to apprehend him.

JUNE 20, 1975

After half an hour, the verdict: Lucan killed her

Lord Lucan was the killer of his children's nanny, an inquest jury decided yesterday. The six men and three women took just 31 minutes to reach the verdict that 29-year-old Mrs Sandra Rivett was battered to death by the earl, who vanished soon afterwards.

The earl's mother, Kaitilin, Dowager Countess Lucan, who gave evidence that suggested her son was innocent, sat with her face downcast, breathing deeply. Coroner Dr Gavin Thurston, who summed up the three days of evidence in 70 minutes before the jury retired, formally announced that 'Richard John Bingham, Earl of Lucan, did on the 7th November 1974, in the City of Westminster, murder Sandra Eleanor Rivett.'

No one to commit

He said it was very rare for a jury to name someone in their verdict and added: 'It is my duty to commit that person for trial to the Central Criminal Court.' But in this case there was no one to commit for trial, and the verdict would remain 'on the file'.

The six men and three women took just 31 minutes to reach the verdict that 29-year-old Mrs Sandra Rivett was battered to death by the earl.

TOP LEFT: Lord Lucan's coronet and peer's robes were auctioned in order to pay the missing earl's creditors.

TOP RIGHT: Lady Lucan with picture of a man held in Australia, who police believed to be Lucan. Since his disappearance on 8 November 1974 there have been many claimed sightings but none these has been verified.

ABOVE: Lady Lucan photographed at home in 1976. Her husband was declared dead by the High Court in 1999. The House of Lords failed to accept there is enough evidence to prove Lord Lucan is dead and has denied his son's request to take his seat in the Upper Chamber.

Declared dead

Since 1974, there have been numerous 'sightings' of Lord Lucan in all corners of the globe, but all the trails turned out to be false. In 1999 the 7th Earl of Lucan was declared legally dead by the High Court, though that wasn't enough to persuade the House of Lords to allow his son to take his seat in the Upper Chamber.

The peer's disappearance left the book open, an invitation to speculators and theorists. Was Lord Lucan a murderer, as the coroner's court found? Did he hire a bungling hitman, who mistook Sandra Rivett for Lady Lucan? Was Lord Lucan the hero of the hour, saving his wife from a vicious attack by an unknown assailant? Did he commit suicide, fearing that he wouldn't be believed? Or is he alive and well, still in hiding?

DR HAWLEY HARVEY CRIPPEN:
Murder at Hilldrop Crescent

The case of Hawley Harvey Crippen has gone down in the annals of the criminal justice system for the part that cutting-edge communications technology played in the arrest. It was the first time that wireless telegraphy had been used to relay information regarding the whereabouts of a murder suspect, information that led to a dramatic chase on the high seas and the apprehension of both the wanted man and his mistress. Less well remembered are the gruesome events that occurred seven months earlier, in January 1910, which precipitated the flight.

ABOVE RIGHT: Dr Crippen, the Camden Town murderer. Crippen went down in history because of the part cutting-edge communications technology played in his arrest.

ABOVE: Crippen's house at number 39 Hilldrop Crescent. He and his second wife Cora took in lodgers to supplement Crippen's meagre income.

Medical training

Crippen was born in Coldwater, Michigan in 1862. He undertook medical training at Cleveland Homeopathic Hospital, taking a sabbatical to gain experience at Bethlehem Royal Hospital in London before graduating in 1885. He would become an eye and ear specialist, but the edges of the medical profession were blurred during that period, and Crippen devoted a considerable amount of his professional career to dispensing patent medicines. He wasn't above penning hard-sell missives extolling the benefits of some miracle cure in an unregulated market that was notorious for the number of quacks it attracted.

Crippen takes a second wife

In September 1892, Crippen married 18-year-old Cora Turner, the daughter of Eastern European immigrants, whose real name was Kunigunde Mackamotzki. He had buried his first wife just eight months earlier, consigning the son from that union, Hawley Otto, to the care of grandparents in California. In 1894 Crippen took up employment with Munyon's Remedies, a patent medicine company that specialised in homeopathic treatments. Around the turn of the century, he was dispatched across the Atlantic to oversee the running of a new Munyon's office in London. That field held little attraction for Cora, who was far more interested in the capital's theatrical set. She soon cultivated many friends from that milieu, and as well as getting some work as a performer, using the stage name Belle Elmore, she also became treasurer of the Music Hall Ladies' Guild, an organisation formed to support female artistes who had fallen on hard times.

39 Hilldrop Crescent

Accounts of Crippen's second marriage vary, from tender to combustible. The doctor was, by all accounts, docile and indulgent, traits that came in very handy when dealing with an ill-tempered wife who had extravagant tastes and lofty theatrical ambitions. Cora was too lacking in refinement to make the impression she craved on the operatic world, despite the image she sought to project. The couple appeared to drift towards a status quo in which they put up a reasonably harmonious public front, while pursuing their separate agendas in private. A house move in 1905 was part of the charade. The Crippens took up residence at 39 Hilldrop Crescent in Camden Town, a property large enough for them not to be under each other's feet, and indeed, large enough to obviate the need for them to share a marital bed.

countenance. In December 1909, Cora gave the Crippens' bank the required 12-months notice for the withdrawal of their funds, some £600. Was this part of a threat to her husband or, as was also suggested, merely the action of a supportive wife seeking to raise capital to fund his various business ventures? At Crippen's trial, the prosecuting counsel would highlight this as a motive for murder, though it appears a somewhat meagre reward for such drastic action.

> The Crippens took up residence at 39 Hilldrop Crescent in Camden Town, a property large enough for them not to be under each other's feet.

Clandestine affair

The care and expense Cora lavished on her own appearance did not extend to the rest of the household. She was happy to leave 39 Hilldrop Crescent a dirty, chaotic mess, but her housekeeping skills – or lack thereof – appeared not to ruffle her husband. When they took in paying guests to supplement their income, it was Crippen who took on most of the domestic chores. It needed more than slatternliness to drive Dr Crippen to murder; namely, the appearance on the scene of a lover.

There is evidence to suggest that Cora was unfaithful many times over, whereas Crippen had but a single grand passion. Ethel Le Neve was the latter's secretary at Munyon's, the two conducting a clandestine affair over several years. Matters came to a head in January 1910, when Ethel celebrated her 27th birthday. Having seen her sister marry at nineteen and produce two children, Ethel yearned to put the mistress's tag behind her and gain the respectability that would attend becoming the wife of respected medical practitioner and businessman Hawley Harvey Crippen. Who knows whether she brought any pressure to bear on the doctor, but what is clear is that they both willed the same end: that Cora Crippen should be an obstruction no longer.

There is a suggestion that Cora discovered the affair and demanded its termination, something Crippen could not

TOP: Miss Ethel Le Neve, Crippen's lover. Crippen claimed that Cora had returned to the United States and had died in California. Le Neve moved into Hilldrop Crescent and began openly wearing Cora's clothes and jewellery.

ABOVE: Mrs Cora Crippen, also known as variety actress Belle Elmore.

LEFT: Miss Smythson and Miss Fawkes, witnesses in the Crippen trial.

Meticulous planning

If Crippen considered taking the more natural option of pressing for a divorce, amicable or otherwise, he obviously soon discounted it. In mid-January he used his professional position to place an order for five grains of hyoscine hydrobromide, which in minute quantities – one-hundredth of a grain - could be used as a sedative. The quantity acquired by Crippen was enough to kill several times over. The fact that the drug was not recorded in any Munyon's ledger was a damning piece of evidence, as was the fact that he obtained it two weeks before Cora's death. This was to be no crime passionel, carried out in a fit of rage. Rather, it was the result of meticulous planning on the part of a man desperate to be rid of a slovenly, shrewish wife so that he could make an honest woman of his long-time mistress.

Murder in mind

On 31 January 1910 Crippen invited friends Paul and Clara Martinetti round to Hilldrop Crescent for dinner and a game of cards. He had murder in mind but wanted witnesses who would be able to attest to a convivial evening, should they be required to do so. Indeed, Paul Martinetti had felt unwell that day, yet Crippen made no offer to release him from the engagement, even though it was a cold winter night. It was around 1.30 am when the party broke up, but Crippen's work was only just beginning. After the hyoscine took its deadly effect on Cora, he dismembered her body, removing all means of identification. Or so he thought.

Many of the body parts, including the head and all the bones, were never found. The likelihood is that some were incinerated – neighbours recalled much waste-burning activity in the back garden – or else deposited in some watery depths. But unaccountably, Crippen chose to bury some tissue in the cellar, covering it in quicklime to hasten the decomposition process. His next task was to account for Cora's sudden disappearance, and that required putting pen to paper.

Crippen wrote to the Music Hall Ladies' Guild – of which Clara Martinetti was also a member – informing them that it might be some time before they saw their treasurer again. 'Please forgive me a hasty letter and any inconvenience I may cause you, but I have just had news of the illness of a near relative and at only a few hours' notice I am obliged to go to America.' It was signed Belle Ellmore, Cora's stage name. It soon emerged that Crippen was behind the letter, for he had misspelt his wife's theatrical moniker, which was written with a single L. He waved that away by saying that he had acted as scribe while Cora was preparing for her hasty departure. It was all very odd, though not unduly suspicious.

JULY 15, 1910

Absconding couple

Yesterday Scotland Yard made a new departure of a most interesting character in their method of crime investigation. The authorities for the first time in their history took the Press into their confidence and issued the following official statement relating to the crime and the steps which led to its discovery:-

Mrs. Cora Crippen, otherwise Belle Elmore, or Belle Mackamotski, an American lady and music-hall artiste, was married some years ago in New York to an American doctor named Hawley Harvey Crippen, alias Peter Crippen, alias Franckel, who for some years represented Munyon's remedies in London, was connected with the Drouet Institute, and has latterly carried on a dental business at Albion House, New Oxford-street, as the Yale Tooth Specialist. Mrs. Crippen was a very charming lady, and was very popular in the music-hall world, and was honorary secretary to the Music-hall Ladies' Guild. They have been in England for some years, and for the past four years they have resided, apparently very happily, at 39, Hilldrop Crescent, Camden Road.

TOP RIGHT: Crippen's house, where police found some remains of a human body buried under the brick floor of the basement. Traces of scopolamine, a calming drug, were also found. The corpse had to be identified from a piece of skin from its abdomen because the head, limbs and skeleton were never recovered. The body was that of Cora Crippen.

FAR LEFT: Witnesses Miss Lil Hawthorne and Mrs Stallon attend the trial.

ABOVE: Chief inspector Walter Dew. Crippen and his lover Ethel Le Neve fled to Brussels after police inquired into Cora's disappearance. Detectives had originally been satisfied with their story but their disappearance aroused suspicion and led to searches of the house on Hilldrop Crescent.

Many of the body parts, including the head and all the bones, were never found. The likelihood is that some were incinerated.

Series of lies

Crippen wasted little time before cashing in some of Cora's jewellery at a pawnbroker's, though first he picked out some pieces for his beloved Ethel. The unseemly speed with which Crippen and Ethel were seen about town, the latter attired in Cora's clothes as well as jewellery, raised eyebrows. Crippen even had the nerve to take her to a ball organised by the Music Hall Ladies' Guild less than three weeks after Cora's sudden departure. In doing so he flaunted his mistress in front of some of his wife's dearest friends. It was a month later, mid-March, that those friends became truly alarmed. Crippen reported that Cora had become dangerously ill with pneumonia, but he showed no inclination to listen to their entreaties and take the next available crossing. On 23 March, the stage publication *The Era* carried the news that Belle Elmore had succumbed to the infection. Crippen packed his bags now, though not for America; he took himself off to France with Ethel. The latter claimed to know nothing of Cora's death at this point, though bizarrely, she spoke of her engagement to Crippen back in January, and now wrote to her family saying that she was a married woman. No wedding took place, but she and Crippen regarded themselves as 'hubby' and 'wifey', as they affectionately called each other.

Cora's friends raise the alarm

Cora's friends, meanwhile, were reeling with the kind of shock that evidently was not afflicting Crippen. They wanted further details of the tragedy but found Crippen vague on the subject. First he said she had died at his son's house in Los Angeles, but a letter from Hawley Otto Crippen said that he was as much in the dark as anyone. All he knew was what his father had told him, namely, that Cora had died in San Francisco. Crippen claimed it was an error born of confusion. He was asked what boat Cora had taken. Crippen blustered. There was no record of Cora, or Belle, on any passenger list. This, along with the evidence of their own eyes watching Ethel Le Neve disporting herself around town with Crippen wearing Cora's finery, was enough to persuade the missing woman's friends to take their concerns to the police.

On 6 July 1910 Chief Inspector Walter Dew paid Crippen a visit, to be informed that Cora had left him, and that the story of the sick relative in America had been fabricated as a face-saving exercise. Ethel was there at the time, introduced to Dew as the housekeeper. Crippen invited the policeman to search the premises, even though he had no warrant to do so, and Dew appeared to be satisfied. The mild-mannered, co-operative physician might have appeared unflappable, but the visit obviously spooked him, for he and Ethel soon hatched their plan for a daring transatlantic escape. First they went to Antwerp, where they boarded the Canada-bound SS *Montrose*.

THE ARREST.

COLLAPSE OF MISS LE NEVE.

INSPECTOR DEW'S DISGUISE.

DRAMATIC SCENE.

CAPTAIN KENDALL'S FULL NARRATIVE.

Dr. H. H. Crippen and Miss Ethel Le Neve were arrested in the Montrose at 9.30 yesterday morning (2.30 p.m. Greenwich time). They were described in the police notice as, "Wanted for murder and mutilation."

Scotland Yard at 4.5 p.m. received the following message from Inspector Dew, who had formally identified them:—

Crippen and Le Neve arrested. Will wire later.—Dew.

This wireless pursuit of Crippen is due alone to the acumen, astuteness, and ability of Captain Kendall, of the Montrose, whose exclusive messages to the "Daily Mail" have been a triumph of detective journalism.

Inspector Dew and the Canadian police were disguised as pilots when they boarded the vessel. Crippen betrayed anxiety as the boat approached, but was taken quite unawares when the police accosted him. Miss Le Neve almost collapsed.

Both were subjected to a lengthy examination by Mr. Dew, and it is understood that Crippen admitted his identity, and said that he was glad that the suspense was over. Several diamond rings were found in his possession.

He is charged with the murder and mutilation of his second wife, Mrs. Cora Crippen, known as Belle Elmore on the music-hall stage. The circumstances of the case are fully told on the next page. The Montrose carried him and the police on to Quebec yesterday. According to cablegrams, he will be sent back immediately.

BELOW: Inspector Dew and C. Denis, disguised as pilots, in a boat. The detectives boarded the SS *Montrose* as it entered the St Lawrence River. At the time Canada was a British dominion and so Inspector Dew was able to act without limitation.

Grisly Secret

Meanwhile, police had discovered that Crippen and his accomplice had flown and were swarming over 39 Hilldrop Crescent. The cellar's shallow grave soon gave up its grisly secret. While forensics experts got to work on the remains, Dew was in hot pursuit of the fleeing couple. Their descriptions had been widely circulated, and Crippen must have thought himself clever to have Ethel decked out in boy's clothes so that they might travel as father and child. The disguise didn't fool the *Montrose*'s captain Henry Kendall for long. There was something not quite right about the 'child's' demeanour or his attitude towards the adult accompanying him. He tested his suspicions by calling out to Crippen by his assumed name, Robinson, and saw that he had to be prompted by his 'son' to respond. Kendall's vessel was fitted with radio communication, then a fledgling technology, and he sent a message to London expressing the belief that the Mr and Master Robinson on his passenger list were in fact Crippen and Le Neve. He had more than half an eye on the £250 reward on offer for information leading to the capture of the two absconders.

Police and press give chase

The police had already learned that Crippen had sent dental technician William Long to purchase a suit of boy's clothes, so the communication from the *Montrose* represented another piece of the jigsaw slotting into place. Dew gave chase aboard a faster ship, the *Laurentic*, which overhauled the *Montrose* a day before the latter docked. A large press pack was in attendance, for the paths of the two vessels had been plotted in the newspapers, which gave acres of space to the gruesome Camden Town murder. Dew wrong-footed the reporters by boarding the *Montrose* via a tugboat on 31 July, and when he bade Crippen good morning by his real name, there was no attempt at dissembling. 'I am more than satisfied,' said Crippen, when asked for an assurance that he wouldn't jump overboard, 'the anxiety has been too awful.' His immediate concern was to protect Ethel, saying she was a complete innocent, and the latter professed to be shocked when told what had been unearthed in the cellar of 39 Hilldrop Crescent.

LEFT: Dr Crippen returns to England to face trial at the Old Bailey. He was found guilty after just 27 minutes of deliberation.

LEFT: Mr Arthur Newton preparing the evidence at his office. During the trial there was a forensic evidence battle over the remains that were found in Crippen's home.

BELOW: Superintendent Frost attending court.

BOTTOM: Witnesses gather at the courtroom. Initially Crippen had told his wife's friends that she had died at his son's house in Los Angeles, but a letter from Hawley Otto Crippen said that he was as much in the dark as anyone. All he knew was that his father had told him that Cora had died in San Francisco.

Experts battle over forensic evidence

Crippen was charged with murder, Ethel with being an accessory after the fact. It was against the husband that the prosecution trained their weapons; they were much less concerned about what Ethel knew and when. The defence counsel contended that there was doubt over the sex of the cellar tissue, let alone that it was the remains of Cora Crippen. One particular piece of skin became the main battleground for rival experts. Eminent pathologists Augustus Pepper and Bernard Spilsbury said it came from the abdomen, and bore a scar of the kind that Cora would have been left with following an ovariectomy some fifteen years earlier. The defence tried to suggest that it was thigh tissue, and a fold in the skin rather than a scar, but Pepper and Spilsbury were imperious in their pronouncements and the experts lined up to oppose them crumbled.

Prosecution toxicologists also won the day, countering the defence's argument that the poison might have been the result of the putrefaction process. They convinced the jury that the deadly hyoscine had to have been ingested by the victim. Crippen had made a vital error in using quicklime to destroy the body, for it acted as a preservative for the hyoscine; without it, the toxicologists would have been unable to pinpoint the cause of death.

The defence tried another tack. Perhaps the remains had been there several years, pre-dating the Crippens' arrival in Hilldrop Crescent? Again the prosecution experts spiked the defence's guns: the remains had been there eight months at most.

The scientific evidence aside, much weight was attached to Cora's supposed decision to leave Crippen for good without taking all her furs, clothes and jewellery, something barely conceivable to members of her class. Crippen's lawyer was left to focus on his client's good character, and the preposterousness of the suggestion that he should have turned into 'a fiend incarnate' on the night of 31 January. The jury believed exactly that, returning a unanimous guilty verdict in barely half an hour.

A week later, Ethel pleaded Not Guilty at her trial, which lasted less than a day and ended in an acquittal. Having nailed Crippen, the prosecution seemed to have no appetite for the battle to prove Ethel's complicity.

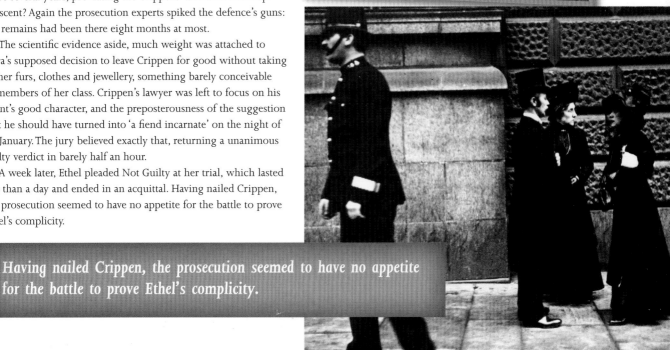

Having nailed Crippen, the prosecution seemed to have no appetite for the battle to prove Ethel's complicity.

Her suit is anything but a good fit. Her trousers are very tight about the hips and are split a bit down the back and secured with large safety pins.

JULY 30, 1910

Captain's telegram: life of the couple on the Montrose'

The man on board the Montrose supposed to be Crippen answers all the descriptions given in the police report, as does also his companion that of Miss Le Neve. I discovered them two hours after leaving Antwerp, but did not telegraph to my owners until I had found out good clues. I conversed with both, and at the same time took keen observations of all points, and felt quite confident as to their identity.

They booked their passage in Brussels as Mr. John Robinson and Master Robinson, and came on board at Antwerp in brown suits, soft grey hats, and white canvas shoes. They had no baggage except a small handbag bought on the Continent. My suspicion was aroused by seeing them on the deck beside a boat. Le Neve squeezed Crippen's hand. It seemed to me unnatural for two males, so I suspected them at once.

Suspicious circumstances

I was well posted as to the crime, so got on the scent at once. I said nothing to the officers till the following morning, when I took my chief officer into my confidence. During lunch I examined both their hats. Crippen's was stamped "Jackson, Boulevard du Nord." Le Neve's hat bore no name, but it was packed around the rim with paper to make it fit. Le Neve has the manner and appearance of a very refined, modest girl. She does not speak much, but always wears a pleasant smile. She seems thoroughly under his thumb, and he will not leave her for a moment. Her suit is anything but a good

fit. Her trousers are very tight about the hips and are split a bit down the back and secured with large safety pins.

Revolver in hip pocket

They have been under strict observation all the voyage, as, if they smelt a rat, he might do something rash. I have noticed a revolver in his hip pocket. He sits about on the deck reading or pretending to read, and both seem to be thoroughly enjoying all their meals. They have not been seasick, and I have discussed various parts of the world with him. He knows Toronto, Detroit, and California well, and says he is going to take his boy to California for his health, meaning Miss Le Neve.

Crippen says that when the ship arrives he will go to Detroit by boat if possible, as he prefers it. The book he has been most interested in has been "Pickwick Papers," and he is now busy reading "Four Just Men," which is all about a murder in London and a £1,000 reward.

When my suspicions were aroused as to Crippen's identity I quietly collected all the English papers on board the ship which mentioned anything of the murder, and I warned the chief officer to collect any he might see.

Captain Kendall's ruse

This being done, I considered the way was clear. I told Crippen a story to make him laugh heartily to see if he would open his mouth wide enough for me to ascertain if he had false teeth. This ruse was successful. All the "boy's" manners at the table when I was watching him were most ladylike, han-

dling knife and fork and taking fruit off dishes with two fingers. Crippen kept cracking nuts for her and giving her half his salad, and was always paying most marked attention.

Watching the wireless

He would often sit on deck and look up aloft at the wireless "aerial," and listen to the cracking electric spark messages being sent by the Marconi operator. He said "what a wonderful invention it was." He said one day that according to our present rate of steaming he ought to be in Detroit on Tuesday, August 2. At times both would sit and appear to be in deep thought.

Though Le Neve does not show signs of distress and is perhaps ignorant of the crime committed, she appears to be a girl with a very weak will. She has to follow him everywhere. If he looks at her she gives him an endearing smile, as though she were under his hypnotic influence.

Crippen was very restless on sighting Belle Isle, and asked where we stopped for the pilot, how he came off, how far from the pilot-station to Quebec, and said he would be glad when we arrived. He was anxious to get to Detroit.

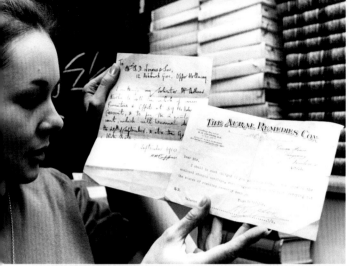

Condemned to death

Hawley Harvey Crippen was hanged at Pentonville Prison on 23 November 1910. In one of his last letters, Crippen gave Ethel his blessing to marry, and she did so in 1915, when she was going by the name of Harvey. For forty-five years, until his death in 1960, Stanley Smith remained unaware that his wife was none other than Ethel Le Neve, mistress of Dr Crippen. Ethel died seven years later, aged 84. Some believe she was an inveterate liar who profited from Crippen's selfless insistence that she was innocent of all wrongdoing, and that the prosecution could have made a much stronger case against her. But a century on, it seems that the precise role Ethel Le Neve played in the events at 39 Hilldrop Crescent on the night of 31 January 1910 will never be known.

Crippen's fate

The jury were out of the box considering their verdict half an hour. It was a quarter-past two when the Lord Chief Justice concluded his powerful and lucid analysis of the grim facts of the trial. The jury took away with them to their deliberations the pyjama trousers belonging to the prisoner, and the pyjama jacket of corresponding pattern and material found among the buried remains of what had been Belle Elmore. At a quarter to three they came back.

The game was up

In the tones in which the twelve answered to the roll call of their names there was the note of consciousness of stern duty done. "Have you agreed upon your verdict?" asked the clerk. "We have," the foreman said. The Lord Chief Justice, in his scarlet and ermine robes, had returned to the Bench, but the prisoner was still in the cells to which when the jury retired he had descended. There was a pause of a moment or two until he re-appeared.

"Guilty"

"Have you agreed upon your verdict?" the Clerk of Arraigns asked again. "We have," the foreman said. A silence of death fell, in which the question was put: "Do you find the prisoner guilty or not guilty?" With emphasis the foreman's answer came: "We find the prisoner guilty of wilful murder."

The little man's intertwined fingers tightened in the effort to preserve his self-command. A pallor spread over his forehead and cheeks. The bald patch at the back of his little, flat head became a dull white. His ears, placed so low that they seem to belong to the neck instead of the head, became transparent as the blood receded. The face showed no expression of emotion, but its look of concentrated attention and purpose ceased now that purpose and effort were no more of value.

Protests of innocence

The question whether he had anything to say why sentence should not be passed upon him received no answer. He stood looking at nothing, his mind blankly revolving. The clerk put the question again. Then, recalling his self-control by a supreme effort, he answered in a perfectly firm, even voice, "Only that I still protest my innocence."

The judge fitted the black cap upon his head and spoke the words of doom; to be hanged by the neck; and the body to be buried within the precincts of the prison, just as Belle Elmore's body had been buried in the house where he had killed her.

He stood motionless, with his clasped hands resting on the ledge of the dock, his head bowed a little and his hairless brows knitted. But no thought came to him to bring back purpose and intelligence to the colourless features till one of the warders touched him on the shoulder. He looked up and realised his position. He could do no more.

Execution of Crippen

Dr. Hawley Harvey Crippen was executed in Pentonville Prison at nine o'clock yesterday morning.

The execution was expeditiously carried out, the time which elapsed from the entrance of Ellis, the executioner, into the condemned cell for the process of pinioning until the complete fulfilment of the sentence being exactly sixty seconds. Crippen had passed a restless night, and he left untouched the frugal breakfast which had been provided for him. He paid the greatest attention to the ministrations of the Rev. Thomas Carey, the rector of the Roman Catholic Church in Eden-grove, Holloway, who was with him from shortly after six o'clock, and went to the scaffold calmly and resignedly, fortified by the last rites of his faith.

No knowledge of any confession

It was officially stated yesterday that the Home Office has no knowledge of any confession having been made by Crippen. The only persons, in addition to the prison authorities, to visit Crippen since his incarceration in Pentonville Prison have been Miss Le Neve, Mr. Arthur Newton (his solicitor), and three Roman Catholic priests connected with the Church of the Sacred Heart, Eden Grove, Holloway.

OPPOSITE TOP LEFT, TOP LEFT & RIGHT: In recent years letters written by Crippen have been sold at auction. These include letters written in his cell whilst he was awaiting trial, a letter to a doctor that was sent shortly after Crippen had murdered his wife and correspondence with Lady Somerset.

OPPOSITE PAGE LEFT: Superintendent Frost and Mr Williamson from the Treasury discuss the case.

OPPOSITE PAGE RIGHT: Inspector Dew gives evidence at Crippen's trial. Dew led the operation that captured Crippen aboard the SS *Montrose*.

OPPOSITE PAGE TOP RIGHT: Dr Marshall attending the inquest to give forensic evidence.

PETER SUTCLIFFE:
'The Yorkshire Ripper'

In the early hours of 5 July 1975, 34-year-old Anna Rogulsky was brutally attacked with a hammer and knife in Keighley, fortunate indeed to survive what was a frenzied onslaught. Three months later, Wilma McCann wasn't so lucky. The 28-year-old mother of four worked the red-light district of Chapeltown, a Leeds suburb. She suffered major trauma to the head and multiple stab wounds, her body dumped on a playing field just 100 yards from her home. It was 30 October 1975; the Yorkshire Ripper's killing spree was under way.

The wave of attacks led to the biggest manhunt in British history, but it would be five years before the killer was brought to justice. In that time, 13 women were butchered, and there were seven more attempted murders. At least, that was the official tally; the actual figures were undoubtedly higher. The mutilation of the victims' bodies inevitably brought forth comparisons with the infamous Whitechapel murders of 1888. The hunt for the Yorkshire Ripper was on.

The man they were looking for was Peter William Sutcliffe. And they found him long before he had claimed his thirteenth victim. Sutcliffe was interviewed on nine separate occasions during the course of the inquiry, but slipped through the net each time. He enjoyed some huge slices of good fortune, and was also helped by an administrative load that swamped the investigating team. Over the five-year period, 250,000 people were interviewed, 30,000 statements taken, 5 million car registrations checked. With computer technology in its infancy, the police database consisted of an unwieldy card index system and shoeboxes filled with documents. It didn't take much for an individual name to be buried in the paper chase, and Peter Sutcliffe profited from the bureaucratic quagmire.

TOP: Peter Sutcliffe at Dewsbury Court where he was accused of murdering 13 women.

ABOVE: Peter Sutcliffe left school at the age of 15 and took on a series of menial jobs. During one spell as a grave digger, he claimed God had spoken to him.

OPPOSITE TOP RIGHT: The house at 90 Kirkgate, Shipley, Yorkshire, where Peter Sutcliffe was born.

OPPOSITE LEFT TOP: Sutcliffe obtained an HGV licence in June 1975.

OPPOSITE LEFT MIDDLE: The sex shop in Bradford where Sutcliffe had an accommodation address. As a young man he frequented prostitutes and it was with them that he began his killing spree.

OPPOSITE LEFT BOTTOM: The Crown Bar in Holytown, Scotland, where Sutcliffe drank.

A target for bullies

Sutcliffe was born in Bingley on 2 June 1946, the eldest of John and Kathleen Sutcliffe's six children. An introverted and sensitive child, he preferred reading and clinging to his beloved mother's skirts to indulging in roughhouse games. At school he was something of a loner, neither joining in with the usual boys' pursuits nor chasing the girls. He was a target for the bullies, which led to bouts of truancy. It was hardly surprising that he left school at 15 with fewer qualifications than his studiousness merited.

Incidents in Sutcliffe's late teens showed that he wasn't just a shy misfit or late developer, but someone with the potential for darker deeds. He struggled to adjust to the world of work, his desultory jobs including a stint as a gravedigger. His workmates recalled his ghoulish penchant for taking trophies from the corpses; and there was also talk of necrophilia. Sutcliffe had his first brushes with the law during this period. There was a string of motoring offences, and he was convicted of attempted theft from a parked vehicle. A foreshadowing of what was to come occurred in 1969, when he was questioned by a policeman after his car was spotted in a red-light area of Bradford. He had a hammer in his possession but it was construed only as an implement that might have been used in the furtherance of robbery. He escaped with a £25 fine.

Police record

Peter Sutcliffe's mugshot, showing a man with dark curly hair, moustache and beard, was now in the system. The word 'hammer' also appeared on the same file under the 'method' heading, though connected with theft, not assault. Over the next six years, there were a number of unsolved attacks on women in the Yorkshire region, several of the victims describing a man whose face was already in the police records. Unfortunately, no one made a connection between the assaults, or spotted that the descriptions matched that of the man convicted of being in possession of an offensive weapon in 1969. It meant that by the mid-1970s Peter Sutcliffe had only a minor record of petty criminality.

Police visit

In the early seventies, Sutcliffe conducted a long, slow courtship with Sonia Szurma, the daughter of Czech immigrants. It almost foundered when Sonia began seeing someone else, and Sutcliffe sought solace in the arms of one of Bradford's prostitutes. He paid ten pounds but couldn't go through with the deal, only to find that her pimp did not deal in refunds. A few weeks later he showed his capacity for violence by clubbing a prostitute over the head with a brick, mistaking her for the woman he believed had cheated him. The victim noted down his licence number and it resulted in a police visit. As the woman decided not to press charges, Sutcliffe escaped with a caution. He would claim his hostility towards prostitutes dated from this period.

Peter and Sonia patched things up and finally tied the knot in 1974. Sonia had trained as a teacher but she was not the most stable companion, having suffered a mental breakdown during which she imagined seeing stigmata on her hands. The couple's prospects appeared much rosier when Sutcliffe gained his HGV licence and they moved into their dream house, a smart property in Garden Lane, in the Heaton district of Bradford. To the outside world Sutcliffe was a hard worker and devoted husband. In fact, he was leading a double life, cruising the local red-light zones, often in the company of long-time friend Trevor Birdsall. On one such occasion, in August 1975, Sutcliffe disappeared for 20 minutes during a night out in Halifax. The next day Birdsall learned of a vicious attack on 46-year-old cleaner Olive Smelt. Sutcliffe had already bragged of one assault and Birdsall harboured grave suspicions regarding this incident. He didn't act on them, but became increasingly troubled by Sutcliffe's fixation regarding prostitutes. Years later, in November 1980, Birdsall would finally take his concerns to the police, but by the time that information was processed Sutcliffe was in custody. And 13 women had been brutally murdered.

PETER SUTCLIFFE:
'The Yorkshire Ripper'

Murder cases linked

Although there were strong similarities regarding the attacks on Anna Rogulsky and Olive Smelt in the summer of 1975, not least the head injuries consistent with hammer blows, many months passed before these were linked, either to each other or to the Ripper inquiry. As far as the police were concerned, Wilma McCann was the first victim. Following her death in October 1975, the police were wrestling with the possibility that there might be no link between the murderer and the victim. An anonymous sexual encounter that had taken a violent turn made their task much more difficult, though there were clues. Wilma had gone clubbing, and was seen trying to hitch a lift home in the early hours of the morning. There were reports of her drunkenly trying to wave down a vehicle to get a lift home, and one mentioned seeing her get into a brightly-coloured fastback car driven by a man with a drooping moustache. At the time Peter Sutcliffe owned a lime-green Ford Capri.

Three months later, in January 1976, 42-year-old Emily Jackson was killed with the same modus operandi: two severe blows to the head and this time over 50 stab wounds. The cruciform shape of the latter injuries suggested that the most likely weapon was a Phillips screwdriver. The killer left the impression of a size-seven bootprint on the victim's thigh, and another in the ground nearby, but it was too common a type to be regarded as a major lead. It transpired that Jackson's husband, Sydney, had driven her to a pub in Chapeltown, leaving her to get on with 'business' while he had a drink. They had arranged to meet later to travel home together, an appointment Emily never kept. There were clear links between the McCann and Jackson cases, and police began issuing warnings for street workers to be on their guard. 'Ripper' headlines began appearing in the press, though it would be a while longer before the term 'Yorkshire Ripper' was coined.

JUNE 27, 1977

Jayne, 16, may be Ripper's victim No.5

A girl of 16 found battered to death yesterday may be the fifth victim of a woman-hating killer. The girl, Jayne McDonald, came from the same road, Scott Hall Avenue, Leeds, as the first victim 20 months ago. Children found Jayne's body in an adventure playground next to the Chapeltown Community Centre in the heart of Leeds's bedsitter land. Three prostitutes have been murdered in the same area over the past 20 months. A fourth victim in Bradford may also have been killed by the same man. All were battered, stabbed and butchered by a brutal killer police have dubbed the 'Ripper of Leeds.'

But police think that Jayne, a supermarket assistant, became a victim by accident. West Yorkshire's assistant Chief Constable, Mr George Oldfield, said: 'Obviously it is too early to speculate but the possibility of a link is very much in my mind.

Terrified

If she is another victim of the same killer then she was probably picked on at random.' Jayne and the first victim, 24-year-old prostitute Wilma McCann, lived only a few doors apart. Neighbour Mrs Violet Webster said: 'We just cannot believe this terrible thing can have happened twice to the avenue. And we cannot help feeling that the killer may live in the area. Women and people with young daughters are terrified by what has happened. Jayne was a very pretty and well brought up, respectable girl. We just pray that the killer is caught before it happens again.'

> 'We just cannot believe this terrible thing can have happened twice to the Avenue. And we cannot help feeling that the killer may live in the area.'

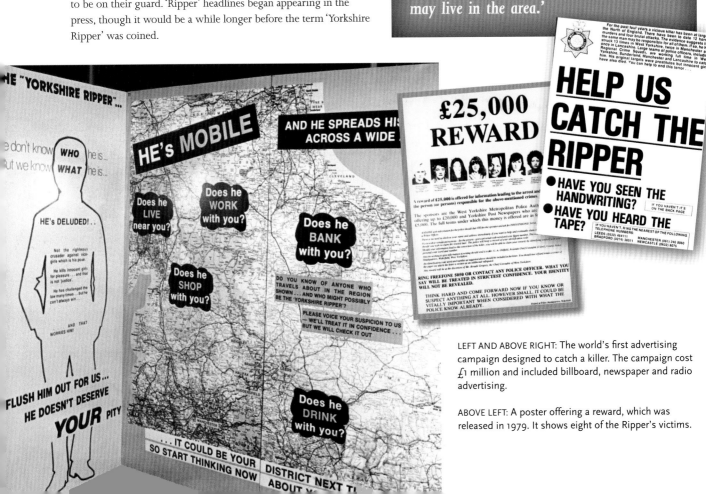

LEFT AND ABOVE RIGHT: The world's first advertising campaign designed to catch a killer. The campaign cost £1 million and included billboard, newspaper and radio advertising.

ABOVE LEFT: A poster offering a reward, which was released in 1979. It shows eight of the Ripper's victims.

Pressure on the police

In February 1977 the body of Irene Richardson was found in Roundhay Park, Leeds, by day a popular swathe of amenity land, by night a popular place for prostitutes to service their clients. Tyre tracks found close to the body were believed to be of the killer's car, potentially a significant breakthrough. A tread pattern was not quite a fingerprint, but the odds of finding a repeat pattern were over 100 million to one against. But first they had to trace the vehicle. The tyres could have come from any one of fifty models, and that left police with 50,000 vehicles to check in the West Yorkshire area. One of those was a Ford Corsair, the car Peter Sutcliffe was now driving. Of course, the suspect car could have had its tyres changed, or been sold or scrapped, but the police began the painstaking elimination process.

Two months after Irene Richardson was killed, the Ripper struck outside Leeds for the first time. The body of Patricia Atkinson was found lying on the bed of her Bradford flat. There was another bootprint, this time on the crumpled bedding, making it more difficult to analyse, but it could have come from a size seven Wellington similar to those found at the scene of Emily Jackson's murder.

The fifth victim was 16-year-old shoe shop worker Jayne MacDonald, whose body was found on a patch of waste ground next to a children's play park in Chapeltown. Distastefully, she was described in some parts of the media as the first 'innocent' victim. Jayne was walking home through a red-light district and it seems Sutcliffe mistook her for a streetwalker. The pressure on West Yorkshire Police to apprehend the killer was ratcheted up another notch, prompting Assistant Chief Constable George Oldfield to take over the running of the inquiry.

Oldfield's problem was the same as that which faced his predecessor, namely, the random nature of the attacks and the lack of connection between perpetrator and victim. And the hunting ground widened in October 1977 when the Ripper crossed the Pennines to claim his sixth victim.

> Tyre tracks found close to the body were believed to be of the killer's car, potentially a significant breakthrough.

Photofits of the Yorkshire Ripper (top: made after Josephine Whitaker was murdered in April 1979. Left: made from a description by Tracey Browne. Above: issued after the attack on Marilyn Moore in December 1977).

BELOW: Sutcliffe's house in Garden Lane, Bradford. He and his Czech-born wife, Sonia, moved there when she qualified as a teacher in 1977.

Fear

The refusal of police to give details of the injuries suffered by the Ripper's victims served to increase the fear among women and led to grotesque speculation. After the rumours, forensic evidence was revealed which suggested the type of weapons the Ripper used – a hammer and a screwdriver. His attacks, according to one detective, came with a blow on the back of the head with the hammer.

In cities, towns and villages throughout the North of England mothers have lectured their daughters, boys have been sure to escort their girlfriends to the doorsteps and women who had to work at night reduced their fear and their earnings by making their journeys in taxis.

Fear also grew into resentment. After the 13th killing, of Jacqueline Hill, in November, feminist groups stormed cinemas in Leeds and Bradford showing films which glamorised violence against women. On college campuses women began to arm themselves against attack with knives, hatpins, scissors and butane gas whistles. Queues of women, from pensioners to teenagers, formed in shops in the Ripper's territory to buy high-pitched pocket alarms.

All the time, the police hunt went on. It cost £4 million, involved 1,000 officers. Now an arrest has been made ... by two uniformed bobbies making routine checks on cars.

The net tightens

Twenty-year-old prostitute Jean Jordan worked the Moss Side area of Manchester and perhaps felt she was safe from the maniac on the loose in the neighbouring county. Or, like many streetwalkers who ignored police warnings, felt she had no choice but to carry on working and take the risk. Sutcliffe was disturbed as he tried to hide Jordan's body in some bushes and was forced to beat a hasty retreat. The body was found over a week later by a man trawling a patch of waste ground for bricks to use in a construction project. His name was Bruce Jones, who would go on to become a household name playing loutish, workshy Les Battersby in *Coronation Street*. The body he lighted upon was in such an horrific state that it could not have lain in the open undiscovered for such a long time. And it hadn't. Sutcliffe had returned to the scene of the crime and moved the body. Why? Because he was searching for the crisp new five-pound note he had paid up front for Jean's services. He feared it was traceable and wanted to retrieve it before the police did. The search proved fruitless, and the note was found in Jean's handbag some 50 yards from the body.

> The body was found over a week later by a man trawling a patch of waste ground for bricks to use in a construction project.

Investigations produced a short list of around 40 companies who might have used the note for payroll purposes. It included the engineering firm Sutcliffe worked for, T & WH Clark. That still meant around 7000 potential suspects but it represented a significant tightening of the net. Sutcliffe was interviewed twice in early November 1977. He said he had no five-pound notes left from his wages of the last week in September. Invited to account for his movements on 1 and 9 October, the days that the Ripper had killed Jean Jordan and returned to the body to search for the banknote, he said he was at home on both occasions, the second of them hosting a housewarming party. Sonia corroborated the story. The officers were satisfied and paid scant attention to the red Ford Corsair parked outside, a vehicle whose tyres would have been a match for those found at the scene of the Richardson murder.

With modern computer technology it would have been a simple task to cross-reference the 7,000 employees who might have received the five-pound note against the 50,000 car owners whose vehicle might have left its mark in Roundhay Park. Sutcliffe's name would have appeared in the results of such an exercise. As it was, the senior investigating officers were forced to concede that the £5 note would not lead them to the Ripper's door.

LEFT: A map showing Sutcliffe's trail of murder across Yorkshire and Lancashire.

TOP RIGHT: The police incident room in Leeds. The volume of paperwork generated by the investigation was immense, compromising the ability of the police to link relevant information.

RIGHT: Chief Constable Ronald Gregory and Detective Chief Superintendent Jim Hobson at the launch of the 'Flush Out the Ripper' campaign.

Sutcliffe's new hunting ground

Just before Christmas there was another breakthrough, an attack in which the victim survived to give a good description of her assailant – a man with dark curly hair, drooping moustache and beard. Dozens of similar descriptions were on file relating to attacks dating back over several years, but because they were not deemed part of the Ripper inquiry – in one case because a different size hammer had been used – the pattern was missed. Not until after Sutcliffe was in jail and the investigation was being reviewed were all these photofit images assembled as a collection. Taken as a group they screamed Peter Sutcliffe, and this oversight would be one of the key points in a damning inquiry into the handling of the case.

In January 1978 the Ripper chose a new hunting ground, Huddersfield. He killed 18-year-old Helen Rytka, who had gone onto the streets with her sister Rita. They got separated and Rita never saw Helen again. Her body was found in a lumber yard where prostitutes habitually took their clients. In May of that year Manchester-based prostitute Vera Millward met her end. Police found tyre tracks that matched those found at the scene of the Richardson murder. Vehicle experts from the Manchester force whittled the list of suspect cars down to just two - Ford Corsair and Ford Cortina Mark 1 – but the hierarchy in that constabulary had by then lost faith in that avenue as a route to finding the killer. Back in West Yorkshire the team persisted with the tyre line of inquiry, but were unaware of their colleagues' findings. By the time Sutcliffe was interviewed as part of the tyre track investigation, he had got rid of the Corsair, and the new owner had changed the tyres.

Police believed the Ripper went to ground after killing Vera Millward, though there were several non-fatal attacks on women in 1978 which were not laid at the Ripper's door. The victims gave the now-familiar description: dark curly hair, drooping moustache and goatee beard. One mentioned a Sunbeam Rapier, the model Sutcliffe had acquired after getting rid of the Corsair. These attacks were not deemed part of the Ripper inquiry.

OCTOBER 4, 1979

Ripper alert as girl dies

The Yorkshire Ripper is feared to have killed his twelfth victim. The blood-covered body of a girl in her early twenties was found yesterday afternoon near a red light district of Bradford. The body of his latest victim, bearing mutilations similar to those which are the killer's trademarks, was found among a dilapidated row of terraced houses at Ash Grove, near the Manningham red light district.

Exhausted

The houses are in a back lane which runs almost to the entrance of Bradford University. The grim discovery was made in the garden of No. 13 by a patrolling policeman. Detectives believe that the girl, as yet unidentified, had lain there since the weekend. The house is unoccupied.

Last night the entire area was sealed off as 100 officers made house-to-house inquiries. A post-mortem was carried out by Home Office pathologist Professor David Gee, the man who has examined all the Ripper's victims. The body was found less than a mile from where two of the Ripper's victims were found.

The man leading the hunt for the Ripper, West Yorkshire's Assistant Chief Constable, Mr George Oldfield, is at present on the sick list after exhausting himself in the search for the psychopath. One of the first officers called to the scene of the new inquiry was Chief Superintendent Jack Ridgway, who is heading the investigation into two Ripper murders in Manchester.

The Ripper last struck five months ago. The majority of his victims had been prostitutes but then he killed 19-year-old building society secretary Josephine Whitaker as she returned home after visiting her grandparents in Halifax.

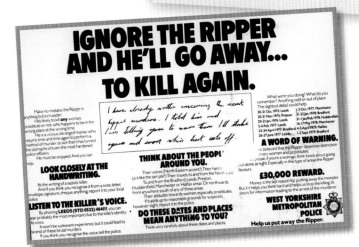

> The victims gave the now-familiar description: dark curly hair, drooping moustache and goatee beard.

TOP RIGHT, LEFT AND OPPOSITE MIDDLE: Desperate to catch the killer, the police launched a massive advertising campaign.

Police on a wild goose chase

1978 provided a major turning point in the investigation, one that saw police veer off in the wrong direction. They were taken in by a number of letters and a cassette tape recording, purporting to be from the Ripper himself. The first letter, dated March 1978, affirmed the writer's desire to rid the streets of prostitutes, and taunted police over their inability to catch him. 'Warn whores to keep off streets cause I feel it coming on again', it ran, though there was remorse over the death of the 'young lassie' Jayne MacDonald, which had been a mistake. It was signed 'Jack the Ripper'. There was a Sunderland postmark, which the writer told them to ignore, but ACC Oldfield and his senior officers came round to the view that that was a double bluff. The focus of the inquiry turned to Sunderland and the search for 'Wearside Jack', as he was dubbed.

This turn of events was disastrous for the inquiry but a boon for Sutcliffe. Had the many assaults on file deemed unconnected with the Ripper investigation been taken into account, they would have suggested that the attacker was a local, not from the north east. The fact that the police believed 'Wearside Jack' was the man they were after had a particular effect on Trevor Birdsall, who put off reporting his suspicions regarding his friend Peter Sutcliffe.

Even as George Oldfield played the tape at a press conference, convinced that the voice and handwriting would lead to an early arrest, there were a few dissenting voices on the investigating team. 'Wearside Jack' had used a lot of phraseology from the original Ripper's correspondence to the police in 1888, and some felt there had to be a possibility that it was an elaborate hoax, taking media reports and feeding them back in the style of the 19th-century serial murderer. The writer had said nothing that could not have been gleaned from the blanket reportage. On the contrary, he gave a clear indication that his only source of information was media accounts, but it took a neat piece of detective work to spot the inconsistency that suggested the road to Sunderland was a wild goose chase.

No Wearside accent

It was down to simple mathematics. In January 1978, the same month that Helen Rytka was killed, the Yorkshire Ripper also picked up 21-year-old Yvonne Pearson from Bradford's red-light

> The search for 'Wearside Jack' was disastrous for the inquiry but a boon for Sutcliffe.

district. Her body lay undiscovered on a patch of waste ground for around eight weeks, and it was this time lag that was key. 'Wearside Jack's' first letter was written after Yvonne Pearson was killed but before the body was discovered. His body count should have included Pearson but it didn't, suggesting he was merely rehashing details already in the public domain. That was confirmed when a subsequent letter, written after Pearson's murder had been reported, now included her in the tally. Failure to spot the anomaly sooner gave Sutcliffe valuable breathing space.

The amount of time and resources devoted to the Northumbria connection made it difficult for the senior investigating team to backtrack; it would have necessitated admitting that many thousands of man hours had been wasted in an inquiry whose costs had already reached astronomical proportions. That blinkered view helped Sutcliffe in the next round of police interviews. His Sunbeam Rapier was logged for making multiple appearances in red-light areas that were under surveillance. Again he successfully fobbed them off, helped by Sonia, who corroborated his every word. Interviewing officers were told to adopt a softly-softly approach in questioning men about repeat visits to red-light districts; they weren't interested in exposing peccadilloes or rocking marital boats. Thus, when Sutcliffe claimed he had travelled through such areas during the course of his work, it was readily accepted. There were no checks to ascertain whether Sutcliffe could have been on legitimate business at the times he was spotted – checks that would have exposed his story as a lie – but thousands of follow-up interviews would have further burdened an inquiry that was already creaking under its own weight. The officers' suspicions weren't totally allayed, but Sutcliffe patently did not have a Wearside accent, which at the time trumped all incriminating evidence relating to tyre tread patterns, five-pound notes and even photofit descriptions.

JANUARY 5, 1981

Ripper - a man is held

Detectives were last night questioning a man in connection with the Yorkshire Ripper murders which have claimed 13 women victims in five years. He will appear in court today on what the police say will be 'a very serious charge.'

In a dramatic statement, West Yorkshire's Chief Constable Ronald Gregory, beaming and linking arms with his senior officers involved in the Ripper hunt, said: 'We are all absolutely delighted, totally delighted with the developments at this stage.'

The man was arrested in the red light district of Sheffield on Friday night as he sat with a woman in a car parked in a dimly-lit alley. Two uniformed policemen, 47-year-old sergeant Robert Ring and probationer PC Robert Hydes, 31, were on vice patrol making routine checks on vehicles in the area. They radioed the registration number of the Rover V8 car to the national police computer. Back came the reply: The number plates had been stolen.

Hoax revealed

Officially, the Ripper resurfaced in Halifax on 4 April 1979, killing 19-year-old building society employee Josephine Whittaker, who was accosted while walking home from a visit to her grandparents. Size seven bootprints were found near the body, and there were also bite marks on the body, made by someone with an eighth-of-an-inch gap between the front teeth. Peter Sutcliffe had such a dental profile.

Barbara Leach, a 20-year-old student at Bradford University, was murdered on 2 September 1979, the 11th Ripper victim. Shortly afterwards, police took a telephone call from Wearside Jack admitting the hoax, and they finally switched their focus back to the hub of the killing ground. An elaborate re-enactment of banking business for the period prior to Jean Jordan's death was staged, in an effort to narrow the field of possible recipients of the five-pound note. That exercise produced a list of 250 people, employees of a dozen firms in the Shipley area. Among those was T & WH Clark. Sutcliffe was interviewed on three more occasions, with no conclusive outcome. He couldn't be ruled out, but there was nothing concrete to tie him to the murders.

Sutcliffe lay low until August 1980, when the body of 47-year-old civil servant Marguerite Walls was found dumped in the grounds of a mansion in Pudsey. She had been garrotted, a change of modus operandi that gave police cause to doubt whether it was the work of the Ripper. The murder of 19-year-old Jacqueline Hill in November saw a return to the normal method of bludgeoning with a hammer and ripping with a knife. The body of the Leeds University student was found close to her hall of residence.

MAY 6, 1981

mission to kill

Yorkshire Ripper Peter Sutcliffe believed he had a mission from God to kill prostitutes, the Old Bailey was told yesterday. And his mission was only partially fulfilled, he told a Home Office psychiatrist.

Before one murder 'there was a voice inside my head saying: Kill, kill, kill. The inner torment was unimaginable.' But long before telling doctors this, a prison warder overheard a conversation between 34-year-old Sutcliffe and his teacher wife Sonia, said Attorney-General Sir Michael Havers, opening the Ripper murder trial. He said he expected to get 30 years in prison but that if he could make people believe he was mad, he would only do ten years in a loony bin.

> *Sutcliffe knew he was in trouble. He managed to get rid of a hammer and knife before he was taken in for questioning.*

Routine police work corners Sutcliffe

It was now that Trevor Birdsall finally took his suspicions concerning Peter Sutcliffe to the police. Before they could be acted upon, the whole case was blown wide open, not by incisive analysis on the part of top detectives but by routine policework from two diligent foot soldiers.

On 2 Jan 1981 Sergeant Robert Ring and PC Robert Hydes were out on patrol in Sheffield when they approached a parked car. They wanted to question the driver and the woman who had climbed into vehicle beside him. The man identified himself as John Williams, but couldn't name his passenger, confirming their suspicions that they had a kerb crawler on their hands. A call to the station revealed that they might have stumbled upon a more serious misdemeanour, for the car had false number plates.

Peter Sutcliffe knew he was in trouble. Under the pretext of wanting to relieve himself, he managed to get rid of a hammer and knife before he was taken in for questioning. There his identity was revealed, and it was found that he had been interviewed a number of times in connection with the Ripper inquiry. At first he admitted only to attaching false plates to his car, and was cool enough to ditch a second knife in the cistern of the station toilet.

The officers were now beginning to think they had caught a much bigger fish. The suspect was whisked away to Dewsbury for questioning by a member of the Ripper team, then Sergeant Ring recalled the roadside comfort break and dashed back to the scene of the arrest. There he recovered the discarded tools of the Ripper's brutal trade. If there was any doubt over who had put them there, it was dispelled after a visit to the Sutcliffes' home. In the kitchen there was a knife block with one of the set missing. The blade that was in police hands fitted the space perfectly.

OPPOSITE TOP: The Ripper tape contained an arrogant but eerie message from the murderer. He said: 'I can't see myself being nicked just yet.'

OPPOSITE ABOVE: Letters sent from the Ripper to the police, including a poem entitled 'Clueless'.

RIGHT: Police at the front door of number 2 Alfred Street in Darlington. The house was brought to the attention of the police when a women looking for her lost child went into the empty terrace house and found an exercise book that contained newspaper cuttings about the Ripper's victims.

ABOVE: A crowd gathered at Dewsbury Court in 1981. Sutcliffe pleaded not guilty to 13 counts of murder but guilty to manslaughter and seven counts of attempted murder.

JANUARY 5, 1981
No Geordie accent

The officers moved in and the man was taken for questioning by detectives. Within hours, they decided to contact the special Ripper Squad Mr Gregory had set up at Leeds, 30 miles away. Detectives from the squad drove to Sheffield and took the man back to Leeds. Later he was moved to a new, top-security police station nearby at Dewsbury. Despite well-publicised police theories, the man has no Geordie accent - he is from Bradford. He is married and in his early thirties. His wife was interviewed by Ripper Squad detectives yesterday and was then taken to Dewsbury to see him.

The man, believed to be a lorry driver, lives in a detached, double-fronted house in the Bradford suburb of Heaton. Neighbours thought his wife was a part-time teacher and said she spoke several languages. One described them as 'an ordinary quiet couple. The woman was very fond of the garden.' The man was sometimes seen repairing cars outside.

Police spent the weekend examining the house and are believed to have taken away several objects in plastic bags. The Ripper's early victims were prostitutes and good-time girls who frequented pubs and clubs. But then, as those murdered came to include a shop assistant, a building society clerk and two university students, it became chillingly clear that no woman, in the Leeds-Bradford area of West Yorkshire especially, was safe from him.

> The jury found Peter Sutcliffe to be sane and answerable for his crimes, convicting him on 13 counts of murder.

Sutcliffe's confession

A confession soon followed, in which Sutcliffe detailed all his grisly deeds, describing himself as a 'beast'. His counsel sought to negotiate a manslaughter charge on the grounds of diminished responsibility, and Sutcliffe now spoke of hearing voices urging him to rid the world of prostitutes. The defence team was content with the plea bargain, but the judge, Mr Justice Boreham, was having none of it. He insisted that the case go to trial to determine whether Peter Sutcliffe was truly mad, or merely bad.

The pre-trial consensus gave way to the normal adversarial court proceedings. The prosecution, led by Attorney General Sir Michael Havers, argued that Sutcliffe simulated symptoms of mental disorder in order to avoid a murder conviction. In doing so he had fooled the psychiatrists who diagnosed that he was suffering from paranoid schizophrenia.

Defence counsel James Chadwin QC called Sutcliffe to give evidence, to allow the jury to hear what he had told doctors and decide for themselves on his state of mind. The court heard of a severe blow to the head, sustained in a teenage motorcycle accident; of the antipathy he bore towards prostitutes after an unsatisfactory run-in with a member of that profession in his youth; and of the divine call which prompted the killing spree. The prosecution established that Sutcliffe had lied to the police and his wife on a number of occasions and had shown himself to be accomplished in that art. Was it not reasonable, therefore, to suppose he had demonstrated that same underhand talent in his conversations with the medical professionals?

Transferred to Broadmoor

The jury found Peter Sutcliffe to be sane and answerable for his crimes, convicting him on 13 counts of murder by a 10-2 majority after seven hours' deliberation. It was 22 May 1981; almost six years had passed since the death of Wilma McCann, officially the Yorkshire Ripper's first victim.

Sutcliffe was sentenced to life imprisonment with a recommendation that he serve a minimum of 30 years. In 1984 Home Secretary Leon Brittan finally bowed to expert medical opinion, accepting that Sutcliffe was suffering from paranoid schizophrenia and allowing him to be transferred from Parkhurst to Broadmoor. Whether Sutcliffe was a delusional psychotic in need of care or a clever manipulator of the system who should be serving time in an ordinary prison remains open to question. Less contentious is the view that he should be held in a secure facility and is unlikely ever to be released back into the community. In May 2008 Home Secretary Jacqui Smith said she could not envisage circumstances in which Sutcliffe – now calling himself Peter Coonan – could be released. It quashed the hopes of the prisoner, whose legal representatives maintained that the 30-year tariff was never formalised and as such constituted a breach of human rights.

Ripper: not guilty plea

Sir Michael told the jury: 'You have to consider whether this man sought to pull the wool over the doctors' eyes. You have to decide whether as a clever callous murderer he deliberately set out to create a cock-and-bull story to avoid conviction for murder.' For none of that detail was ever told to the police.

Before the jury was sworn in, Sutcliffe's 30-year-old wife Sonia, who had been sitting to the right of the dock with her mother Mrs. Maria Szurma, left the court escorted by a policewoman and did not return. She is thought to be a defence witness. Sutcliffe stared straight ahead and did not even give a fleeting glance towards his wife as she left the famous No. 1 court with her mother.

Luck

Last week, he pleaded not guilty to the murder of 13 women but guilty to manslaughter on the grounds of diminished responsibility. He admitted attempting to murder seven other women. But the Judge, Mr. Justice Boreham, expressed 'grave anxieties' about the pleas and decided a jury should be empanelled.

Only once did a flicker of expression cross Sutcliffe's bearded face. He smiled when a juror named Sutcliffe was called into the box. Then for 4¹/₂ hours Sir Michael recounted in harrowing and grisly detail the Ripper's catalogue of 'sadistic' killings and attacks on women.

Incredibly, last Christmas he even walked past one of his victims who had survived, Mrs Maureen Long. He recognised her instantly but she walked by. It was the kind of luck which had enabled him to escape arrest for five years. Sir Michael revealed yesterday that Sutcliffe was questioned nine times because his car was seen in red-light districts in the North. But each time he was let go.

Throughout his 'crusade' Sutcliffe, a Bradford lorry driver, believed he was being protected by God - and even claimed the fake letters and tapes sent to police were the work of God to mislead police.

2006 DNA test

The Byford Report into the conduct of the Ripper inquiry was extremely critical of West Yorkshire police. It highlighted procedural lapses, systemic failures and ill-judged decisions, all of which meant that Sutcliffe remained at large longer than he should have. One of the gravest miscalculations surrounded the 'Wearside Jack' hoax. That mystery was cleared up in March 2006, when the hoaxer's identity was finally revealed. A DNA sample from saliva deposited on one of the envelopes was matched to a Sunderland resident who had been convicted on a drunk and disorderly charge. Forty-nine-year-old John Humble was an alcoholic loner and social inadequate with a record of petty crime dating back to his teens. He was given an eight-year prison sentence for perverting the course of justice, closing the book on one of the most infamous cases in criminal history.

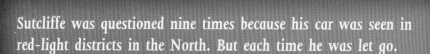

Sutcliffe was questioned nine times because his car was seen in red-light districts in the North. But each time he was let go.

LEFT AND OPPOSITE BELOW: Sutcliffe in January 1981 as he is taken to court to face the charges brought against him for the murders of 13 women.

OPPOSITE TOP: Sutcliffe leaves the Old Bailey in a police van after he received a life sentence. He was found guilty on all 13 counts of murder and seven attempted murders.

TOP: Sutcliffe pictured as he leaves court in Newport, Isle of Wight, where he appeared after being attacked at Parkhurst Prison by fellow inmate James Costello.

THE KRAYS:
Rulers of the East End Underworld

'I'm not going to waste words on you. The sentence is that of life imprisonment. In my view, society has earned a rest from your activities and I recommend that you be detained for at least 30 years.'

With those words, uttered by Mr Justice Melford Stevenson at the Old Bailey on 5 March 1969, the curtain was brought down on the reign of the Kray twins, rulers of the East End underworld for over a decade. Remarkably, not everyone bade good riddance to gangland's most notorious figures. Stories

of Ronnie and Reggie Kray's charitable giving were legion; they were ever willing to dip into their pockets in response to a hard-luck story, or fund a Christmas party for local pensioners. The streets, it was said, were far safer when the Krays ran the show. They also looked after the families of the 'aways', the euphemism given to their acolytes who were serving time. Both twins' funerals brought thousands out onto the streets of the capital; theirs was a tight-knit community that looked after its own. Yet the Krays' story was no romantic tale in which the only victims were hardened criminals who got what they deserved. Ronnie and Reggie built their empire on violence and intimidation and maintained it through fear, emulating the Mafia-style level of control that they had set out to achieve.

East Enders

The twins were born 24 October 1933 to Charles and Violet Kray, who already had a six-year-old son, named after his father. The boys' father was a peripheral figure during their upbringing, for he roamed the country as a travelling salesman. Not that Charles Snr would have made much of a role model, for he was a hard-drinking gambler who consorted with the local villains when he wasn't out on the road. He also showed his mettle when he was called up for military service, choosing to go on the run rather than fight for King and country.

At school Ronnie and Reggie were willing and co-operative, showing little indication that they would veer badly off the rails. They did show themselves to be handy with their fists, but initially that was in the controlled environment of the ring. The boys were keen and able boxers, inspired to put on the gloves by their maternal grandfather, who had fought under the name Jimmy 'Cannonball' Lee. They were treading a well-worn path, for many East Enders took up boxing as a way of channelling their aggression, and as a possible escape route from an impoverished existence in an unemployment blackspot.

The highlight of their boxing career came in 1951, when they fought on the same card in a junior championship staged at the Royal Albert Hall, but by then the twins had revealed that they weren't averse to a rather less noble art, with the gloves off. Two years earlier, they found themselves up on a GBH charge following an incident outside a dance hall. The twins were acquitted through lack of evidence, which would become a recurring theme over the next 20 years. It was no easy task to find someone willing to testify against the Krays, even in their teenage years.

'The Firm'

One of the early money-making scams they became involved in was sham auctions, where their muscle and boxing prowess came in handy. Stooges in the crowd ramped up

> 'The Firm' was the name given to the organisation that would rule the East End roost and to whom others paid their protection dues.

prices before an unsuspecting purchaser secured his 'bargain'. When the penny dropped either they disappeared shamefacedly, not wanting to admit they had been taken for a ride, or, if they chose to confront the rogue operators, one of the Krays would be pressed into service. A favourite trick of Reggie's was to wait until the victim was remonstrating in full flow, then deliver a vicious uppercut. A blow to a slack jaw inflicted horrific injuries.

The boys' boxing careers came to an end when they were claimed for National Service in 1952. Army life didn't agree with them, and they spent much of the time incarcerated at Shepton Mallet military prison for absconding and a string of other misdemeanours before being dishonourably discharged in 1954. They took over the Regal billiard hall in Mile End, and after a few run-ins with the local hard cases, slowly established 'The Firm', the name given to the organisation that would rule the East End roost and to whom others paid their protection dues – if they knew what was good for them. Thuggery attracted thugs, and the twins brought some of them into their circle. Their timing was perfect, for the mid-fifties saw the retirement of Billy Hill and Jack 'Spot' Comer, two of the most notorious gangsters of the day. The Krays were ready and able to step into the vacuum created, though they had to see off several other contenders for the underworld crown.

APRIL 6, 1965

Boxers who became club owners

The Kray twins, ex-professional boxers, have run clubs in both the East End and the West End of London. As lightweights they won their first professional fights in July 1951. They were 17.

From the East End clubs they owned, The Double R, in Bow Road, and the Kentucky, in Mile End Road, the Krays organised concerts and parties in aid of the aged and crippled. They gave television sets to old people's homes; money to a Bethnal Green Darby and Joan club. Bethnal Green councillor Mr.

Bob Rosomond said: "When I was mayor I often met the Kray brothers at charity functions. On one occasion Ronnie Kray came to the town hall with Winifred Atwell, the pianist. He was showing her round the East End."

Two years ago the Krays took over Esmeralda's Barn, a rendezvous for debutantes and their escorts in Wilton-place, Knights-bridge. The twins - in frilly toreador dress shirts and black ties - moved into the "high life." They have been frequent callers backstage at West End theatres. At first nights, big boxing promotions and film premieres the Krays are always to be seen.

OPPOSITE: The three brothers Reggie, Charles and Ronnie in a handclasp of friendship.

TOP: Reggie Kray outside his house in Bethnal Green with his grandfather, Jimmy. He and Ronnie had just been acquitted of attempting to obtain protection money from Soho club owner Hew McGowan.

ABOVE: The twins flank mother Violet who was always a stalwart supporter of her boys. Ronnie and Reggie Kray were born on 24 October 1933 in Hoxton, East London, to Charles and Violet Kray. The couple already had a six-year-old son, also called Charlie, who was born on 9 July 1927.

Loose cannon

Ronnie was the dominant partner in The Firm, styling himself as the 'Colonel' in their military-style operations. He was also unhinged, his psychosis diagnosed during a seven-year stretch he was given for violent assault in 1956. Ronnie had to be restrained with a straitjacket while serving at Winchester Prison, and was eventually certified insane and transferred to Long Grove Mental Hospital, Epsom. His grip on reality was tenuous and he suffered acute paranoia, at one time saying he was convinced that Reggie was a Soviet spy. Even so, Ronnie showed enough improvement to get himself released after serving half his sentence, or, at least, convinced the doctors that he was well enough to be given his freedom. In fact, he was dangerously psychotic, and even Reggie regarded him as a loose cannon whose wild unpredictability was having a damaging effect on their business interests.

Untouchable

The Krays made a fortune from extortion and fraud, and operated illegal gambling dens. As well as taking regular protection payments, they also engaged in the practice of 'nipping', where members of the gang made random visits to premises they were 'securing' and helped themselves to some of the proceeds. One of their favourite scams was the 'long firm fraud'. Companies were set up, premises obtained and goods ordered from suppliers. Bills were paid promptly to begin with in order to increase their credit rating, at which point a huge order was placed and the operation closed down. The premises were often torched before the disappearing act.

These clubs attracted numerous celebrity patrons, and the twins enjoyed being photographed with stars from the world of sport and entertainment.

On the surface, the Krays liked to present themselves as respectable businessmen, acquiring interests in several nightclubs, including Esmeralda's Barn in the upmarket West End, a stone's throw from Knightsbridge. These clubs attracted numerous celebrity patrons, and the twins enjoyed being photographed with stars from the world of sport and entertainment. One David Bailey photoshoot produced stark monochrome images that acquired iconic status, on a par with Twiggy and The Beatles in capturing the 60s zeitgeist. The Metropolitan Police Force knew that the empire was propped up by violence and intimidation, but proving it was another matter entirely. And events that occurred in the mid-sixties convinced the Krays even more that they were untouchable.

Scandal surfaces

Ronnie Kray was a known homosexual, and in 1964 the Mirror Group broke a sensational story linking a gangster with a Tory peer. The paper had photographic evidence of the liaison, but concerns over a possible lawsuit led the editor to run a tantalising headline: 'The Picture We Must Not Print'. The German magazine *Stern* had no such qualms and named Ronnie Kray and Lord Boothby as the protagonists in the story. The *Mirror* then backed down, issuing open apologies to both parties, and thereafter Fleet Street was pragmatically circumspect in its reporting of the capital's gangland ringleaders.

TOP, ABOVE AND BELOW: The Kray brothers. When the twins attended Wood Close Primary School in Brick Lane there was no hint of their future criminal tendencies and they got on well with teachers and other pupils. The influence of their grandfather, Jimmy 'Cannonball' Lee, soon led both boys into amateur boxing, at that time a common pastime for working-class boys in the East End. However, by the time the boys turned professional they had already been in trouble with the law.

Kray twins go free

Ronald Kray, 31, grinned at his twin brother Reginald outside their parents' home in London's East End yesterday and said: "Definitely it's the quiet life for us now." They had just left the dock at the Old Bailey's No. 1 Court. There they were cleared of charges of attempting to obtain protection money from a Soho club owner. The Krays, who had been in custody for three months after their arrest, were acquitted with a third man on the sixth day of a retrial after a jury in the first trial failed to agree.

The Krays, in blue Italian-cut suits, struggled through a crowd of their friends as they left the court. A bronze Jaguar took them to their lawyers' office and then to their parents' home in Vallance Road, Bethnal Green. There the two East Enders, who used to own the fashionable Esmeralda's Barn nightclub in Knightsbridge, were hugged and cheered by neighbours.

Their mother, Mrs. Violet Kray, ran out of the terrace house saying: "I'm almost crying, I'm so relieved." Reginald brought his typist girlfriend Frances Shea, 21, out of the house and hugged her. He said: "We're hoping to get married this week."

A representative of his firm of solicitors said: "Don't say anything." Then he turned to questioners and said: "Reginald has not made his mind up yet." Cars arrived and men hurried into the Kray house. A man from the solicitors' office opened the door from time to time. He said: "They're just having a quiet drink in the peace of their own home after the ordeal."

> Their mother, Mrs. Violet Kray, ran out of the terrace house saying: 'I'm almost crying, I'm so relieved.'

Krays' trial collapses

That same year, one club boss decided to call the Krays' bluff and go to the police instead of paying for the 'door services' offered. When Hew McCowan made a statement detailing how the Hideaway Club in Gerrard Street had been targeted by the Krays, it must have been music to the ears of Detective Superintendent Leonard 'Nipper' Read, the man tasked with breaking the stranglehold The Firm exerted on the capital. Unfortunately, it was not the hoped-for breakthrough. McCowan's manager, Sidney Vaughan, was to be a key witness, but he changed his story, telling Read he had had some kind of epiphany and that his original statement was false. Even worse, witnesses came forward to testify that McCowan had tried to suborn them into giving false evidence against the twins. There was a hung jury, and a retrial was ordered. That failed to go the distance, Mr Justice Lyell halting the proceedings and finding the defendants not guilty. It was partly in response to this case that the Labour government passed the 1967 Criminal Law Act, which allowed for 10-2 majority verdicts. Under the new system at least three jurors would have to be 'got at' to secure an acquittal, though that was of small comfort to DS Read when the case collapsed in 1965.

ABOVE RIGHT: The tenacious characteristics shown in the boxing ring were to be seen later on in the Krays' business activities with devastating effects. By the time Reggie and Ronnie finished their years of National Service in 1954 they were already immersed in a seedy world of criminal activity which would see them in court for the first of many appearances.

ABOVE LEFT AND TOP LEFT: Shortly after the case against the brothers collapsed at the Old Bailey in April 1965, Reggie married his girlfriend, Frances Shea. The wedding photographs were taken by the celebrated photographer David Bailey. As West End nightclub owners at this time the Krays mixed with many well-known people, which gave them an air of respectability and in the 1960s they became celebrities in their own right, even appearing in interviews on television.

'Most clubs are very respectable'

The twins celebrated by rubbing McCowan's nose in it, hosting a victory party at the Hideaway Club, which they had acquired and renamed El Morocco. The acquittal even brought them a platform on the BBC, where they gave a sanitised view of their business dealings. The occasional patron might overindulge and have to be dealt with, they said, but apart from that 'most clubs are very respectable'. Reggie took the opportunity to publicly announce his forthcoming nuptials, and in April 1965 married Frances Shea, whom he had known since she was a 16-year-old schoolgirl. It was a stormy relationship, Frances soon buckling under the stifling oppression of having every facet of her life ordered by her husband. After two months she left and returned to her family home, the marriage, apparently, never consummated. Reggie certainly shared his brother's homosexual predilections, and in local circles they were irreverently known as 'Gert and Daisy', though, naturally, not to their faces. In June 1967 Frances took an overdose of phenobarbitone, perhaps realising that there was only one sure way of walking out on the Krays.

First victim

It was murder, not extortion that finally proved the Krays' undoing. Their first victim was George Cornell, a member of the South London Richardson gang, long-time enemies of the Krays. However, it wasn't a turf war that caused Ronnie Kray to go looking for Cornell on 9 March 1966. It was a matter of honour and respect, for Cornell had unwisely called Ronnie a 'fat poof'. It was also rumoured that he had shot a cousin of the Krays during a bar-room fracas, but the insult alone was enough for Ronnie to seek retribution. The showdown took place at the Blind Beggar public house in Aldgate. Ronnie and one of his lieutenants, John 'Ian' Barrie, confronted Cornell, who seemed unfazed, remarking, 'Well, look who's here.' They were to be his final words, for Kray unceremoniously put a bullet through his head. He had hardly chosen a remote location for the revenge killing – there were over two dozen people in the pub – yet the police struggled to find a single witness. East Enders were reticent enough to inform on one of their own, and fear of reprisals made it doubly difficult for the police to build a case against the Krays.

> They were to be his final words, for Kray unceremoniously put a bullet through his head.

JANUARY 10, 1969

Rivals in violence

The Kray twins' rivalry in violence linked two terror murders committed 20 months apart, an Old Bailey jury was told yesterday. Mr Kenneth Jones, QC, prosecuting, said: 'During that intervening period arguments took place from time to time between Ronald and Reginald Kray... In the course of these arguments Ronald would say to his brother: "I have done my one, it is about time you did yours."'

Twenty months after the first murder, the second man was stabbed to death. Mr Jones said the reason for this murder was not hard to seek. 'Reginald Kray had decided to show that he was equal to his twin brother in violence and that he could kill too.'

ABOVE AND RIGHT: Reggie married his childhood sweetheart Frances Shea at St James the Great with St Jude church in Bethnal Green on 19 April 1965. Veteran boxer Ted 'Kid' Lewis and former champions Terry Spinks and Terry Allen were among the guests. The marriage was short-lived, lasting only eight weeks, although it was never formally ended.

LEFT: Frances died in June 1967 after taking an overdose of barbiturates. Reggie attended the hearing at St Pancras Coroner's Court with elder brother Charlie. The inquest ruled that that she had committed suicide.

Second murder

In December that year the twins committed their second murder. The victim was another villain, Frank Mitchell, a brute of a specimen known as the 'Mad Axe Man'. Mitchell was sprung from Dartmoor Prison, perhaps to help in a possible turf war with the Richardson mob, or maybe simply to keep a promise or render a favour. The escape plan went smoothly enough, and Mitchell was whisked away to a flat in London to lie low. But he became restless, and it seems the twins turned on the man they now regarded as a liability. On Christmas Eve 1966, Mitchell was told he was being taken to another safe house in the country, but as he piled into the waiting van he was shot at the Krays' behest by two of their henchmen. The body was never recovered and it remains, officially, an unsolved murder.

TOP LEFT: The Kray brothers arrive for a hearing at Bow Street Magistrates' Court. On 8 May 1968 the Krays were arrested when police raided their mother's flat in Braithwaite House, Old Street. Sixteen members of their 'firm' were detained on the same day. Their arrest and incarceration before their trial helped to loosen the grip of fear they had on the community and many witnesses started to come forward.

ABOVE INSET: After the failure of the prosecution in May 1965, Inspector Leonard 'Nipper' Read tackled the problem of convicting the twins with renewed vigour. He frequently came up against the East End 'wall of silence', which discouraged anyone from providing information to the police.

BELOW: Members of the Kray gang return to the Old Bailey in an armoured van to receive their sentences.

Butchered

Ronnie was becoming increasingly unstable. He had upped the ante dramatically with the cold-blooded execution of George Cornell, and wanted Reggie to show the same murderous intent. Following Frances's death, the bond between the brothers was deeper than ever, and Reggie was more than willing to put himself on the same bloody footing. All that was needed was a suitable victim.

The initial target was Leslie Payne, the financial brains of the outfit who oversaw the long-firm cons and looked after The Firm's business interests. He was suspected of trying to cut a deal with the police and small-time crook Jack McVitie was recruited as hit man, paid a £100 retainer to do the job. McVitie was universally known as 'The Hat' for he was never seen without his trilby, which he wore to hide his receding hairline. His bald spot became the least of his problems when he not only failed to carry out his mission, but also let slip in an unguarded moment that he had ripped off the Kray twins and might kill them instead. With that he effectively signed his own death warrant. Ronnie and Reggie installed themselves at a Stoke Newington flat and told underlings to put the word out for McVitie to come and join the party. Jack walked right into the trap, and after a failed attempt to escape by jumping through a window, he faced the merciless wrath of the Kray twins. Told by Ronnie to take his death like a man, McVitie replied: 'I'll be a man but I don't want to die like one.' It made no difference, for Reggie butchered him with a carving knife, egged on by his brother. While they cleaned themselves up, some of their lieutenants got rid of the body, perhaps in deep water, perhaps in the foundations of some civil engineering project. It was never recovered.

> Ronnie was becoming increasingly unstable. He had upped the ante dramatically with the cold-blooded execution of George Cornell, and wanted Reggie to show the same murderous intent.

058111 REG.KRAY

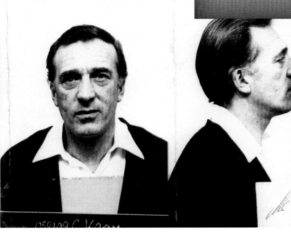

> Terrified, bathed in sweat, like a caged animal, he tried to escape. He threw himself at the window and smashed it, but Reginald Kray and Ronald Kray pulled him back.

058110.RON KRAY

ABOVE: Mug shots of the Krays. Once the gang members were in custody it was relatively easy to gain a conviction. The murder trial began on 8 January 1969 and lasted for 40 days.

Tongues finally loosened

The wall of silence surrounding the Krays now began to crumble. All three murders had been gratuitous and irrational, leaving insiders fearing their turn might be next. Some thought the twins were now out of control, and were unnerved enough to want to see them toppled. That was the breakthrough Read had been waiting for. Until then no one dared speak out against the Krays while they were at large, and they would remain at large until someone spoke out against them. This Catch 22 cycle was broken in 1967, when two members of The Firm implicated the Krays after being arrested on other charges. Paul Elvey was carrying dynamite when he was taken into custody, and told police that the Krays intended to use it to blow up the house of one of their enemies. Elvey dragged Alan Cooper's name into it, and the latter, faced with a charge of conspiracy to murder, told police that he had been hired as a hit man by the Krays.

At 6 am on the morning of 8 May 1968 the police launched a co-ordinated sweep, hauling dozens of gang members into custody. Read himself arrested Ronnie and Reggie Kray. His hope that having all the villains out of commission might loosen a few tongues proved correct. Those with a grievance who now felt able to air it included Leslie Payne, who was aware of the threats against him and wanted out. He gave details of The Firm's fraudulent activities. Albert Donoghue, another trusty lieutenant, spilled the beans regarding the death of Frank Mitchell, while Ronnie Hart, a cousin to the Krays, gave chapter and verse on the events surrounding Jack McVitie's demise. John Dickson, who drove Ronnie and Ian Barrie to the Blind Beggar on the night George Cornell was gunned down, also jumped ship. With gang members turning tail, the Blind Beggar barmaid, who had insisted she'd seen nothing at the time and lived in fear for three years, now found the courage to come forward.

JANUARY 10, 1969

'The last brutal sequence of this whole foul incident was then enacted in the living room. McVitie was at last fully aware of what was to happen to him. This was no party. Terrified, bathed in sweat, like a caged animal, he tried to escape. He threw himself at the window and smashed it, but Reginald Kray and Ronald Kray pulled him back and started belabouring him with their fists. Then Ronald Kray, who had done his, held McVitie from behind, pinning his arms. Reginald Kray took up the knife, stabbed McVitie in the face, punched him over the heart and plunged the knife repeatedly into McVitie's body with his twin brother saying over and over again, "Kill him, Reg."

As he said the words 'Kill him, Reg!' Mr Jones' voice dropped to a hoarse whisper. He went on: 'McVitie fell to the floor gravely wounded, gasping for breath. The butchery was not complete. Reginald Kray stood astride him and plunged the knife into his neck twice, twisting it to make sure its deadly work was done.' Then, said Mr Jones, Ronald Albert Bender, one of the Krays' associates, felt McVitie's heart and pronounced him dead.

Mr Jones said that some weeks after the McVitie murder Ronald Kray told a man that if two women who knew that violence had been done said anything they would be 'done.' 'He enlarged just a little on this,' said Mr Jones. He said: "I've got a woman who could do this. I had her ready for Cornell's old woman."'

Longest murder trial

The Old Bailey trial began 8 January 1969 and ran for 40 days, the longest murder trial in British legal history. There was huge media interest, and black market tickets for the public gallery changed hands for £5 as everyone waited to see whether the prosecution, led by Kenneth Jones QC, could finally secure a conviction against the Krays. Albert Donaghue pleaded guilty to being an accessory to the murder of Jack McVitie, leaving the fate of ten men to be decided by the court. Mr Justice Melford Stevenson wanted to simplify the proceedings by numbering the defendants. Ronnie and Reggie were having none of that and the judge relented, though that would be their only victory during the proceedings.

The twins were volatile throughout. In one outburst Ronnie called the chief prosecuting counsel a 'fat slob' when he didn't like the line of questioning being pursued with one particular witness. To see an all-powerful underworld figure reduced to playground-style name-calling was an indication that the Krays were emasculated, their reign of terror over. On 5 March 1969 Reggie and Ronnie were both found guilty of the murder of Jack McVitie, and the latter was also convicted of murdering George Cornell. Of the other eight men in the dock only one walked free. Charlie Kray was found guilty on an accessory charge and given ten years.

ABOVE RIGHT AND INSET RIGHT: Charlie Kray is driven away from Maidstone Jail in 1975 after serving seven years of his ten-year sentence. After leaving prison he lived in Benidorm and tried to build a property development business. However, he was once again imprisoned in 1997 for 12 years after he was found guilty of masterminding a drugs deal. After suffering with chest pains he was taken from Parkhurst Prison on the Isle of Wight to hospital, where he died on 4 April 2000 aged 73.

BOTTOM RIGHT: Reggie arrives at the Old Church in Chingford for the funeral of his mother Violet, who died of cancer in August 1982. The notorious East End gangsters arrived separately – each handcuffed to a prison guard and flanked by police officers. Ronnie Kray was brought from Broadmoor Hospital for the criminally insane in Berkshire.

Ronald Joseph Hart stood in an Old Bailey witness box for 150 minutes yesterday and calmly told the Kray case jury that he saw Reginald Kray knife Jack 'The Hat' McVitie to death.

JANUARY 18, 1969

Jack the Hat said 'I don't want to die'

Ronald Joseph Hart stood in an Old Bailey witness box for 150 minutes yesterday and calmly told the Kray case jury that he saw Reginald Kray knife Jack 'The Hat' McVitie to death. He claimed that he helped the Kray twins to drag McVitie from a window as he tried desperately to escape being killed. His evidence brought an outburst from Reginald Kray in the dock. He stood up, pointed to Hart in the witness box and shouted: 'If there was any stabbing done, it must have been done by you.'

Hart, 26, who was allowed to keep his address secret, said Ronald Kray posted him at the front window of a flat in Evering Road, Stoke Newington, London. It was his job to shout down when McVitie arrived. He followed McVitie and the escort of four men who had brought him into a basement room. He added: 'I saw Reggie Kray get McVitie up against the wall. McVitie had Reggie Kray's arm trapped under his arm. Reggie Kray was holding a gun in the hand that was trapped.

Then McVitie ran out into the passage. Ronnie Kray got hold of him, pushed him against the wall near the telephone and said: "Come on, Jack, be a man." McVitie said: "Yes, I'll be a man but I don't want to die like one." They went back into the room. McVitie was pushed into the settee. Reggie Kray tried to shoot him. Reggie pointed the gun at him and pulled the trigger. Nothing happened. McVitie made a run for the window. Reggie gave the gun to Ronnie Bender. Next thing I remember, Reggie and McVitie were up against the wall. Ronald Kray was trying to push the carving knife into McVitie's back. It was bending.

'McVitie ran across the room and smashed the window. Ronald Kray, Reggie Kray, Ronnie Bender and myself pulled him back. Then Reggie Kray got hold of the knife and stuck it in McVitie's face. Reggie punched him in the chest and started to stick the knife into his stomach about three or four times. Ronnie Kray was holding McVitie's arms from behind. McVitie was telling them to stop. Ronnie Kray was saying: "Kill him, Reg. Go on, Reg." Then McVitie fell on the floor. He was dying then ... Reggie Kray stood astride him and stuck the knife through his throat.'

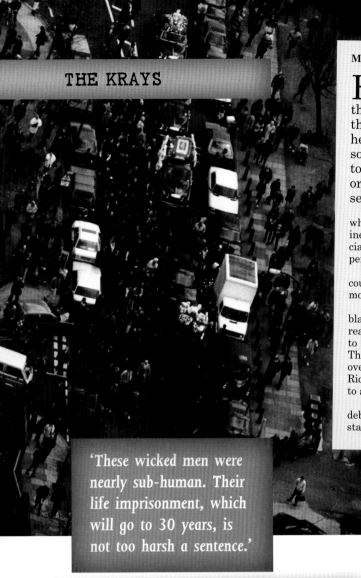

> 'These wicked men were nearly sub-human. Their life imprisonment, which will go to 30 years, is not too harsh a sentence.'

MARCH 6, 1969

Separate jails for the Krays

One hundred and fifty-nine years in jail. That was the total of the sentences passed and recommended at the Old Bailey yesterday for the Kray twins and members of their 'murder firm.' The twins, Ronald and Reginald, now 35, will be old-age pensioners when they are released if the judge's proposals in his report on the case to the Home Secretary are carried out.

For Mr Justice Melford Stevenson sentenced them to life for murder and recommended that each twin should be kept in prison for 30 years. Four others found guilty of murder were jailed for life. The judge recommended two should serve 20 years and two 15 years. There would be no remission for good conduct for the twins.

Some of the Great Train Robbers who got 30-year sentences will serve a maximum of 20 with good conduct. The Kray sentences are among the longest given at the Old Bailey since the war.

ABOVE AND RIGHT: Ronnie Kray was given a traditional send-off, with six black-plumed horses and a glass-sided hearse following his death in Wexham Park Hospital, Slough, on 17 March 1995. The infamous gangland killer died in hospital of a heart attack two days after collapsing at Broadmoor where he was serving a life sentence for murder. Ronnie's twin brother was allowed out of Maidstone Prison for the day, handcuffed and accompanied by three prison guards. Thousands of mourners lined the funeral route waiting for the hearse and entourage of 20 black Daimlers to make its way from the funeral directors W. English and Son, past Vallance Road, where the twins were brought up, to St Matthew's Church, Bethnal Green.

MARCH 6, 1969

HONEST citizens – and a few dishonest ones – will sleep more peacefully now that justice has overtaken the Kray gang. The enormity of their crimes, especially those of the killer twins, almost passes belief. We have heard of murder as a business, but this was murder as a sort of family competition. 'I've done mine,' says Ronald to Reginald, 'now it's your turn.' The court story of the ordeal of Jack McVitie, stabbed to death in cold blood, sends shivers down the spine.

These wicked men were nearly sub-human. Their life imprisonment, which will go to 30 years, is not too harsh a sentence. This outcome will inevitably lead to a renewal of the debate on capital punishment, especially when it is recalled that the taking of lives has earned the same penalty as that of the Great Train Robbers for the taking of property.

It is not often that so much unrelieved evil is disclosed in the British courts. But the disturbing thing is that the gangster has become much more common in this country than he used to be.

At one time the protection racket prospering on the proceeds of vice, blackmail, and armed menace was unknown here. It was something to read about under a Chicago date-line. But since the war it has grown to ugly proportions, and there is even talk of the Mafia muscling in. The gun, which was also rare in our underworld, is increasingly taking over. Punishment such as given to the Krays and to the leader of the Richardson 'torture gang' who got 25 years in 1967, should give pause to any who feel like emulating them.

But the only real deterrent is an alert and devoted police force, the debt to whom, as Mr Justice Melford Stevenson said, cannot be over-stated or ever discharged.

30 years

The twins began their 30-year stretch in different prisons, Ronnie at Parkhurst, Reggie at Leicester. After representations from mother Violet, Reggie joined his brother at the Isle of Wight facility in spring 1971. Their first outing came 11 years later, to attend Violet's funeral. Charles Snr died shortly afterwards, in February 1983. By then they were separated again, Ronnie having been transferred to Broadmoor.

Reggie's third outing in 26 years came in March 1995, this time to attend the funeral of his twin brother, who had suffered a fatal heart attack. He was 61. Reggie spent five more years behind bars, and had just exceeded the minimum recommended term when he was released on compassionate grounds. He was suffering from terminal bladder cancer and enjoyed only a month of freedom before the disease claimed his life on 1 October 2000, three weeks short of his 67th birthday.

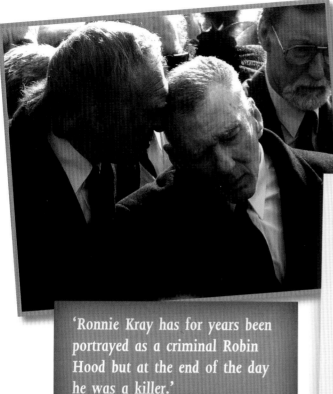

'Ronnie Kray has for years been portrayed as a criminal Robin Hood but at the end of the day he was a killer.'

MARCH 18, 1995

Ronnie Kray, killer with a fan club, dies in agony

Ronnie Kray, the East End gangster who attracted both hatred and respect, died of a heart attack yesterday. While friends and former enemies queued to praise a 'villain of honour', others dismissed him as nothing more than a cold-blooded murderer.

Kray, 61, a paranoid schizophrenic with a history of heart problems, died at the Wexham Park Hospital in Slough shortly after 9am. He had collapsed two days ago in Broadmoor, where he was serving a life sentence imposed in 1969 for the murder of George Cornell and Jack 'The Hat' McVitie.

Reggie's fury

Reggie Kray, who is also serving a life sentence for murder, is furious at finding out about his twin brother's death from an inmate who heard the news on a radio in Maidstone Prison. He said: 'I learned he was dead not from prison authorities, police or the hospital but from a fellow inmate. He knocked on my door and gave me the news and I collapsed in horror. I could not believe it.' Friends believe the death will add impetus to the campaign for his release on parole, possibly as early as this year.

The twins ran a brutal gang in London's East End during the late 1950s and 1960s which netted them a fortune and allowed them to live a life of luxury. They were local celebrities - liked by some, feared by many. Since their conviction, an industry has grown around them with books, T-shirts, television specials and a film starring pop star twins Gary and Martin Kemp of Spandau Ballet.

Reaction to the death was polarised. Actress Barbara Windsor said if the brothers had been judged by today's standards they would have been released a long time ago. 'They weren't menacing and did a lot for charity. They were charming with old people and women and they've been badly misrepresented for over 30 years. People could walk the streets in the East End in those days. It was a safer place.'

'Mad' Frankie Fraser, 70, a member of the notorious Richardson gang in the 1960s, said: 'He had very good principles. Women and children - he loved them. And he was very honourable.'

But reformed robber John McVicar said the twins were just hoodlums. 'I think it was significant that at their trial more people from their "firm" were prepared to give evidence against them than for.'

Laurie Johnson, deputy chairman of the Metropolitan Police Federation, said: 'Ronnie Kray has for years been portrayed as a criminal Robin Hood but at the end of the day he was a killer.'

TOP RIGHT: The Krays reached iconic status, revered and honoured by some and scorned and hated by others. Father Christopher Bedford, leading the funeral service, said: 'I feel that everybody has to be given a Christian burial and commended to God's mercy.'

MIDDLE LEFT: Charlie helps carry the coffin of brother Ronnie. Both Charlie and Reggie died in 2000 and joined Ronnie in the family burial site. Reggie had originally purchased the plot back in 1967 as a resting place for his first wife, Frances Shea, and subsequently his mother, father, elder brother

and then Ronnie were buried there. Reggie had become ill while in Norfolk's Wayland Prison and was diagnosed with inoperable cancer of the bladder. Jack Straw, the British Home Secretary, approved his release from prison on compassionate grounds in September 2000. He died peacefully in his sleep on 1 October, one month after his release.

TOP LEFT: Charlie and Reggie share a quiet moment at the graveside of brother Ronnie as he was buried with all the pomp and sentiment only the East End can muster.

JOHN CHRISTIE:
10 Rillington Place

John Reginald Halliday Christie will forever be associated with the murderous spree he embarked upon between 1943 and 1953, crimes so heinous that the infamous address where they occurred, 10 Rillington Place, was expunged from the record, renamed Ruston Mews when the row of unprepossessing three-storey houses in Notting Hill was demolished.

ABOVE LEFT: This picture of John Christie, issued by Scotland Yard on March 27, 1953, started a nationwide manhunt. Christie was educated at Halifax Secondary School, where he excelled at mathematics. He was skilled with his hands and had a high IQ. He sang in the choir and became a Scout, but he was never popular with his classmates.

BELOW: Crowds gathering in Rillington Place. Despite a change of street name the address would never lose its sinister associations.

An impotent loner

Christie was born in Halifax on 8 April 1898. His father was authoritarian and abusive, while his mother and sisters were overprotective and bossy. The young Christie was a good scholar, a choirboy and Boy Scout, though something of a loner and given to flights of hypochondria. He cast himself as something of a ladies' man, yet he was taunted following a disastrous early sexual liaison. It was an unsympathetic response to the impotence that would afflict him throughout his life. Scarred and humiliated by the experience, he would find nefarious ways to demonstrate his potency in the years ahead.

By 1920, aged 22, Christie recovered confidence enough to marry Ethel Waddington, a homely type of woman who would be less likely to undermine his performance. The marriage endured sexual failure and a lengthy separation, during which time Christie moved among the seedy strata of London society. He had a number of brushes with the law that led to custodial sentences, his transgressions including petty theft and a violent attack on a prostitute. The latter incident was a portent of what lay ahead, and an indication of his attitude towards women.

In 1933 Christie attempted to put his dubious past behind him by taking a position as a clerk and seeking a reconciliation with Ethel. The couple moved into the cramped ground floor flat at 10 Rillington Place in 1938, and Christie's credentials for respectability received a further boost the following year, when he was appointed a special constable, the vicissitudes of war causing his criminal record to be overlooked.

> Christie had a number of brushes with the law that led to custodial sentences, his transgressions including petty theft and violence.

TOP: Christie on Brighton pier. During the 1920s Christie was convicted for petty criminal offences. These included three months' imprisonment for stealing postal orders while working as a postman in 1921. He served another three months in 1933 for stealing a car from a priest who had befriended him.

ABOVE: Ethel Waddington from Sheffield married Christie on May 10, 1920 in Halifax. She separated from her husband after four years and Christie moved to London while Ethel went to live with relatives. They were reconciled after his release from prison in November 1933.

LEFT: Police guard the entrance to the house where the bodies had been found.

JOHN CHRISTIE: 10 Rillington Place

RILLINGTON PLACE W.11

J. TAMBLY

LEFT AND OPPOSITE BELOW RIGHT: Crowds gather in Rillington Place. Timothy Evans and his pregnant wife, Beryl, moved into the top-floor flat of 10 Rillington Place in April 1948.

BELOW LEFT: Muriel Amelia Eady was Christie's second victim. He promised to cure her bronchitis with a 'special mixture' he had concocted, but in fact he used domestic gas, which contained carbon monoxide that would render a person unconscious. Once Eady was knocked out, Christie choked her to death.

BELOW RIGHT: Christie murdered his wife in bed on the morning of December 14, 1952. She was last seen alive two days earlier.

BOTTOM: Three of Christie's eight victims: Rita Elizabeth Nelson and Kathleen Maloney were both killed in January 1953 and Hectorina McKay MacLennan was murdered on or about February 27.

Modus operandi established

It was during a tour of duty in 1943 that Christie met Ruth Fuerst, a 21-year-old munitions worker and part-time prostitute. He lured her back to 10 Rillington Place, safe in the knowledge that Ethel was away visiting her parents. Fuerst became his first victim, raped and strangled to death. Sex and strangulation would be his modus operandi, which next accounted for Muriel Eady, whom he met in the factory where both were employed. She met her end in October 1944, Christie later bragging about the ingenious way in which he drew her into his web with the offer of an efficacious inhaler that would benefit her bronchial condition. The tubing was linked to the gas supply, which rendered his victim semi-conscious and unable to resist his sexual and physical assault. He would say that the lifeless naked bodies of Fuerst and Eady thrilled him; he exerted power over them, with no threat of rebuke. Both women were buried in the tiny back garden of 10 Rillington Place.

Christie claims a mother and her daughter as his next victims

Christie's murderous proclivities were held in check for four years, until Timothy John Evans and his teenage wife Beryl took possession of the second-floor flat in the spring of 1948. Evans, who came from Merthyr Vale, was an illiterate, feeble-minded fantasist who just about managed to hold down a job as a delivery driver. Christie ingratiated himself with his new neighbours, focusing his attention on Beryl, who was heavily pregnant with their first child. Baby Geraldine was born in October, but not into a happy home. Her parents were struggling financially, and the arguments over money threatened to worsen when Beryl found herself pregnant once again. She was adamant that she did not want another child, which was music to the ears of John Christie when news of the predicament filtered down two floors. He had little trouble passing himself off as a one-time medical student who had experience of terminating unwanted pregnancies.

The date set for the proposed procedure was Tuesday, 8 November. Christie primed the hapless Evans for the bad news that would follow by spelling out the chances of the mother dying during the operation. Christie later described his failed attempt to have intercourse with the unconscious Beryl. He then strangled her and waited to give Evans the bad news.

Christie suggested concealing Beryl's body in one of the outside drains and having the motherless infant adopted by acquaintances of his. Evans went along with it. No doubt the confused, distraught simpleton, faced with the consequences of abetting a criminal act, was easily persuaded to take on the role of co-conspirator. He was also fearful of Christie, who would boast of his ability to manipulate his intellectually impaired neighbour.

Two days later, Evans arrived home to find that his daughter had departed to her new family. In reality, she, too, had been strangled and the body put with that of her mother in an outhouse. Evans believed that his wife had died during an abortion and that his daughter had been taken in by another family. He was soon to learn the terrible truth.

Guilt forces Evans to go to the police

On Monday 14 November, a furniture dealer cleared out Evans's flat, and Evans himself took a train to his home in South Wales, where he spent the next two weeks visiting relatives. He would give differing accounts of his wife and child's whereabouts, at one time saying they were holidaying on the south coast; at another that they had relocated to Bristol, where he was to join them; and even that the marriage had foundered over Beryl's infidelity.

On 30 November Evans could bear the guilt no longer. He walked into the Merthyr Tydfil police station and confessed to murdering his wife, telling officers he had put her body into the drain outside 10 Rillington Place. In his initial statement Evans said that Beryl had been depressed at becoming pregnant again and told her husband she wanted an abortion. Evans had procured the necessary medication, and when he arrived home from work on Tuesday 8 November, he found his wife's lifeless body and disposed of it in the property's drainage system.

Evans's story unravelled as soon as police examined the drains of the London property and found no body. He then changed his story, saying that his original statement had been tailored to protect his neighbour, John Christie. This time he related the truthful tale of Christie's offer to perform the abortion, and his arrival home on the night of 8 November to be informed that the procedure had gone wrong. The two men had hidden the body, Christie telling Evans he would dispose of it in the drains at a later date. A more thorough search of 10 Rillington Place was conducted, and the bodies of Beryl and 14-month-old Geraldine were found in the outside washhouse. Both had been strangled.

In yet another statement, Evans confessed to both murders. This was the first time that he had mentioned the death of the child, and it was that crime on which the police decided to proceed. In their view, Evans was guilty of a callous double murder, but a conviction for killing his young daughter was all that was needed to send him to the gallows. And the confession meant that he was damned by his own hand, an open and shut case.

Protests of innocence go unheard

But there was a problem. Some of the language used in the confession was far too sophisticated for its illiterate author, and it was also said that the use of numbers in the subscript to indicate the time and date of the statement would have been beyond his capabilities. In short, there were strong grounds for thinking that Evans had been manipulated by the presiding officers, just as he had been manipulated by Christie. Indeed, he retracted the confession, implicating Christie in Geraldine's death, the only possible perpetrator. But this was an amendment too far for the jury, who decided it was a desperate effort to shift the blame elsewhere. During the trial, Evans insisted that Christie had committed both crimes, and that the confession had been gained through intimidation. It was to no avail. The jury believed the star Crown witness, John Christie, a man who had received commendations for his wartime service as a special constable. What possible motive could he have for killing Geraldine? As well as giving a bravura performance in denying all knowledge of the abortion and Evans's version of subsequent events, Christie ensured that Evans remained firmly in the frame by highlighting the couple's stormy relationship.

The jury took just forty-five minutes to return a guilty verdict, and Timothy Evans went to the gallows at Pentonville Prison on 9 March 1950, protesting his innocence to the last.

DECEMBER 16, 1949

Murder Charge No. 2

Timothy John Evans, 25-year-old motor driver, was remanded for a week at West London yesterday, accused of murdering his wife Beryl, 19, at Rillington Place, West London, on November 8. There was a new charge against him of murdering his 14-month-old child on November 10.

JANUARY 14, 1950

Man with Two Bodies on his Hands

The man who "lied and lied and lied" was sentenced to death at the Old Bailey yesterday for the murder of his 14-month-old child. This comment by Mr. Justice Lewis referred to an allegation by Timothy John Evans, 25-year-old long-distance lorry driver, that his wife and child were killed by another man.

The bodies of 20-year-old Beryl Susanna Evans and the child were found trussed up in a washhouse at their home in Rillington Place, Notting Hill, West London. But for the fact that Evans had been sacked by his employer for disobedience, it seemed that he was going to use his lorry to take the bodies away. Evans sold his wife's wedding ring for 6s. to a South Wales jeweller and also sold all the furniture in the house for £40.

Later he told the police at Merthyr Tydfil, where he had gone to live with a relative, that he had put his wife's body in a drain. A search was made and the bodies were discovered at his home.

MARCH 25, 1953

Three women die in murder house

The boarded-up bodies of three women were found last night hidden behind gay, new wallpaper in the scullery of the ground-floor flat at 10, Rillington Place. Notting Hill, West London. So triple murder came to the tall Georgian house which had already been the scene of a double murder in 1949.

Mr. Beresford Brown, a Jamaican, uncovered the secret. He was moving from the top floor flat to the vacant ground floor flat, and began to examine the scullery. He wanted to install a bath, noticed that a part of the wall looked different. He tapped, and there was a hollow echo. When he pulled the wallpaper off he found a cavity, roughly boarded up. Behind the boards were the remains of the three women.

Last night Chief Superintendent Beveridge, of Scotland Yard, put out a country-wide request for the previous tenants of the flat, Mr. John Christie and his middle-aged wife, Ethel, to come forward, in the hope that they might be able to help with the inquiry.

TOP: Chief Superintendent Peter Beveridge entering 10 Rillington Place where the new tenant, Beresford Dubois Brown, discovered bodies hidden in a wallpapered-over panel in the kitchen. Pathology tests later revealed carbon monoxide in their bodies. A nationwide manhunt for Christie ensued on March 25, 1953.

LEFT: Holes in the ground of the garden at 10 Rillington Place. Following the discovery of the bodies inside the house, the search was extended to the garden. Detectives drove stakes into the earth in order to search for more bodies.

ABOVE AND OPPOSITE PAGE: Police search through weeds, rubbish and neglected shrubs for clues in the derelict garden behind number 10. The bones of Fuerst and Eady were discovered, taking the body count to six.

MARCH 25, 1953

Riddle of identity

With Dr. F. E. Camps, Home Office pathologist, and Chief Inspector Low, of the finger-print department, he was working until the early hours today, to identify the dead women and form an opinion of the probable dates of their deaths. It was established that the tragedy has no link with the murder of 19-year-old Mrs. Beryl Evans and her 14-month-old daughter Geraldine, who were found strangled at the same address in 1949. Mrs. Evans's husband, Timothy Evans was hanged for the murder of his child.

Mr. Christie, a British Road Transport clerk, employed at the Shepherd's Bush depot, had lived for about 15 years in the ground-floor flat with his wife. About two months ago, said Mrs Doreen Lawrence, a neighbour, Mrs. Christie disappeared. Mr. Christie stayed on alone with his dog, but was not seen much. "He said his wife had gone to her sister's at Birmingham," Mrs. Lawrence added.

Flat sub-let

"Last Thursday Mr. Christie left the flat. Before going he sub-let to a young Irish couple without the knowledge of the landlord. He did not give them the key and when they arrived they had to put their furniture in through the window. But on Saturday the landlord made them leave because he had arranged to let Mr. Brown have the flat."

Mr. Christie was last seen having a meal at a fish and chip bar at the top of the road. He said then that he was going to have his dog "done away with." Mr. Christie was a special constable at Harrow Road police station during the war, and police in the Notting Hill area know him well. Recently he had visited the local police station to lodge complaints about coloured residents in Rillington Place. He was one of the principal witnesses at the murder trial of Timothy Evans.

'Last Thursday Mr Christie left the flat. Before going he sub-let to a young Irish couple without the knowledge of the landlord.'

The net finally closes in on Christie

Following Evans's death the matter rested for the next three years, until 10 Rillington Place's ground-floor flat had a change of tenant. In clearing out the apartment prior to occupation, the new occupant discovered a deep alcove that had been papered over. There he found a woman's body, and the subsequent police search uncovered two more cadavers in the alcove, another under the floorboards, and bones enough to form two skeletons buried in the garden – the remains of Fuerst and Eady.

The hunt was on for Christie, who appeared to realise the net was closing in when he quit his job, sold his possessions and papered over the alcove before illegally sub-letting his flat. He made little effort to flee, however. On 31 March 1953, he was apprehended by police on Putney Bridge, near the embankment where he had been sleeping rough. Under questioning he related the details of his ten-year killing spree.

Christie had murdered Ethel in December 1952, placing her body under the floorboards, and in his final months of freedom claimed three more victims, those whose bodies were hidden in the alcove. Prostitutes Kathleen Maloney and Rita Nelson were each subjected to the same gassing treatment, their unconscious or lifeless bodies subjected to a sexual assault. His last victim, Hectorina MacLennan, represented a departure from his usual choice of target. She was searching for accommodation when the two struck up a conversation at Ladbroke Grove Station in March 1953. Christie offered to help, but his plans were thwarted when MacLennan arrived at 10 Rillington Place with a boyfriend in tow. He allowed them to stay for three nights before asking them to leave. He followed the couple and caught MacLennan alone, inviting her to return home with him. She met the same fate as the others, and Christie coolly dealt with the concerned boyfriend who turned up at the door in search of a partner who appeared to have vanished into thin air.

John Christie was tried and convicted for the murder of Ethel, the jury rejecting his plea of insanity as they reached a guilty verdict after barely an hour's deliberation. He was executed at Pentonville Prison on 15 July 1953.

TOP LEFT: A copper boiler from the scullery of 10 Rillington Place is placed in a police car and taken to Scotland Yard.

MIDDLE LEFT AND BOTTOM LEFT: The spot, near Putney Bridge, where Christie was found by P.C. Thomas Ledger. The constable had stopped Christie and asked him who he was. Subsequently Christie was taken away to be questioned and the manhunt for the Rillington Place murderer came to an end.

ABOVE: The police station where Christie was detained. After word got out about his capture, crowds gathered outside the building.

OPPOSITE: Christie was driven from Notting Hill Police Station to West London Magistrates' Court to appear on charges of murdering his wife. From there, as crowds began to gather, he was taken to Brixton Prison.

Christie charged with murder of his wife

Behind the drawn blinds of a ground floor room in Notting Hill police station, West London, last night, John Reginald Halliday Christie, 55-year-old haulage clerk, was charged with the murder of his wife, Ethel Christie, of 10, Rillington Place, Notting Hill. He was charged by Detective-Inspector Griffin, who since Tuesday has been investigating the mystery of the house.

The charge as read to Christie was "that on or about December 14 at 10, Rillington Place you murdered your wife, Ethel Christie, aged 54." Christie was brought to Notting Hill police station from Putney, where he was arrested at 9 o'clock yesterday morning. He was to remain at Notting Hill police station overnight and appear at West London Magistrates' Court today.

'Excuse me, but who are you?'

Police Constable Thomas Ledger, of Putney, is 6ft. 3in., aged 43, and holds a Long Service Medal, a Good Conduct Medal, and a Commendation. He gained these awards in years of dutiful but rather uneventful service.

At nine o'clock yesterday morning he was patrolling near the point where Lower Richmond-road joins the embankment at Putney. There, leaning on the embankment railings, watching men unload some barges, he saw a dishevelled-looking man. In the memory and in the notebook of every policeman in the country was the description of John Reginald Halliday Christie. P.C. Ledger had also a photograph and this he took out of his pocket.

Challenge

Then, as Christie turned and was about to walk away, he found Ledger barring his path. The policeman gave the challenge that has been repeated all over the country during the week that Christie was sought for interview - a challenge which has seriously embarrassed many hundreds of men with thinning hair and spectacles, and an air of gentility.

P.C. Ledger asked: "Excuse me, but who are you?"

He was answered. Then he invited the bespectacled man with three days' growth of beard to walk with him to a police call-box. There the officer telephoned Putney Police Station and stood waiting until a van arrived with two other policemen. Christie was driven to Putney Police Station. Deputy Commander Rawlings hurried there from Scotland Yard and Chief Superintendent Barratt and Chief Inspector Griffin went from Notting Hill five miles away, where they had been working on the Rillington Place murders.

Then Chief Superintendent Barratt sent an official message to Scotland Yard calling off the nation-wide search for Christie. Shortly afterwards he sent another message announcing that Christie had been charged with the murder of his wife, and would appear at West London Magistrates' Court. Hundreds of men, women, and children gathered outside the police station at Putney, and later at Notting Hill Police station, in the hope of catching a glimpse of Christie.

> The charge as read to Christie was 'that on or about December 14 at 10 Rillington Place you murdered your wife, Ethel Christie.'

Evans case reopens

Christie's confession inevitably cast doubt on the conviction of Timothy Evans, not least because he included Beryl Evans in his list of victims, though he vehemently denied any culpability regarding the fate of Geraldine. The Howard League for Penal Reform pressed for the case to be reopened, and Labour MP George Rogers took up the issue. Home Secretary Sir David Maxwell Fyfe acceded, and the events of November 1949 were re-examined, in camera, in an inquiry headed by Mr John Scott Henderson QC. Remarkably, that inquiry found the case against Evans to be overwhelming, and that no miscarriage of justice had taken place. Christie's inclusion of Beryl Evans in his confession was discounted as a device to help his own defence. This meant that according to the official version of events, there were two unconnected stranglers operating out of 10 Rillington Place in the autumn of 1949. Many thought such a coincidence stretched credulity to breaking point, but another twelve years would pass before the recently elected Labour Government ordered yet another re-examination of the Evans case.

ABOVE: The crowds outside Putney Police Station try to catch a glimpse of Christie. Elaborate police precautions prevented them from doing so.

TOP RIGHT: Dr Nickolls, head of the Science Laboratory (wearing a hat) attempts to make his way through the crowds queueing outside Clerkenwell Magistrates' Court. They were hoping for seats at Christie's hearing.

ABOVE RIGHT: People queueing outside the Old Bailey the day before the Christie trial opened. Miss Joan Elton was the first to arrive – she had prepared food

and brought a blanket for her overnight wait.

OPPOSITE BOTTOM RIGHT: A deck chair is carried into the Old Bailey as evidence in Christie's trial.

RIGHT: Crowds outside the Old Bailey after the verdict. Christie's attempt to plead insanity failed and he was sentenced to death after not even an hour's worth of deliberation.

OPPOSITE BOTTOM LEFT: The sentence notice that was put up outside Pentonville Prison on 4 July 1953.

Two MPs and mother of hanged man demand new inquiry

Immediately after John Christie was sentenced to death last night, the mother of Timothy John Evans, hanged in Pentonville three years and three months ago, called on the Home Secretary, Sir David Maxwell Fyfe, to reopen her son's case and hold a public inquiry. She charged that her son had been hanged for a murder he did not commit - the strangling of his baby daughter, 14-month-old Geraldine, found dead at 10, Rillington Place, the Christie death-house, with her mother.

Christie, who appeared to be weeping as he left the Old Bailey dock for a condemned cell at Pentonville, said during his trial that he strangled Mrs. Evans. But he strenuously denied killing Geraldine. Backing up Evans's mother in her demand are two M.Ps - Mr. George Rogers, North Kensington, and Mr. Sydney Silverman, who are trying to table questions in the House - and the Howard League for Penal Reform. Mr. Rogers wants to ask: Was there a miscarriage of justice; will the Home Secretary order an inquiry?

The League wants a public inquiry too, and in a letter to the Home Secretary, says: "Although Evans was only charged with the murder of his child, evidence regarding the murder of his wife was part of the case for the Crown. Within the last few days, however, statements have been made which throw doubt on that evidence. The whole of the evidence then available must have been considered by the Home Secretary [Mr. Chuter Ede] in deciding how to advise his late Majesty on the exercise of the royal prerogative of mercy. There is, therefore, a possibility that

such advice may have been based on incorrect information."

What is there now to help the Home Secretary make his decision on whether or not to reopen the case?

Baby's bottle still Half-full

First, there are the Evans family - his mother, Mrs. Probert, and his sister, Mrs. Eleanor Ashby, who live in St. Mark's Road, a few hundred yards from 10, Rillington Place, where Timothy Evans had a flat. Mrs. Ashby said last night of her 25-year-old lorry-driver brother: "Tim did not know his baby was dead until he arrived at the police station in Notting Hill. He told me that after he was charged. We now know that when the police searched at Rillington Place they found all Geraldine's belongings hidden in a cupboard in Christie's front room Her clothes, her pram, and even her feeding bottle, half-filled with milk, were there. No one has mentioned these facts before."

Devoted to his daughter

Now for Evans's aunt - Mrs. Violet Lynch of Mount Pleasant, near Merthyr Tydfil. He went to her home after leaving Rillington Place. Of those days she said: "His life was devoted to Geraldine and he would not have harmed a hair on her head. When on trial Timmy swore to me over and

over again that a man named Christie had promised to take the child to a safe home. What a terrible man he was to have sat there after murdering Beryl, Timmy's wife, and yet saying nothing as he watched Timmy being sent to the gallows."

There will also be before the Home Secretary the report of the Evans trial, where it was first alleged that Christie knew something about the deaths of Mrs. Evans and the baby. Then there are Christie's admissions at his own trial, and the questioning there of Chief Inspector Albert Griffin.

Sir Lionel Heald, the Attorney-General asked the inspector: "Have you any ground for believing that the wrong man was hanged in the Evans case?" Inspector Griffin: "None."

'It is possible'

Sir Lionel; "Is one possibility that two men were concerned with the death of Mrs. Evans?" Inspector Griffin: "It is possible. I do not know." And, yesterday, the judge said of the Evans murder: "It is foolish for us to pretend it may not be a matter of disturbing interest."

There is, too, the view of the Home Secretary at the time, Mr. Chuter Ede. He said last night: "I am making no comment on this matter. Whether more is heard of it rests with his successor, Sir David Maxwell Fyfe, who will have before him today these final words from the Penal Reform League: It is imperative that public confidence in justice be maintained."

'Have you any ground for believing that the wrong man was hanged in the Evans case?' Inspector Griffin: 'None.'

Crowds Wait As Christie Dies

Two hundred people outside Pentonville Prison yesterday watched the posting of the notice announcing the execution of John Reginald Halliday Christie, the mass murderer of Rillington Place. The crowd which included women and children, surged across the road to read the notice which was posted at 9.06 a.m.

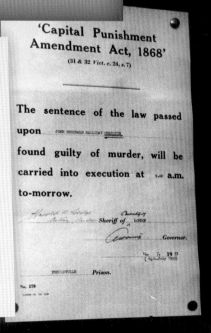

'Capital Punishment Amendment Act, 1868'
(31 & 32 *Vict. c.* 24, *s.*7)

The sentence of the law passed upon JOHN REGINALD HALLIDAY CHRISTIE found guilty of murder, will be carried into execution at 9.00 a.m. to-morrow.

Sheriff of LONDON

Governor.

19 53
(15 July 1953)

PENTONVILLE Prison.

No. 278

Posthumous free pardon for Evans

In October 1966, High Court judge Sir Daniel Brabin delivered a report which endorsed the findings of the Scott Henderson inquiry. Like his predecessor, Brabin found the thought of an egregious miscarriage of British justice an unconscionable proposition. In his view, the balance of probability suggested that Christie killed Geraldine Evans, and the child's father, therefore, was hanged for a crime he didn't commit. But the inquiry also concluded that Evans's confession regarding the death of his wife was genuine, not the misguided gesture of a remorseful husband who had allowed her to die at the hands of an illegal abortionist. In other words, the charge sheet may have been wrong but Evans was still a murderer who had received the appropriate come-uppance. Brabin subscribed to the fanciful view that two men, each responsible for killing women by means of a ligature, were living under the same roof. The report's author met the charge head on, commenting: 'It is no solution to the problem of the coincidence to ignore the evidence which points to the coincidence being a fact.'

Within a week, Home Secretary Roy Jenkins gave his verdict on the coincidence theory, eliciting cheers from the benches of the House of Commons when he granted Timothy John Evans a posthumous free pardon. Evans's remains were exhumed from Pentonville Prison and reinterred on consecrated ground, and the case was instrumental in the decision to abolish the death penalty, but it didn't quite represent the closing of an unseemly chapter in British legal history. The pardon exonerated Evans only from the charge on which he was convicted, that of killing his daughter. In 2004 family members failed in their bid to have the case referred to the Court of Appeal, and although it is widely accepted that Evans was innocent of all wrongdoing, the findings of the two official inquiries have left a cloud hanging over his name.

ABOVE: The front cover of Ludovic Kennedy's book. Sir Hugh Lucas-Tooth, Under-Secretary at the Home Office at the time, was of the opinion that the book contained no fresh evidence and had misled a great number of M.P.s: 'The book provides a flattering picture of Evans and damns Christie on every possible occasion.'

OCTOBER 13, 1966

'Speculative'

Mr. Ludovic Kennedy, author of a book about the Evans case, described Mr. Justice Brabin's findings as "speculative." He was surprised, he said, that the judge should have treated the murders of the wife and baby as separate transactions, whereas they had previously been treated as one transaction.

Mr. Kennedy said that he thought Mr. Justice Brabin had said three fairly significant things. "One is that no jury would have convicted Evans, in his opinion, if they had known what we know now. The second is that he is not satisfied of Evans's guilt beyond reasonable doubt. The third is that he thinks it improbable that Evans killed the baby. All these things taken together make it in my view possible for the Home Secretary to grant a free pardon. If people say that there is no precedent for this, I would say that this case is entirely without precedent."

> Evans's remains were exhumed from Pentonville Prison and reinterred on consecrated ground, and the case was instrumental in the decision to abolish the death penalty.

ABOVE: Justice Brabin said that he wasn't satisfied of Evans's guilt beyond reasonable doubt while his mother said: 'I don't believe my son did either of these murders. Christie did them both.'

TOP: The grave of Mrs Beryl Evans and her baby Geraldine in Gunnersbury Cemetery. Their bodies were found in the wash house of 10 Rillington Place.

OPPOSITE TOP AND MIDDLE: Rillington Place, where the remains of Christie's victims were discovered, had to be renamed Ruston Close to throw sightseers off the scent. Later the buildings were demolished; a new housing complex was built and named Bartle Road.

OPPOSITE BOTTOM: Christie and Ethel.

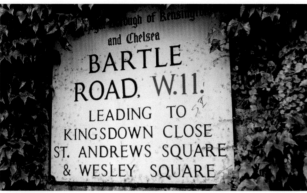

> 'No jury would have convicted Evans if they had known what we know now'.

Evans 'hanged for the wrong murder'

Timothy Evans was probably hanged for the wrong murder. That is the main conclusion in Mr. Justice Brabin's 156-page report on his inquiry into the murders at 10, Rillington Place, Notting Hill, 16 years ago. Evans, a 25-year-old illiterate van driver, was hanged at Pentonville Prison, London, in 1950 for killing his 14-month-old daughter, Geraldine.

That killing, the judge says, was probably done by John Reginald Christie, Evans's landlord at Rillington Place, who three years later, was revealed as a mass-murderer. Evans was also accused of killing his wife, Beryl, but never stood trial for it. That killing, the judge concluded, probably was done by Evans. The inquiry was commissioned by the Government after intense pressure on the then Home Secretary, Sir Frank Soskice, to clear up the question of Evans's guilt or innocence.

For almost a year, Mr. Justice Brabin studied and heard more than a million words given in evidence. The time lag, blurred memories, the tangle of lies, confessions and denials from both Evans and Christie made it impossible for him to nail down the complete truth of whether there were one or two killers living in the same house. But the judge's personal view is that there were.

He says: "It is a coincidence which it is claimed cannot be accepted in fact," but adds: "In human affairs few things are surprising." He sees events at Rillington Place like this:

Evans killed his wife after a violent row. He may have confided in Christie, who promised to dispose of the body, then fled to Wales. Christie, with two undetected war-time murders already committed, then killed Geraldine. Evans, in giving himself up, confessed to the murder of his wife. But, for some unknown reason, Christie managed to persuade Evans not to implicate him in the killing of Geraldine.

Mr. Justice Brabin's report completely overturns the ruling of the Scott Henderson inquiry, which was set up after the murders of Christie came to light. This inquiry reported that there had been no miscarriage of justice in the Evans case. But the true story will never be known, as the judge makes clear in an explanation of the difficulties he faced in making the investigation.

Findings

He says: "One fact which is not in dispute, and which has hampered all efforts to find the truth, is that both Evans and Christie were liars. They lied about each other. They lied about themselves."

The report points to differences in the killing of Mrs. Evans and Christie's victims. Evans had a violent temper and had struck his wife on various occasions. A pathologist's findings showed injuries to her head caused by hand or fist blows about 20 minutes before her death. But none of Christie's victims showed any sign of violence other than strangulation.

The report says: "If Christie was to strangle for the sake of strangling, it would be likely that he would do so immediately after striking her and not wait for 20 minutes or five minutes when screams might be heard."

In 1953 Christie had sexual intercourse with three women - later found in the house - and gassed them. But there was no evidence of this murder pattern in the murder of Beryl Evans. It goes on: "The evidence further satisfies me that the only person who mentioned that Beryl Evans had been strangled with a rope was Evans himself. "He could only have known this because he used a rope or because he saw a rope used or saw one on his wife's neck or because Christie told him that a rope had been used. "speculative ."

Mr. Justice Brabin found Geraldine's death "more perplexing." He says: "I do not believe that he who killed Beryl Evans must necessarily have killed Geraldine. They were separate killings done, I think, for different reasons. The wife was killed in anger. Her daughter died because her crying might have got on the nerves of her father." Geraldine is believed to have been murdered 48 hours after her mother.

"It is not possible to know how Christie became aware of the killing of Beryl Evans. Whether he discovered it after hearing yet another row, or whether Evans sought his help after he had killed his wife, cannot be known."

Clever

"In any event with Beryl Evans dead, Christie, who was staying at home, would have become aware that Geraldine was alone in the flat and thereby would learn that her mother was at least missing and might well have discovered her death. Christie knew everything that went on in that small house. He was known to creep about the stairs and landings."

Mr. Justice Brabin says he is sure that Christie would never have allowed two bodies to remain in his home "unless he was himself involved in the killing of one or both persons." He describes the killing of Geraldine as "in cold blood" and says Christie would be more likely to do it. "Christie denied that he killed Geraldine until the end of his own trial because he was clever enough to know that to admit killing her would have inflamed any jury against him - first because Evans had been hanged for her death and secondly because it was the deliberate killing of a baby in cold blood."

His mother says: I'll fight on

Mrs. Thomasina Probert, Evans's 65-year-old mother, said last night: "I don't believe my son did either of these murders. Christie did them both. I want to continue the fight until I clear my son's name."

GERAGHTY AND JENKINS:
Charlotte Street Robbery

'I did my best,' said the dying man, who had a history of stepping into the breach to help others, heedless of the risk to himself.

Too young to hang

Many will recall the infamous Bentley-Craig case of 1952, in which Christopher Craig's age saved him from the rope, leaving Derek Bentley to answer for the murder of PC Sidney Miles, killed during a rooftop showdown following a bungled robbery. It was not a unique case. Five years earlier, three young men were convicted of murder following a botched raid on a jeweller's shop. Two hanged for their part in the crime, while the third member of the gang, a 17-year-old youth, escaped with a custodial sentence.

Jeweller's shops targeted

On Friday 25 April 1947, three men robbed a jeweller's shop next to Queensway Tube station, Bayswater, and made off with goods worth £4,500. Guns were trained on staff during the raid, though it was clear that their sole purpose was to deter any heroic act, for manager Stanley Coleman reported that one of the masked raiders specifically instructed his accomplices not to shoot.

BELOW: A police car leaves Marlborough Street police station on 21 May 1947, as the crowds push forward to try to catch a glimpse of the men charged with the murder of Alec de Antiquis. The father of six was shot while trying to prevent the escape of three men who had attempted to rob a jeweller's.

ABOVE: A few days earlier one of the accused, his face covered by the jacket of one of the accompanying detectives, had attended a hearing at Tottenham Court Road police station.

Three perpetrators

The police inquiry was still ongoing when another London jeweller's, Jay's in Charlotte Street, W1, was hit four days later. Once again there were three perpetrators, masked and armed, but any similarity to the previous week's crime ended there. For the trio who burst into Jay's on the afternoon of 29 April 1947 it was all about to go horribly wrong. Firstly, managing director Alfred Stock had the presence of mind to slam shut the open door of the safe. A scuffle ensued between Stock and one of the raiders, who used the butt of his pistol to reinforce his demand that the safe be opened. The shop manager then weighed in, hurling a chair in the direction of the other attackers. It missed, but provoked a retaliatory burst of gunfire that left a bullet embedded in the woodwork. The commotion brought other backroom staff running and the alarm was sounded. The raiders panicked and fled empty-handed, piling into a Vauxhall saloon parked outside. The alarm was raised on the streets, too, and the cry went up to stop the car and apprehend its occupants. A van driver responded to the rallying call by blocking the vehicle's path. The three men clearly thought their best chance of escape was on foot, for they abandoned the car and took flight.

> The raiders panicked and fled empty-handed, piling into a Vauxhall saloon parked outside.

Father of six shot dead

The hue and cry attracted the attention of motorcyclist Alec de Antiquis, a 34-year-old garage owner and father of six, who rode his machine onto the pavement and blocked the thoroughfare. It was a brave gesture, but should have been no more than that, for it was no difficult task for the fugitives to sidestep the obstruction. Indeed, two of the men did just that, but the third chose to vent his fury at this latest effort to thwart his intentions. He raised his weapon and shot at Mr de Antiquis, who sustained a fatal head wound. 'I did my best,' said the dying man, who had a history of stepping into the breach to help others, heedless of the risk to himself.

There followed a further struggle with another have-a-go hero, this time without a firearm being discharged. The men then melted into the afternoon throng, with nothing to show for their efforts other than the fact that they had avoided capture.

> The hue and cry attracted the attention of motorcyclist Alec de Antiquis who rode his machine onto the pavement and blocked the thoroughfare.

TOP: Passers-by try to comfort 34-year-old mechanic Alec de Antiquis as he lies dying on the pavement. De Antiquis was on his way to collect some parts he needed for his small repair shop when he came face to face with three armed men running directly towards him. (Copyright G H Higgins).

ABOVE AND LEFT: The broken goggles, split glove and bloodstained army haversack belonging to Alec de Antiquis were picked up from the gutter in Charlotte Street and piled onto the saddle of his motorcycle before it was wheeled away by a local bobby.

No clues

Leading the police investigation was Chief Inspector Robert Fabian, who had spent a quarter of a century cleaning up the streets of the capital and would be immortalised in the 1950s TV series *Fabian of The Yard*. Fabian's detection rate was legendary, and it looked as if the Charlotte Street robbery would tax his powers to the limit. The Vauxhall, stolen shortly before the robbery, provided no clues. A .32 calibre bullet had killed Alec de Antiquis, while the one recovered from the shop's woodwork came from a .455 calibre revolver. A third gun dropped at the scene had a set of fingerprints on it, but these failed to match any on police files. The amateurishness with which the job was carried out suggested it was the work of young tearaways, and there were plenty of those who had yet to acquire a rap sheet. There were a number of eyewitnesses, but with handkerchiefs covering the men's faces that proved to be a fruitless line of inquiry. There were even wild discrepancies over the visible features, such as height, build and the apparel they were wearing.

Breakthrough

A breakthrough came after three days, when taxi driver Albert Grubb reported a contretemps with a man who jumped onto the running board of his cab and tried to force his way into the vehicle. Grubb got the better of the exchange and he watched as the man and a companion entered Brook House, an office building in Tottenham Court Road. When the pair emerged a few minutes later, one was minus the raincoat he'd been wearing. A sweep of the building turned up not only that garment – stuffed at the back of a caretaker's cupboard – but also a knotted scarf that had been used as a facemask. A key that fitted the stolen car was also found.

The Montague Burton coat was common enough and held no clues other than the batch number. Records kept by the well-known firm of gents' outfitters showed that it would have been sold at one of their London shops. Fabian and his team were helped by the fact that clothing was still subject to rationing. As a hedge against the use of counterfeit coupons, retailers logged sales against the name on the ration card supplied by the purchaser. That gave police a long list to work through, and they set about the painstaking task of eliminating possible suspects one by one. Eventually, they lighted upon Thomas Kemp, who had bought a raincoat of the required type from the Deptford High Street store the previous December. Kemp had no convictions but he was related by marriage to some unsavoury characters well known to the police. These were his wife's brothers, Tommy and Harry Jenkins.

> *There were a number of eyewitnesses, but with handkerchiefs covering the thieves' faces that proved to be a fruitless line of inquiry.*

ABOVE: The published sketches played a significant role in apprehending the criminals – particularly the raincoat which proved pivotal in solving the crime.

RIGHT: One of the suspects is pictured arriving at Tottenham Court Road police station on 17 May, following his arrest in Plumstead the previous day.

APRIL 30, 1947

The amateur killer

The minutes went by. Gunman No. 3, in the Vauxhall outside - right opposite a poster advertising "Odd Man Out" - became scared. He ran - and took the ignition keys of the car with him. Then out came Gunmen Nos. 1 and 2. They could not start the car, so they, too, ran. At that moment Mr. de Antiquis came along Charlotte Street on his big, red Indian motor cycle. He was wearing a leather jerkin and a crash helmet. He tried with his powerful machine to intercept the running pair.

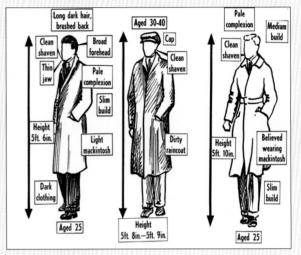

The watchers

One of the men stopped, aimed and fired a shot which hit Mr. de Antiquis in his left temple. He fell dying on the corner. It was here last night, in the dusty road, that a woman dressed in black placed a rough cross and an arum lily. Round this wreath gathered all the black men, the yellow men, and the seedy white men who make up the street boys in this crowded corner of London. Strange crowds - and strange names on the shops along the street. Barba-Yanny, the restaurant, for example; Mr. Tong, the barber; Chinese signs on a cafe; Jinghi, the fur dealer; Mystic, the woman who reads your hands.

Inside Jay's, the police were working late. Chief Inspector Robert Fabian, ex-chief of the Flying Squad, was there in charge. With him were Divisional Detective-Inspector "Bob" Higgins, and fingerprint experts, Superintendent F. Cherrill, with his assistant, Chief Inspector S. Birch.

In their search for clues, walls were stripped, counters and fittings unscrewed, or sawn off. There will be no business at Jay's today.

It was motor bikes, and his unceasing hunt for spare parts for them, that led Alec de Antiquis to the back streets of Tottenham Court Road yesterday. To earn a living for himself, his wife, and their six children in his little repair shop in High Street, Colliers Wood, Alec had to find spares where he could.

Suspects hauled in

Tommy Jenkins was serving time for a smash-and-grab raid on a jeweller's in 1944, a robbery in which a naval officer who tried to intervene was run over and killed by the getaway car. The driver, Ronald Hedley, was given the death sentence, later commuted to life imprisonment. Jenkins was found guilty of manslaughter and given eight years. Police strongly suspected that his younger brother Harry was also involved in the heist but couldn't prove it. Harry had since had a spell at Borstal, released just a week prior to the Charlotte Street raid.

Fabian's first port of call was the home of Thomas and Vera Kemp. Thomas Kemp wasn't in so Fabian questioned his wife about the raincoat. She said it looked similar to one her husband had lost. Fabian left, but the house was kept under surveillance and Mrs Kemp was soon on the move. She led the police straight to the Jenkins' abode and Fabian knew he was onto something.

Under questioning Thomas Kemp admitted that the raincoat had not been lost but lent to his brother-in-law Harry Jenkins. That was enough to haul Jenkins in, and the police also rounded up some of his known confederates. They included 20-year-old Christopher Geraghty and 17-year-old Terence Rolt, both of whom claimed to have been at home ill on the day of the robbery. Jenkins also denied involvement, though he refused to disclose his alibi. Even at 23 he was well versed enough in police procedure to know that they had to prove he was involved; he didn't have to prove he wasn't. Jenkins remained ice-cool when Fabian put him in an identity parade in front of 27 eyewitnesses, including four who had seen the unmasked visages of two of the gang when they ducked inside the office block. None pointed Jenkins out. It later came to light that he pulled a classic trick to throw the witnesses off the scent. Before the parade he had idly asked for a copy of the morning paper, which he stuffed into his pocket when he took his place in the line-up. It gave the impression that he had been out on the streets mid-morning, hauled in at the police's request to make up the numbers and therefore not the prime suspect.

TOP RIGHT: 23-year-old lighterman Harry Jenkins from Bermondsey is pictured travelling in a police car from Tottenham Court Road police station on his way to Marlborough Street Court.

LEFT: Jenkins was remanded in custody for a week with 20-year-old labourer Christopher Geraghty (pictured) and 17-year-old warehouseman Terence Rolt. The three Londoners were charged with 'being concerned with intent to commit an armed robbery and also being concerned in the murder of Alec de Antiquis'.

TOP LEFT AND ABOVE: As Harry Jenkins leaves Tottenham Court Road police station in an open-necked shirt, he is surrounded by some of the detectives who had been involved in the investigation. The leading detective was Chief Inspector Robert Fabian, who would later be immortalised in the TV series *Fabian of The Yard*.

Confessions

Jenkins was off the hook for the time being, and even tossed the police a lead. He said he had given the raincoat to another career criminal, Bill Walsh, whose name was in the frame for the Bayswater robbery on 25 April. The hunt for Walsh ended on Plumstead Common on 16 May. Visibly shaken at the prospect of being implicated in a murder inquiry, Walsh readily confessed to participating in the Queensway raid. His role had been lookout, he insisted; the actual robbery was carried out by Jenkins, Geraghty and a third man later identified as Michael Gillam. Walsh also admitted to 'casing' the Charlotte Street jeweller's on behalf of Jenkins, Geraghty and Rolt. There was obviously crossing and double-crossing going on between the band of thieves, but Walsh had a solid alibi for the Charlotte Street robbery and Fabian was inclined to believe his version of events.

Rolt was picked up again and this time the youngest member of the gang cracked under pressure. He admitted driving the stolen vehicle for the Charlotte Street raid and named Geraghty and Jenkins as his accomplices. Geraghty later admitted he fired the shot that killed Alec de Antiquis, disposing of his gun in the Thames. It was found by some children playing on the river bank, ballistics experts confirming it as the murder weapon. Harry Jenkins continued to maintain that he was elsewhere at the time the crime was committed.

JULY 29, 1947

Antiquis: Two will hang

Ninety days after Alec de Antiquis was shot dead after a daylight "hold-up" in a crowded Soho street - a crime which shocked Britain - three men were found Guilty at the Old Bailey last night of his murder. Two were sentenced to death - Christopher James Geraghty, 20-year-old labourer, who fired the shot, and Charles Henry Jenkins, 23-year-old lighterman. The third, 17-year-old Terence John Peter Rolt, warehouseman, was saved by his youth; the death sentence cannot be passed on anyone under 18. Mr. Justice James Hallett ordered that Rolt should be detained during the King's pleasure, and gave the opinion that he should not be released for at least five years.

The jury of nine men and three women returned just before 6 p.m., after an absence of 50 minutes. There was deathly quiet as they returned their verdicts of Guilty against all three.

As the tension in the famous court eased slightly, the judge instructed a warder to send Rolt below.

'Their duty'

Geraghty and Jenkins stood impassive. Then Mr. Justice Hallett, wearing the black cap, passed sentence of death on them both. "The jury have in my judgment merely done their duty." he said, "a duty which they owe to the community whose representatives they were. For the crime of which you have been found Guilty there is only one sentence known to law."

Jenkins and Geraghty turned smartly about and, silent, hurried down the steps to the cells below. As Jenkins disappeared he gave a quick glance round and smiled at relatives.

In his summing-up, Mr. Justice Hallett said: "It is not every day, thank God, that innocent people are shot down in the streets of London in circumstances such as occurred here. It is not every day even that hold-ups by three men, armed with guns, occur in London, though naturally this case has attracted a great deal of public notice. I described this affair as an outrage. I do not know whether you were surprised when Mr. Russell Vick (K.C. who defended Jenkins) protested against that description but I shall continue to so describe it."

TOP LEFT: Harry Jenkins arrives back at court for the resumed hearing of the murder charges in May 1947. He had completed a spell in borstal just one week before the Charlotte Street robbery took place.

LEFT: Once again a large crowd gathers to see the notorious felons Jenkins, Geraghty and Rolt, as they leave Marlborough Street Police Station.

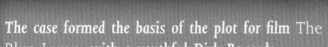
The case formed the basis of the plot for film The Blue Lamp, with a youthful Dirk Bogarde.

Murder charge upheld

On 21 July 1947 the three men took their place in the dock at the Old Bailey, each pleading not guilty to the murder charge they faced. The fact that each of them was carrying a loaded weapon ensured that their fates were intertwined, and any hopes that the shooting might be downgraded to manslaughter owing to a lack of premeditation were soon dashed. Trial judge Mr Justice Hallett said that citizens doing their duty in trying to apprehend fleeing felons were accorded special protection in the eyes of the law, a tradition dating back almost three hundred years. If the felon meted out violence resulting in the death of the citizen, he was liable to a murder charge even if the outcome was unintended. That statement alone was enough to counter Geraghty's claim that he had meant only to scare Mr de Antiquis, and the defendants' prospects were dealt another blow when it was pointed out that firing at the head at close range could hardly be construed as a warning shot.

Neither Geraghty nor Rolt took the stand but Jenkins did testify. He finally provided the long-awaited alibi, which family members and acquaintances endorsed, but to the jury it had the hollow ring of fabrication. After a week-long trial, it took them less than an hour to find all three guilty. Jenkins and Geraghty were given the death sentence, and after all appeals failed the two were hanged at Pentonville Prison on 19 September 1947. Rolt, being aged under 18 at the time of the crime, was detained at His Majesty's pleasure with a recommendation that he serve a minimum term of five years. In fact, he served nine years, released in June 1956.

The case formed the basis of the plot for the 1949 film The Blue Lamp, with a youthful Dirk Bogarde playing the callow hoodlum who guns down a man standing in the way of his escape following a robbery. Some details were changed, notably that the murder victim was not a passing motorcyclist but a serving police officer, PC George Dixon. Actor Jack Warner famously came back from the dead to reprise the role in a long-running TV series Dixon of Dock Green.

TOP LEFT, BOTTOM LEFT AND ABOVE: There were many court appearances before the case finally reached the Old Bailey in July 1947, when the trio of perpetrators were charged with the murder of Alec de Antiquis. After a week-long trial the jury needed less than an hour to find all three men guilty. As Rolt was under 18 at the time of the crime, he was ordered to be detained at His Majesty's pleasure for a minimum of five years. Jenkins and Geraghty (seen getting into a police car) were both sentenced to death by hanging. Christopher James Geraghty and Charles Henry Jenkins were hanged in a double execution at London's Pentonville Prison on 19 September 1947. Terence Rolt was released from prison on licence in June 1956 after spending nine years in jail.

DONALD NEILSON:
The Black Panther

On the morning of 14 January 1975, Dorothy Whittle made the shocking discovery that her 17-year-old daughter Lesley had been abducted during the night from their comfortable home in Highley, Shropshire. Three messages imprinted on Dymo-tape were found in the lounge, leaving no doubt over the explanation for Lesley's disappearance.

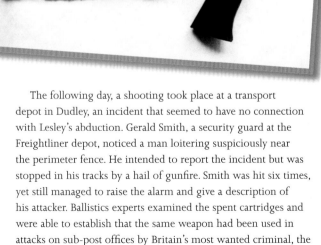

Ransom demands

One of the messages set out a ransom demand of £50,000, which was to be taken to a telephone box at Swan shopping centre, Kidderminster, that evening. The bag-carrier would receive a phone call with further instructions. The tape message carried a dark warning: 'From the time you answer you are on a time limit. If police or tricks death.'

The kidnapper had chosen his target carefully. Lesley's father had built up a thriving coach company, and on his death in 1970 had left £82,000 in trust for his teenage daughter. This information had featured in the press, and obviously one criminally-minded media watcher had seen it as an opportunity for a big payday.

Lesley's 31-year-old brother Ronald kept the phone box appointment, though he had not complied fully with the kidnapper's request, for he was in two-way radio communication with the police. A news blackout was vital to the success of the operation but the story leaked out and the assignation was aborted. The Whittle family faced an anxious wait for the kidnapper to make further contact.

The following day, a shooting took place at a transport depot in Dudley, an incident that seemed to have no connection with Lesley's abduction. Gerald Smith, a security guard at the Freightliner depot, noticed a man loitering suspiciously near the perimeter fence. He intended to report the incident but was stopped in his tracks by a hail of gunfire. Smith was hit six times, yet still managed to raise the alarm and give a description of his attacker. Ballistics experts examined the spent cartridges and were able to establish that the same weapon had been used in attacks on sub-post offices by Britain's most wanted criminal, the Black Panther.

Sub-post office raids

There had been a spate of sub-post office robberies over recent years, the perpetrator often making off with paltry sums. One such raid in 1972 had resulted in the postmaster being shot. He was a lucky survivor, but over the previous twelve months three more have-a-go heroes had been fatally wounded. Donald Skepper was shot dead when his Harrogate premises were hit in February 1974; Derek Astin suffered the same fate during a robbery in Accrington the following September; and two months later, Sidney Grayland died from gunshot wounds after he struggled with the interloper at the sub-post office run by his wife in Langley, West Midlands. The Post Office had put up a £25,000 reward for information that led to the killer being brought to book, but thus far he had eluded the long arm of the law. The 'Black Panther' tag wasn't just a reference to his hooded appearance; it also encapsulated the stealthy, feline quality he seemed to possess for melting away after committing a crime.

Police make links

Meanwhile, there had been significant developments in the abduction case. On 16 January, the Whittle family received a call containing a recorded message; it was Lesley's voice with instructions from the kidnapper regarding payment of the ransom. Ronald Whittle followed a Dymo-tape trail that led to Bathpool Park, near Kidsgrove. He was to look out for a flashing torch, the signal from the kidnapper. While Whittle was still struggling to find the park in the darkness of the small hours, a courting couple pulled up at the appointed place. The lovers were spooked by the flashlight and drove off, and the kidnapper also retreated, thinking it was a police trap.

A few days later, police discovered a link between the Black Panther's latest attack and the Whittle inquiry. They ran a check on a Morris 1300 saloon that had been left near the Freightliner depot and found that it had been stolen. Inside the vehicle was the gun that had shot Gerald Smith, a cassette tape of Lesley's voice and a pair of her slippers. There were also some numbered envelopes containing Dymo-tape messages that obviously formed a ransom trail. The investigating officers now knew that the men wanted for the post office homicides, the shooting of Gerald Smith and the abduction of Lesley Whittle were one and the same: the Black Panther.

> The lovers were spooked by the flashlight and drove off, and the kidnapper also retreated, thinking it was a police trap.

OPPOSITE LEFT: Britain's most wanted man, Donald Neilson, commonly known as 'The Black Panther'. Born Donald Nappey on 1 August 1936, Neilson was jailed for life in July 1976 for the murder of 17-year-old Shropshire heiress Lesley Whittle and three sub-postmasters in post-office robberies.

OPPOSITE RIGHT: Chilling reminders of the secret life of Neilson: one of his sinister, trademark hoods and his sawn-off shotgun were found among an assortment of equipment when police searched his Bradford home following his arrest in the Nottinghamshire village of Rainworth in December 1975.

TOP RIGHT: A 'For Sale' notice marks the home of Neilson in Grangefield Avenue in Bradford, Yorkshire, where the jobbing

builder lived with his wife, Irene, and 14-year-old daughter Kathryn. He had married Irene in 1955 and it was she who persuaded him not to pursue a career in the armed forces, but to settle down in Bradford.

ABOVE: Neilson had enjoyed the discipline and routine of National Service when he was a teenager. Although he did not join the army on a permanent basis, he continued to indulge his interest in the outdoor life and often took his wife and daughter on camping trips and outings involving survival activities and manoeuvres.

LEFT: The locked attic in Neilson's house where police found a stash of guns and a recording of Lesley Whittle's message giving instructions for the ransom payment.

Underground tunnels

It wasn't until 6 March that police made a thorough search of Bathpool Park. By then some schoolboys playing in the area had already made two important discoveries. They found the kidnapper's torch and a Dymo-tape message that read: 'Drop suitcase in hole'. After an intensive overground search of the park, police turned their attention to what lay beneath their feet. Where was the 'hole' referred to in the message? They learned that there was a network of underground tunnels, built to carry storm water from the surrounding hills. At the bottom of one 60-foot shaft leading down to one of the culverts, they found a platform which had obviously been used as a camp, for there was a sleeping bag, food and drink. They also found Lesley Whittle's lifeless naked body, with a wire ligature round her neck. The post mortem revealed that she had died of vagal inhibition, not asphyxiation. The vagus is a cranial nerve that regulates heartbeat and breathing; Lesley had died from shock before the noose had done its work. The time of death was estimated to be within days of the abduction.

Diligent policework

The police drew a blank trying to trace where the goods recovered from the Morris 1300 and the underground camp might have been bought. Photofit images and the taped voice of the Black Panther drew a huge response when they were screened on television, but produced no significant lead. Months passed and it seemed that the trail had gone cold, the Black Panther once again showing his talent for going to ground. The breakthrough, when it came, was the result of diligent police work on the part of two young constables on Panda patrol in the Nottinghamshire village of Mansfield Woodhouse. PC Stuart McKenzie and PC Anthony White decided to question a man carrying a holdall who was loitering suspiciously in the vicinity of the local post office. He produced a sawn-off shotgun and forced the officers into the patrol car. McKenzie took the wheel while the gunman occupied the passenger seat, pointing his weapon at the constable's ribs. White was in the back of the vehicle.

As they passed through the village of Rainworth, the officers made their play. McKenzie braked hard and White grabbed the shotgun, which discharged, injuring his hand. Two men queuing in a nearby fish and chip shop rushed to the officers' assistance and the gunman was soon overpowered. McKenzie and White didn't know it yet but they had arrested the Black Panther.

FEBRUARY 15, 1975

Do you know him?

The police have nicknamed him the Black Panther - unconsciously, perhaps, giving him a touch of glamour his exploits hardly deserve. He is Britain's most wanted man - suspected of the kidnapping of 17-year-old heiress Lesley Whittle and the murders since 1971 of three sub-postmasters and another 20 or so raids on post offices around the country. The police cannot definitely put a name to him.

Astonishing dossier

But they have built up an astonishing dossier of the personality, background and appearance of the man they cannot name. Oddly, perhaps, in a man who is a merciless killer, he has shown compassion for women. And that fact alone leads the police to believe that Lesley Whittle may still be alive. One instance was during an armed robbery when he loosened the bonds on a woman after she complained that they were too tight. In another case he covered a woman with a blanket when she told him she was cold.

Other clues have formed a general profile of the kidnapper. The cloth cap and anorak or coat he wears may be part of a disguise. But police are convinced that he is a Black Country man. Witnesses have described him as about 35 to 40 years old, with black, wavy hair, not too long and from new trousers found in the abandoned stolen car police know he is between 5ft. 4in. and 5ft. 6in. tall and wears clothes with 29in. legs and a 32in. waist. He may have been in the Services. He has been seen carrying a large blue RAF webbing pack and walks in a brisk, military fashion.

LEFT: A police search of the Black Panther's lair in the attic of his Bradford home yielded a haul of army accessories including knives, guns and ammunition. Some wire which matched that used to tether Lesley in the underground drainage shaft was also discovered.

ABOVE AND RIGHT: It was a chance breakthrough that led to the arrest of Neilson and the subsequent search of his family home. He had been spotted acting suspiciously outside a post office near Mansfield by two patrolling policemen. As they questioned him, he pulled out a gun and forced them to drive him away. Following a violent struggle he was brought under control and detained, although at this stage the police still were unaware exactly who they had just captured.

Hideout

Every hour of the murder hunt now strengthened police theories that the Panther was an itinerant construction worker who had helped to tunnel the drainage scheme where he made his hideout. Nine years before British Rail had driven a tunnel and line through the park and fresh drains were built with the scheme. These carried surface water from the park and the overflow from its lake. They were added to a maze of existing drains – some 8ft. high – which served nearby sewer works and a canal. There were several entrances to the complex and in one part an underground canal. The whole area beneath the park was criss-crossed by tunnels, some of which police did not suspect existed but which the killer used freely.

Rage

It seemed that he forced Lesley into the shaft, dressed only in her nightclothes. Then he tied her up and returned to the surface to await the arrival of her 31-year-old brother, Mr Ronald Whittle, with the £50,000 ransom. But when things went wrong the Panther returned in a rage to kill the girl, who had been left standing on the ledge with her hands bound. The ransom money was to be thrown down the shaft where Lesley's body was found. Her killer would have collected it and run off into the maze of tunnels, leaving Mr Whittle to discover his sister.

Tough

Mr Jack Trow, of Long Row, Kidsgrove, who worked on the drainage scheme as a ganger, said: 'There were some tough types on the job. I thought about it and a couple might have fitted the bill from the impression I have of the Panther. There was one gang of tunnel men from Scotland who were very tough, and there were also quite a few from the Black Country.'

Police examined a number of things found in the shaft. They included changes of clothing, Lesley's candlewick dressing gown, and a sleeping bag. They also examined the underside of a manhole cover leading to the hideout on which the word 'death' had been scrawled. The cover was beneath one which marked the entrance to the shaft where Lesley's body was found. The scrawl was believed by detectives to be the Panther's sick postscript to his hideous crime.

TOP: More items discovered in the police search included a wire saw from an RAF survival kit, a leather cosh, a cigarette lighter with a razor blade and a toggle cord.

ABOVE: Neilson was wearing some of the pictured clothing, including an anorak and cap, when he was arrested. It was only when his car and home were searched that police realised the person they had arrested was the Black Panther, the man responsible for the murder of the Shropshire student and three postmasters.

RIGHT: A police reconstruction of how the Black Panther appeared to his victims. Neilson's first casualty, Lancashire postmaster, Leslie Richardson, had given the police an accurate description after he was shot in the first of the violent robberies in February 1972.

MARCH 10, 1975

Lesley died of fright

Fear killed Lesley Whittle after her kidnapper tethered her by a wire cable to a ladder in the blackness of a 60ft. deep drainage shaft. The 17-year-old heiress died of fright when she plunged 45 feet down the shaft from a ledge near the top. She was found hanging from the wire which had been fixed round her neck. Lesley is believed to have been pushed off the ledge by her killer. A five-hour post mortem disclosed yesterday that Lesley died of vagal inhibition - a massive shock to the heart brought on by fear. Police now believe that she died within days of being kidnapped more than seven weeks ago by the vicious Black Panther, wanted for the murder of three sub-postmasters.

The Panther - the most dangerous man in Britain - used the shaft as the entrance to his hideout in a labyrinth of drainage tunnels below the Staffordshire beauty spot of Bathpool Park, Kidsgrove. He forced the terrified girl into his subterranean world after driving her 70 miles from her home in the village of Highley, Shropshire, where he had snatched her at gunpoint.

Arsenal of weapons

The man identified himself as Donald Neilson, a 39-year-old self-employed builder who lived in Grangefield Avenue, Bradford, with his wife and daughter. The holdall he was carrying when challenged contained two of his trademark hoods, and a search of his house revealed all the Panther paraphernalia, including an arsenal of weapons, a press for making false number plates and wire of the type that had been used to tether Lesley Whittle by the neck. These were kept in a locked attic, away from the prying eyes of his family, who were unaware of the double life Neilson was leading.

Details of the Black Panther's history emerged. Donald Neilson was born 1 August 1936, growing up in Morley, near Leeds. His family name was actually Nappey, which made him the butt of schoolboy jokes during his impressionable years. His home life was hardly any happier, and he suffered a major blow at the age of 11 when he lost his mother to cancer. By the time he reached adulthood – and rid himself of the surname that had blighted his formative years – Neilson was a loner with a chip on his shoulder. He married mill worker Irene Tate in 1955, the union producing one daughter, Kathryn. Neilson did his National Service in the King's Own Yorkshire Light Infantry, and although he had an undistinguished record as a soldier, he developed an obsession with the trappings of the military lifestyle. His forte was survival techniques, and he would even take his wife and child out on manoeuvres. Neilson tried his hand at several lines of work, none of which brought him much success or satisfaction. When he chalked up yet another failure in the building trade, he turned to armed robbery, planning his crimes with military precision. A feature of his preparations was choosing hides where he could go to ground until the heat was off, surviving on meagre rations. As far as his family and neighbours were concerned he was busy working away from home.

Years of planning

The post office raids had not been very lucrative, and reading about heiress Lesley Whittle had given him the idea for a big score. He had spent over two years planning the operation. The original ransom trail was to have led to the Freightliner depot; the altercation that led to the shooting of Gerald Smith caused him to abandon that plan and choose Bathpool Park as the drop-off point instead.

Tethered

The spot included two shafts, one down which Lesley's 31-year-old brother Mr Ronald Whittle was instructed to throw £50,000 ransom and 150 yards away the 62ft. deep one where the girl was held prisoner, tethered to a platform by a wire rope round her neck.

His forte was survival techniques, and he would even take his wife and child out on manoeuvres.

LEFT: A signed receipt from Neilson's struggling business. By the time Neilson kidnapped the teenage heiress in 1975, he was already a multiple murderer, having previously supplemented his limited earnings as a builder by robbing post offices at gunpoint. The non-fatal shooting of postmaster Leslie Richardson was followed by more violent robberies and three other postmasters were shot dead in similar incidents.

ABOVE: Police issued a re-constructed image of the kidnapper – 'Britain's Public Enemy Number 1' during the hunt for the abductor of the teenage schoolgirl. Neilson had carefully chosen his victim who had been left a five-figure sum by her deceased father in his will.

MARCH 17, 1975

How kidnapper outwitted the police

This is the underground hide-out of the Black Panther, part of a damp and stinking maze of tunnels where he kept heiress Lesley Whittle a terrified prisoner and finally killed her. It was an ideal hiding place. Few had any idea of the existence of the labyrinth more than 60ft. below the ground ... and more important for the man who knew he would be hunted by hundreds of police, it had four escape routes.

But before he could use them the Panther had to ensure that the 5ft. high drainage tunnels beneath Bathpool Park at Kidsgrove, Staffordshire, would not be flooded. The way he did this - and the careful selection of his hideaway - has convinced police that he has an intimate knowledge of the drainage system, and probably helped to construct it.

Some time before 17-year-old Lesley was kidnapped from her home in the village of Highley, Shropshire, in January, the Panther turned off the valves which allowed overflow water from a reservoir half a mile away to escape into the drainage tunnels. At this time of year the hideout is normally up to 5ft. deep in floodwater. With the valves off the killer reduced the depth to a mere two inches. Only a man familiar with the system could have known how to do it. Only a man familiar with the system could have picked such a superb hiding place among the maze of underground piping. It was no random choice.

The quiet odd-job man from Grangefield Avenue

The arrest of odd-job man Donald K. Neilson, the family man with a daughter he adored, has shocked his neighbours in a city suburb. Today Neilson, 35, will be accused in connection with the murder of 17-year-old Lesley Whittle, whose body was found in a drainage shaft last March at Kidsgrove. He ran his builder's and joiner's business from three garages behind his house in Grangefield Avenue, Thornbury, two miles from Bradford city centre.

Yesterday detectives were still in the stone-built terraced house on the main Leeds-Bradford road, 72 hours after he was detained at Mansfield, Nottinghamshire. His wife and daughter have been taken away by police who have been involved in Britain's biggest-ever manhunt.

'Castro'

Neilson was known as 'Castro' to the man who knew him better than anyone. Mr Keith Walker, 38, who lived next door to him for ten years until a few months ago, said: 'I gave him the name because of the clothing he always wore – a jacket, jeans and boots. I don't think he was ever in the Army, although he looked every inch a part-time paratrooper and drove about in a Champ, a military Land-Rover.

He was an odd-job man who occasionally helped me on jobs when I had a building business. He was a fantastic worker, tireless and utterly fearless. I've seen him walk up and down a roof and swing down a rope lowered round the chimney. He kept himself very fit with swimming and hiking. His only amusements were swimming and going to the pictures regularly. He liked good westerns. He was also fond of music, mainly film themes. His favourite record was *A Fistful of Dollars*. He idolised his daughter and took her everywhere with him. He took her swimming and to a disco dance once a week.

I felt a chill down my spine when I heard he was the man detained in connection with Lesley Whittle's death.' Mr Walker said Neilson told him he had bought a house in Pudsey when he put his home up for sale a few months ago. He added: 'I'm probably the only person who became friendly with him and got close to him but I still only went in his house twice in ten years and have no idea about his background before I knew him. From his accent I'd place him coming from somewhere in the Midlands on the Shropshire side. His wife spoke with a Yorkshire accent although I sometimes wondered if they were actually married because to me they acted more like brother and sister.'

TOP RIGHT: Neilson's van photographed at his home in Thornbury, Bradford.

MIDDLE RIGHT: The van alleged to have been used by the Black Panther when he kidnapped Lesley Whittle. Neilson had earned this sobriquet from the media because of his practice of wearing a dark-coloured balaclava during the post-office robberies.

BOTTOM RIGHT: The Mercedes believed to have been used by Donald Neilson.

> He looked every inch a part-time paratrooper and drove about in a Champ, a military Land-Rover.

DONALD NEILSON: The Black Panther

'We know that nothing can bring Lesley back, but until her killer is arrested, charged and convicted there must always be a feeling of gloom.'

BOTTOM: A crowd of 300 jeered and shouted as 39-year-old Donald Neilson was driven to court. Extra police with their dogs had been brought in to control the hostile mob.

OPPOSITE LEFT: Covered by a plaid blanket Neilson cowers in the back of one of the convoy of five police cars which drove him to court. He was to be charged with four murders, as well as the serious offences of attempted murder, GBH, robbery, kidnapping and possession of firearms.

LEFT: Neilson being taken down a flight of steps on his way to court. He was led handcuffed into the dock of the packed courtroom by Detective Inspector Wally Boreham and Detective Chief Inspector Len Barnes.

DECEMBER 15, 1975

Callous

He made concrete blocks and for a time rented a garage to make wooden sheds. But nothing seemed to work out right for him and even his taxi business folded up after only nine months. He often went off camping in his hiking gear and would take his wife and daughter with him. He called me Kiddo but for a time we fell out because of the way he treated one of his dogs, a mongrel bitch, which was killed because he let it roam the streets. I found it dead in the road, put it on his doorstep and told him it would remind him of being callous when he claimed he loved dogs.

My wife saw him on Thursday night when they caught the same bus to Leeds.' Another neighbour said: 'His wife and daughter also kept themselves apart. I never knew the child to have playmates when she was younger. Mrs Neilson had a job as a cleaner at a city centre store.'

Neilson had a quick military-style walk. He once owned two Alsatians which he had referred to as 'Army dogs.' About six years ago he changed his name by deed poll from Nappy. 'I think he felt it was embarrassing, particularly for his daughter,' said a neighbour. He ran an old van and Land-Rover. But six weeks ago he bought a new Toyota van from the garage across the road.

Scientists and detectives have been working behind the blue venetian blinds at Neilson's house for nearly two days and have taken away clothing, papers, cameras, torches, and a mattress. Detectives at Kidsgrove will hold a top-level conference today. One thing that will be discussed is when an identification parade is to be held. It will be attended by security guard Gerald Smith, shot six times by a man at the freightliner depot in Dudley, Worcestershire.

Cloud lifts for a village

Ron Whittle smiled for the first time in 11 months yesterday, and spoke of the cloud that has lifted from the village of Highley in Shropshire. At the same time the Vicar, the Rev John Brittain, who declared that the Devil himself had trod the village, told parishioners that their prayers had been answered.

Mr Whittle, a coach proprietor, is 32, but grey streaks in his black hair betray the agony the family has been through since his sister Lesley was kidnapped on the wild, windy night of January 14. Yesterday a brief phone call from Detective Chief Superintendent Bob Booth, head of the West Mercia CID, told him that 'the hunt for the kidnapper and the murderer was at an end'. Mr Whittle said: 'The news was the best Christmas present that anyone could wish for. We know that nothing can bring Lesley back, but until her killer is arrested, charged and convicted there must always be a feeling of gloom.' Finally, Mr Whittle – recalling that he had been under suspicion among some members of the public because of his likeness to an artist's impression of the ruthless kidnapper-killer – said: 'I hope the news will put paid to any rumours.'

FAR RIGHT: The frenzied crowd hammer their fists on the outside of the van which ferried the Black Panther to his trial at Oxford Crown Court which started on June 14, 1976.

BOTTOM: A blanket covering her head, Mrs Irene Neilson leaves Stone police station with her solicitor. She was taken to the station 24 hours after her husband was jailed for life for murdering three sub-postmasters and heiress Lesley Whittle and seven offences in connection with the thefts from post offices.

Neilson escaped a fifth murder charge because of an ancient statute which stated that a victim had to succumb to injuries within a year and a day for it to be deemed murder.

Neilson pleads not guilty

Neilson was tried at Oxford Crown Court, as it was decided that feelings were running so high in the Black Panther's target territory that he could not be guaranteed a fair trial. He accepted the kidnapping charge but pleaded not guilty on the four counts of murder. There were also charges of attempted murder in relation to Gerald Smith and Anthony White. Smith died four months before the case went to court, but Neilson escaped a fifth murder charge because of an ancient statute which stated that a victim had to succumb to injuries within a year and a day for it to be deemed murder. The law has since been amended.

Neilson maintained that the gun had been fired accidentally in the struggles that took place in the post offices, and that Lesley had lost her footing on the platform when he returned from the abortive meeting with Ronald Whittle. The prosecution maintained that he felt angry and cheated when he returned to the culvert empty-handed and pushed her off the ledge in a fit of rage. The jury agreed. Donald Neilson was sentenced to life imprisonment by Mr Justice Marr-Jones, who recommended that in this case the tariff should be interpreted literally. Successive home secretaries have endorsed that decision, and Neilson died of motor neurone in disease 2011, one of Britain's longest-serving prisoners.

DEREK BENTLEY:
'Let him have it, Chris!'

'That night I was out to kill, because I had so much hate inside me for what they had done to my brother.' Those words were spoken by 16-year-old Christopher Craig on 2 November 1952, the night he shot PC Sidney Miles during a botched raid on a warehouse with his 19-year-old accomplice Derek Bentley. The crime resulted in a murder conviction and an execution, but it was not Craig who went to the gallows. Derek William Bentley, who was already in custody when the fatal shot was fired, was hanged for the killing of PC Miles.

Officers on the scene

The Derek Bentley case sparked a campaign for justice that lasted over 40 years; it also marked a watershed moment in legal history for the part it played in removing capital punishment from the statute book.

On the night of 2 November at around 9.15 pm Croydon police station received a telephone call from a woman stating that she had witnessed a break-in. She reported seeing two men climb the gateway entrance to the premises of Barlow & Parker, a confectionery warehouse situated in Tamworth Road, Croydon. Several officers were dispatched to investigate, arriving in two squad cars. By the time they reached the scene, the would-be thieves had made it onto the building's flat roof.

LEFT: Barlow & Parker, the confectionery warehouse in Croydon which was the scene of the shooting.

ABOVE: PC Sidney Miles, the officer shot dead during the break-in.

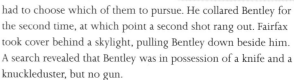

A knife and a knuckleduster

PC Frederick Fairfax was the first to challenge them, having reached the roof via a drainpipe. A disembodied voice gave a belligerent reply: if he wanted them, he'd have to come and get them. Fairfax ran to the lift stack behind which they had taken cover and grabbed one of the men, whom he later discovered to be Derek Bentley. Still maintaining his hold on Bentley, the officer rounded the stack, hoping to apprehend the accomplice, Christopher Craig. Fairfax and Craig came face to face, and Bentley seized the opportunity to break away, shouting, 'Let him have it, Chris.' There was a flash and a report, and Fairfax fell to the ground with a gunshot wound to the shoulder.

Bentley and Craig ran off in different directions, and Fairfax had to choose which of them to pursue. He collared Bentley for the second time, at which point a second shot rang out. Fairfax took cover behind a skylight, pulling Bentley down beside him. A search revealed that Bentley was in possession of a knife and a knuckleduster, but no gun.

Another officer, PC Norman Harrison, had been trying to reach the scene by edging his way along a sloping roof that abutted the flat roof, but Craig spotted him and fired off two shots, forcing Harrison to retreat. Further reinforcement arrived in the shape of PC James Macdonald, who had taken the same drainpipe route as Fairfax, and he joined his fellow officer in restraining Bentley. They asked the detainee about Craig's firearm, to be told that it was a Colt 45 and that he had plenty of ammunition.

RIGHT AND BOTTOM RIGHT: Nine-year-old Edith Ware and her mother who lived in Tamworth Road, Croydon. Edith had been looking out of her bedroom window when she saw two men climbing over the warehouse gates. Her father rushed to the nearest phone box to alert the local police.

BELOW: DC Fairfax (second from left) was the first officer to arrive on the scene. He challenged the two men, apprehending Derek Bentley on the roof.

TOP RIGHT: Despite being shot, DC Fairfax was able to continue chasing Bentley and after apprehending him found a knife and a vicious spiked knuckleduster but no firearms.

ABOVE: Christopher Craig was 16-years old at the time of the shooting and still a minor. After Craig had shot Fairfax, PC Sidney Miles, who had obtained keys to the building, tried to gain access to the roof using the stairs but as soon as the door was opened Craig shot him between the eyes, instantly killing the officer.

ABOVE (INSET): Derek Bentley was 19 years old. He had suffered a serious head injury after an accident during the Second World War and this had left him with permanent brain damage. He suffered from epilepsy and had a very low IQ.

'Come on coppers, I'm only sixteen'

Keys to the premises had been obtained, and officers who had taken the internal staircase could now be heard on the other side of the door that led out onto the roof. One was PC Sidney Miles, the other PC Harrison, who had taken the stairs after his abortive attempt to reach the scene via the adjoining roof. Fairfax shouted to his colleagues to advise them on the position of the gunman, to the left of the door. It made little difference, for as soon as Miles burst through the opening he fell to the ground, shot between the eyes.

Harrison hurled his truncheon, a bottle and a block of wood in Craig's direction and managed to join Fairfax and Macdonald. A fourth officer, PC Robert Jaggs, had also made his way up the drainpipe.

Craig was now ranting, making reference to his elder brother Niven, who had just been sent down for a 12-year stretch for armed robbery. He apparently wanted to take that conviction out on those before him, for he taunted them by yelling out: 'Come on, coppers! I'm only sixteen!'

Much would be made of that remark. Was it a sneering jibe, that a group of police officers oughtn't to have much trouble arresting one youth in his mid-teens? Or was Craig telling them that he was too young to hang, and could therefore act with impunity?

ABOVE RIGHT: Police guard the entrance to the factory after the shooting. During the chase on the factory roof, Craig had jumped 20 feet into a neighbouring garden, sustaining multiple injuries.

BELOW RIGHT: Mrs Miles, widow of the murdered policeman. PC Miles was posthumously awarded the King's Police and Fire Service Medal.

Multiple injuries

Bentley was ushered down the stairs, informing Craig of what was happening by calling out: 'They are taking me down.' When Fairfax returned from handing over the prisoner, he was now armed with a revolver. He told Craig to put down his weapon, but the latter was in no mood to go quietly. 'Come on, copper, let's have it out,' came the reply, accompanied by another shot. Fairfax launched an assault on Craig, making an arcing run and discharging two covering shots as he ran. Craig's weapon clicked, later found to have misfired, for there were two live cartridges still in the chamber. To evade capture Craig dived headlong into a garden 20 feet below. He sustained multiple injuries but remained conscious during his arrest, and lucid enough to express the wish that he was dead and that he had taken the officers with him.

While Craig was being transported to Croydon Hospital for medical attention, Bentley was taken to the local police station. He told officers he knew Craig had a gun but didn't think he would use it. As far as he was concerned, robbery was to have been the extent of their illicit deeds that night.

Both Illiterate

The history of the two youths then emerged. Bentley and Craig had attended the same school, Norbury Secondary Modern, though the three-year age gap meant that their paths didn't cross much during that period. When they did begin hanging around together, it was Craig who assumed the dominant role. Both were illiterate, but Bentley, an epileptic with an IQ of 66, was especially susceptible to the malign influence of the other. His parents recognised the fact and forbade Derek from consorting with Craig, but to no avail.

TOP RIGHT: All four officers involved in the incident received awards from the Queen. (Left to right) Detective Sergeant Fairfax (George Cross), PC James MacDonald (George Medal), PC Norman Harrison (George Medal) and PC Robert Jaggs (British Empire Medal).

ABOVE: Frederick 'Fairy' Fairfax pictured with wife Muriel the day after the shooting.

OPPOSITE LEFT: The now promoted Detective Sergeant Fairfax shows his son Allen the George Cross, presented to him at Buckingham Palace.

RIGHT MIDDLE: (Left to right) PC Macdonald, DC Fairfax and PC Jacks pictured during the court case.

LEFT: Detective Sergeant Fairfax and his wife arrive at the Old Bailey at the start of the trial. Bentley and Craig were charged with murdering PC Sidney Miles and with the attempted murder of DS Fairfax.

TOP LEFT, MIDDLE LEFT, ABOVE AND ABOVE RIGHT (INSET): During the trial several photographs of Bentley's home, including his collection of china, were released. Shots of the back room and the garden shed showed the equipment he used for repairing television and wireless sets.

ABOVE RIGHT: The Home Secretary's flat in Great Peter Street. Crowds often gathered outside after the trial had finished in an effort to influence his response.

Equally culpable

The trial opened at the Central Criminal Court on 9 December, 1952, Craig and Bentley jointly charged with PC Miles's death. Both entered pleas of Not Guilty. Prosecuting counsel Mr Christmas Humphreys made it clear from the outset that while Craig's finger was on the trigger of the murder weapon, Bentley had incited his partner-in-crime and was equally culpable. It made no difference, he argued, that Bentley was already in police hands when the shooting took place. In law Bentley was party to the murder, though common sense was all that was needed to reach that conclusion.

It emerged that Craig had been fined for possession of a weapon a year earlier, and that he harboured ambitions of becoming a gunsmith. The younger defendant certainly had a chip on his shoulder, having been ridiculed during his time working in the storeroom of an engineering firm for his inability to read. The cultivation of the 'hard man' image was a way of acquiring status and covering up for his inadequacy.

But the rooftop bravado deserted Craig in the witness box, where he claimed he had shot PC Miles by accident. His passion, he said, was collecting weapons, disassembling them and putting them back together. He said he was not a good shot, and that he had fired aimlessly in a bid to scare the police officers away. Craig maintained he had no recollection of saying that he was filled with hate and was out to kill someone that night. He even had an answer for the rooftop dive, saying it was out of remorse for having injured an officer. Mr John Parris, acting for Craig, asked the jury to accept that he had not intended to kill Miles, citing the fact that he had been within a few feet of PC Fairfax, yet that officer had received only a flesh wound to the shoulder. He was not seeking an acquittal, but a verdict of manslaughter was appropriate in this case.

Craig: 'One of the most dangerous criminals'

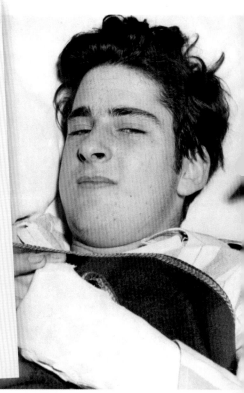

Christopher Craig, the 16-year-old gun-boy, and Derek William Bentley, 19, his fellow street-corner thug, were found guilty at the Old Bailey yesterday of the murder of P.C. Sidney Miles. Craig, too young for the death sentence, was ordered to be detained until the Queen's pleasure be known. Bentley was sentenced to death. In his case, the all-male jury, who were 77 minutes reaching their verdict, made a recommendation for mercy. When the verdict had been given the Clerk of Arraigns asked Craig and Bentley whether they had anything to say. Both looked down at the dock rail before them - and said nothing.

Lord Goddard, the Lord Chief Justice, had the black cap placed on his head. He said to Bentley: "You are 19 years of age. It is, therefore, my duty to pass on you the only sentence which the law can pass for the crime of wilful murder." Bentley raised his head only once as the sentence was read. He glanced at the judge when Lord Goddard came to the closing words, "May the Lord have mercy on your soul." The black cap was removed. Bentley was hurried below by two warders.

Craig stood in the dock with three warders. "Christopher Craig, you are not 19, but in my judgment, and evidently in the judgment of the jury, you are the more guilty of the two," said Lord Goddard. "Your heart was filled with hate and you murdered a policeman without thought of his wife or family or himself. Never once have you expressed a word of sorrow for what you have done. I can only sentence you to be detained until Her Majesty's pleasure is known. I shall tell the Secretary of State when forwarding the recommendation in Bentley's case that in my opinion you are one of the most dangerous young criminals that has ever stood in that dock."

Deliberate act

Bentley maintained that he didn't know Craig had a gun, and denied saying 'Let him have it, Chris.' Summing up on his behalf, Mr F H Cassels said that the jury had to be sure that there was a prior agreement with Craig to use violence to resist arrest, and that Bentley had incited him to discharge his weapon. It was pointed out that Bentley showed no aggression towards the police officers, or any inclination to make a run for it. Surely he could have escaped the clutches of the injured PC Fairfax and rejoined Craig, had he wished to. Was it tenable that this same desperado who allegedly incited the shooting of PC Miles also meekly accepted his own capture?

In his summing up, presiding judge Lord Goddard all but ruled out the possibility of accidental death and a manslaughter verdict, directing the jury in the matter of the special protection accorded to the police: '...if a police officer has arrested, or is endeavouring to arrest, and that includes coming on the scene for the purpose of arrest, a person, and the arrest if effected would be lawful, and that person for the purpose of escape or of preventing or hindering the arrest does a wilful, that is to say an intentional act which causes the death of an officer, he is guilty of murder whether or not he intended to kill or cause grievous bodily harm.'

The Lord Chief Justice emphasised that while the outcome may have been accidental – the death of PC Miles – the perpetrators were still guilty of murder if the weapon had been deliberately discharged. The only leeway offered to the jury was if they found that the firing of the gun was itself accidental. But since Craig had emptied the revolver and reloaded, Lord Goddard opined that it was hard to see this as anything other than a deliberate act.

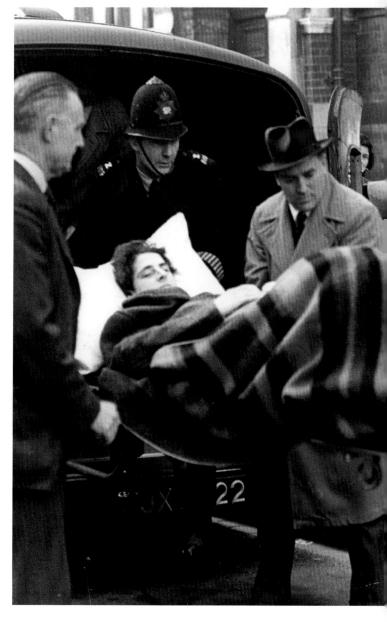

ABOVE AND BELOW: During the court case which opened on 9 December 1952, Craig was transported between Brixton Prison hospital and the Old Bailey by stretcher. During the fall from the roof he had broken an arm and fractured his spine. Giving evidence at the trial, his father told the court that Craig had left school at 15 unable to read or write due to word blindness and had often been ridiculed because of this. He also had an obsession with firearms.

Death sentence passed

Turning to the case against Bentley, the judge stressed that if he was aware that Craig was carrying a gun, and there was an understanding that violence might be used to resist arrest, he was equally guilty of murder. It was no defence to say that he didn't believe his accomplice would use the weapon, or go to the lengths he did. The judge declared that it hardly seemed credible that Craig, a braggart with a passion for firearms, would not have shown Bentley the weapon he was carrying. But the crucial piece of evidence against Bentley was the utterance 'Let him have it, Chris', attested to by Fairfax, Macdonald and Harrison. Could it be that three brave public servants, who had demonstrated such admirable devotion to duty that night, had all been mistaken, or made sworn statements they knew to be untrue? And if Bentley did utter those words, it showed that he knew Craig had a gun and was urging him to use it.

Some seventy-five minutes later, a Guilty verdict was returned on both, with a recommendation for mercy in the case of Bentley. Craig, the guiltier party according to the judge, was over the age of criminal responsibility but not old enough to receive a capital sentence. He was given an indeterminate jail sentence. The jury's wishes regarding Bentley were overlooked as a death sentence was passed.

ABOVE: A detective carries baskets of exhibits into court. Jumbled together were PC Miles's cap and Craig's trilby alongside a knife, a mask and some ammunition.

ABOVE RIGHT: Bentley tries to hide his face as he is driven away from court.

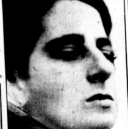

Maxwell Fyfe stands by decision after appeal by 200 MPs

Derek William Bentley will be hanged at Wandsworth Jail at nine o'clock this morning for his part with 16-year-old Christopher Craig in the murder of P.C. Sidney Miles. Shortly before 11 o'clock last night the Home Secretary finally refused to recommend a reprieve. It was the third time in a few days that Sir David Maxwell Fyfe had said "No reprieve."

He gave his decision in a letter to Mr. Aneurin Bevan, who led a party of six Socialist M.Ps to interview him at the Home Office earlier last night and present him with a last-minute appeal signed by 200 M.Ps. Sir David's letter stated that he had given "very anxious consideration" to the case the M.Ps put up.

He fully appreciated the further points of emphasis they had presented and had considered them with an open mind. But he had decided there was no sufficient reason for him to change his mind. The balance, he felt, was still the other way. Consequently his decision must stand.

Five hours earlier he had sent a similar "No" by special Home Office messenger to the Bentleys' home at Norbury.

The fight for a life

For seven hours yesterday the Bentley case dominated the House of Commons.

Here is a brief time schedule of events:

4.30 p.m. After an hour's discussion Speaker W.S. Morrison ruled that in matters touching the prerogative a death sentence cannot be debated until it has been carried out.

5.30: Mr Silverman drew up an appeal begging the Home Secretary "even now" to recommend a reprieve.

6.30: About 100 Socialist M.Ps had signed this appeal. The Bentleys arrived at Westminster. Mrs. Craig and her daughter were also there.

8.30: Another 100 signatures had been added and the Socialist deputation were grouped around Sir David's desk on the softly carpeted floor of the draughty great room.

9.15: The deputation left - and at **10.45** they heard the decision.

Father holds back news from his wife

In the great Central Lobby of the House of Commons, stage of many stirring appeals, there has probably never been a more moving sight than that of last night when hundreds of people came in to urge their M.Ps to fight for Bentley. The atmosphere was hopeful then. Every moment it was expected that a reprieve would be announced.

But just before the House rose, the Home Secretary's private secretary, Mr. Whittock, arrived with a letter, handed it to Mr. Harry McGhee, one of the M.Ps who had formed the delegation. It was the Home Secretary's decision.

Tried everything

Mr. Bentley, who was sitting at a table drafting another telegram to the Queen, was called over by Mr. Tom Driberg, M.P., and given the news. Mr. Bentley moved away as though stunned. Then, speaking as casually as he could, he shepherded his wife and daughter out - he said he thought they had better go home as the House had risen.

After they had gone home, still talking hopefully of a reprieve, Mr. Bentley said: "All we can do now is pray. We have tried everything and it has failed." He was crying.

A friend telephoned to the Queen the telegram they had been drafting: "There is still time to save my son. Please help me" - Mrs. Lilian Rose Bentley. Earlier a telegram had gone to the Duke of Edinburgh from Mr. Niven Craig, father of Christopher Craig.

Derek Bentley saw his family for the last time from 3 p.m. to 3.30 p.m. yesterday. His mother brought him three last gifts: a photograph of his three dogs, Bob, Judy, and Flossie; a rosary; and a letter from a girl friend.

OPPOSITE BELOW RIGHT: Newspaper headlines after the verdict of guilty had been passed reflect the fact that both men were accused of murder – but because of the difference in their ages Bentley would hang, despite a recommendation for mercy from the jury. Craig was given an indeterminate sentence.

TOP RIGHT: Detectives pack up the evidence used during the trial. There was an immediate outcry after the verdict as many members of the public voiced their disagreement with the judge's decision.

RIGHT: In a wave of emotion, Bentley's father William protests at the verdict.

Clamour for reprieve

There was a clamour for Bentley to be reprieved. Hundreds of MPs were incensed at the prospect of a man said to have the mental age of an 11-year-old being hanged for a crime that was committed when he was already in custody. Their hands were tied by the Speaker, who ruled that the case could not be debated in the House until the sentence was carried out. Even Lord Goddard, who would be severely criticised for his partial handling of the trial, believed that Bentley would be reprieved. But Home Secretary Sir David Maxwell Fyfe ignored all petitions, and the convicted man went to the gallows at Wandsworth Prison on 28 January 1953.

Bentley's execution provoked considerable outrage. For almost forty years critics focused on the ambiguity of the words ascribed to Bentley on which the case against him turned. Might he not have been urging Craig to surrender the weapon instead of fire it? Remarkably, the defence made nothing of the possible dual meaning at the trial; only later did that linguistic uncertainty add further weight to claims that a miscarriage of justice had occurred.

Then a darker picture emerged, calling into question whether the words had been spoken at all. Bentley had denied ever saying 'Let him have it, Chris', and his rebuttal of the official version of events was supported by Craig. That had been construed as felons sticking together, but in 1989, their story was backed up by PC Claude Pain, who was also on the roof at the critical moment but not called as a witness. Fairfax, Harrison and Macdonald may not have been guilty of deliberate fabrication. They had to make ordered sense out of confusion and panic, piecing together their reports while traumatised by the death of a colleague. Having convinced themselves that the fateful words had been spoken, the officers perforce had to repudiate any counter-claim. The three men denied that Pain had been in the vicinity, and the latter, troubled by the events but nearing retirement and fearing the consequences of impugning the reputations of his colleagues, remained silent.

TOP: The Home Secretary refused to overturn the ruling and at 11 pm, the night before Bentley was due to hang, crowds gathered outside the Home Office demonstrating against his decision. Inside six MPs including Aneurin Bevan were pleading with the Home Secretary to change his mind.

ABOVE: Telegrams sent to Bentley's parents from Winston Churchill and the Home Secretary, Sir David Maxwell Fyfe following appeals to overturn the judge's decision.

RIGHT: The notice of execution outside Wandsworth Prison announcing that Derek Bentley would hang at 9.00 am the following morning.

OPPOSITE ABOVE RIGHT: William Bentley and his daughter, Iris, arrive at the Home Office bearing packages that contained 6,800 signatures begging for a reprieve.

OPPOSITE ABOVE LEFT: The following morning crowds gathered in silence outside Wandsworth Prison at 9.00 am, just as Bentley was sent to the gallows.

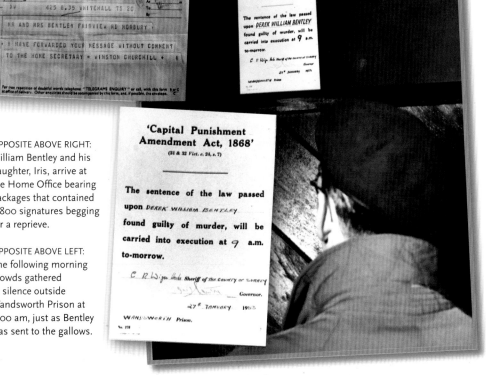

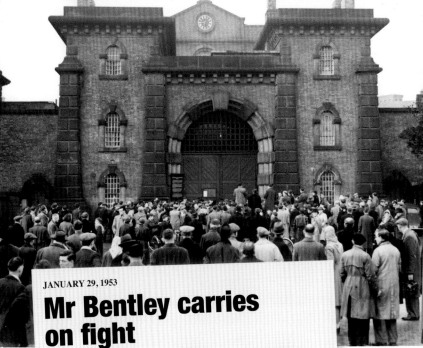

JANUARY 29, 1953

Mr Bentley carries on fight

Mr. William Bentley, father of 19-year-old Derek Bentley who was executed yesterday, said last night: "I am going to fight on to get the law changed. "A lot of people are with me. Nearly 30,000 people signed for a reprieve for Derek. Like me, they cannot understand why a boy who was in custody when the murder was done should die, and the man who fired the shot should live." Sixteen-year-old Christopher Craig, found guilty with Bentley of the murder of P.C. Miles at Croydon, was sentenced to be detained during the Queen's pleasure.

Mr. Bentley said his wife and daughter will probably go to St. Leonards-on-Sea to the home of a sympathiser who has offered them a holiday. On Sunday afternoon he will drive to Marble Arch to join a demonstration which has been organised by Miss Anne Doran, a 25-year-old actress, and Mr. Darell Sykes, a 22-year-old salesman. After the execution yesterday Miss Doran went home to get a few hours sleep before going to the Gateway Theatre for the first night of a play. She takes the part of a murderess.

About 500 people were outside Wandsworth Jail when the notice of Bentley's execution was posted. Mr. Bentley drove through the crowd and collected some of his son's personal effects including his new overcoat. He went home and told his wife he had not yet been able to get the rest of Derek's clothes.

Hospital visit

At the inquest two hours later Dr. David Haler, a pathologist, said his examination had shown that Derek Bentley's brain was normal. When Mr. Bentley heard this he went to Guy's Hospital, where his son had once been treated, and got a medical report. "I handed this to a solicitor," said Mr. Bentley. "It shows my son's brain was not normal."

BOTTOM LEFT: A prison official emerged from the gates at 9.10 am to post up another notice. Protestors immediately began to shout and throw missiles as police officers struggled to control the crowds.

BELOW: Officers lead away one of the protestors. By the time of Bentley's execution the crowd outside the prison had swelled to more than 500 people.

ABOVE RIGHT: During the commotion the glass over the notices was smashed. Behind the broken shards the announcement of the execution and the doctor's confirmation of his death can be seen.

RIGHT: William and his wife Lillian on the day of their son's execution

BELOW: Bentley's father and sister Iris stand grim-faced. They immediately began a campaign to clear his name.

JANUARY 29, 1953

Bentley and Craig: Comment

Derek Bentley, aged 19, who was hanged yesterday for murder, was made to suffer the ultimate indignities by so-called "friends."

Most people will regard the scuffling and hysteria of the small crowd of notoriety-hunters outside the prison gates as highly distasteful. The condemned youth might have been spared a brawl over his body. He might have been allowed to pass from the world in decent silence. Instead, coins were thrown, glass smashed, and there were shouts of "Murder" and "Save him" – as though he were a national hero.

He was not. The hero in this case was Police Constable Miles, who was shot dead while protecting his fellow citizens. Having said this, we recognise and respect the large body of opinion which held that Bentley, who had not fired the fatal shot, and who had been recommended to mercy, should not have been executed.

Verdict

We commend the sincerity of the 200 M.Ps who signed a last-minute appeal for a reprieve, and of the six who, as a deputation, sought to persuade the Home Secretary to change his decision.

But we think they were wrong. They said that a new factor, "public reaction," had appeared and that the great majority of Bentley's fellow-countrymen thought that to hang him would be contrary to fair play and natural justice. The appellants, however, had no means of assessing the size of the majority (if any) which favoured a reprieve. Nor can we agree that "fair play" or "natural justice" should supersede the law. If this were admitted the courts would be robbed of their function – which is to reach a verdict in accordance with the evidence.

Conviction quashed

Iris Bentley, Derek's sister, campaigned tirelessly to clear the stain on the family name. A partial victory was achieved in 1993, when Home Secretary Michael Howard accepted that a limited pardon was appropriate, on the grounds that a capital sentence should not have been passed. He refused to budge on the issue of the verdict, however, which he deemed correct. That wasn't enough for the Bentley family, who took the case to the Court of Appeal, where the conviction was quashed in July 1998. Lord Goddard came in for severe criticism over his handling of the trial. He was self-avowedly on the 'hang 'em and flog 'em' wing of the judicial spectrum, and his direction of the jury was interpreted as a determined effort to ensure that someone paid the full price for the death of PC Miles. Craig might have been able to avoid the noose; Bentley wouldn't.

The ruling came too late for Iris Bentley, who lost her battle against cancer a year earlier. Christopher Craig, who spent ten years behind bars for his part in the events of 2 November 1952, emerged from the shadows to place on record his own deep remorse and pass comment on the decision that exonerated his teenage friend. 'Today, after 46 years, the conviction of Derek Bentley has been quashed and his name cleared. While I am grateful and relieved about this, I am saddened that it has taken those 46 years for the authorities in this country to admit the truth.'

> A limited pardon wasn't enough for the Bentley family, who took the case to the Court of Appeal, where the conviction was quashed in July 1998.

OPPOSITE BOTTOM: William and Iris arriving at the Cambridge Theatre in London for the opening night of *Murder Story* written by Ludovic Kennedy. The plot of the play bore a very close resemblance to the crimes committed by Bentley and Craig.

OPPOSITE TOP: Bentley's father and sister Iris worked tirelessly to have the verdict overturned.

She had some success in 1993 when Home Secretary Michael Howard gave a limited pardon, agreeing that the execution should not have taken place. The case was taken to the Court of Appeal and in July 1998 the conviction was quashed. Lord Goddard, the judge that made the original decision, also received severe criticism for his handling of the case.

JANUARY 29, 1953

Justice
Courage

In politics "public reaction", can be a valuable guide. But it can all too easily pervert the course of justice. Derek Bentley had justice.

He was properly tried and sentenced. He appealed, but his appeal was dismissed. What the M.Ps endeavoured to do, in effect, was to re-open the case; but it is not for the House of Commons to re-try criminal causes.

The law in the matter under discussion is clear. It says that if two or more persons set out on a foray which is likely to end in murder, and murder results, all are equally culpable. It was established that Bentley knew his companion, Craig, to be armed. It was also stated that during the struggle with the police on the warehouse roof he shouted to Craig: "Let him have it, Chris!" Those five words proved his guilt.

This is generally admitted. But many people thought that since Craig - who killed the policeman - was too young to be hanged, Bentley - who did not - should also have escaped the gallows. But if this argument were admitted there would be nothing to stop any older man giving a lethal weapon to a boy in some burglarious enterprise, knowing that if murder were done neither of them would hang. In any case, Bentley's guilt was not made less by the fact that Craig was younger.

In all this sorry business tribute must be paid to Sir David Maxwell Fyfe, the Home Secretary, who has carried out a difficult and distressing task with courage and dignity. We should all remember that he has stood fast not merely in a blind adherence to the letter of the law but so that the interests of the community shall be served.

BELOW LEFT: William, Lillian and Iris Bentley made the journey to Wandsworth prison 20 years after Derek's execution to place wreaths in his memory

BELOW: In 1991 Craig agreed to take a lie detector test on television to help secure an official pardon for Derek Bentley. When asked if Bentley had shouted 'Let him have it, Chris' he replied 'No'. The machine clearly indicated that he was telling the truth. Craig had eventually spent ten years in prison and after his release led a quiet, law-abiding life (bottom).

JAMES HANRATTY: The A6 Murder

James Hanratty was hanged for murder on 4 April 1962, one of the last men to be given a capital sentence before that sanction was removed from the statute book. The Hanratty case became a cause célèbre as a phalanx of campaigners joined the family's fight to have the verdict overturned.

Over the next forty years, home secretaries of both political hues were exhorted to re-examine the case that resulted in James Hanratty being sent to the gallows. It seemed that scientists had provided the definitive answer when they subjected key evidential artefacts to DNA analysis in 2002. However, the possibility that the samples were contaminated left many still steadfast in their belief that the twenty-one-day court proceedings – at the time the longest murder trial in British history – produced an unsafe conviction.

Tap on the window

The victims of the crime for which Hanratty was executed were 36-year-old physicist Michael Gregsten and 22-year-old laboratory technician Valerie Storie. They were colleagues at the Road Research Laboratory in Slough, and were also lovers. Gregsten was married with two young children, and although his wife knew of the affair, he and Storie had to use discretion to snatch their moments of intimacy.

On the night of 22 August 1961 the couple were ostensibly planning the route for a staff car rally. After visiting a pub in Taplow, they drove to a lay-by in a cornfield near Maidenhead, where their amorous pursuits were interrupted by a tap on the window of Gregsten's Morris Minor. He wound down the window to find himself staring down the barrel of a handgun. The man pointing the weapon said it was a hold-up and that he was on the run from the law. Initially, he had a handkerchief covering the bottom half of his face, but that was removed when he climbed into the back seat and ordered Gregsten to drive. There followed a circuitous two-hour journey, which included a stop for petrol. With a gun pointing at his back, Gregsten couldn't alert anyone at the service station, though he did try to attract attention by flicking his reversing lights on and off. Some motorists would recall seeing the haphazard flashing, though none thought enough of it at the time to take any action.

ABOVE LEFT: James Hanratty, the notorious A6 murderer. Hanratty was a professional car thief, convicted of the murder of Michael Gregsten at Deadman's Hill on August 22, 1961.

ABOVE RIGHT: The car that Hanratty hijacked after shooting Gregsten and Storie was found outside Redbridge Underground Station near Ilford.

Murder then rape

The journey ended some sixty miles away, on a stretch of the A6 near Luton called Deadman's Hill. The gunman ordered Gregsten to pull into a lay-by. He had said he was hungry as he hadn't eaten for some time, but now sleep appeared to be the priority. He said they would be tied up while he rested, and bound Storie's hands to the door handle, though so inexpertly that she claimed she was soon able to free herself. Gregsten then made a sudden movement which panicked the gunman into firing his revolver twice. Both bullets struck Gregsten in the head, almost certainly killing him instantaneously.

Storie was then raped, after which she begged the man to take the car and leave her with Gregsten. He appeared to consent to this and asked her to help in getting Gregsten's body out of the car. He also made her run through the car's controls, and took a small amount of money proffered by Storie. She had caught but a fleeting view of the attacker, when his face was illuminated in the headlights of a passing vehicle, but he wasn't taking any chances. He fired a number of shots, hitting Storie five times. Assuming that he had done for both eyewitnesses, the murderer and rapist drove off in the direction of Luton.

Murder weapon found

It had not been so difficult for Storie to feign death as she had spinal injuries that would leave her paralysed from the waist down. She was very much alive, though she had no idea whether she would survive the night. Storie later said that she thought of using stones to spell out 'blue eyes, brown hair' to help identify the attacker if she didn't make it, but couldn't find any within easy reach. In the event, she had to wait until 6.45 the next morning before a farm worker came to her rescue.

The Morris Minor was found later that day in Ilford, some 40 miles from where the shooting took place. The murder weapon was also soon in police hands. The Enfield .38 revolver that killed Michael Gregsten and maimed Valerie Storie was discovered under the seat of a London bus, along with sixty rounds of ammunition. An identikit picture of the wanted man was produced, based on Storie's fleeting view of the assailant. Apart from that, and the gunman's voice, there was precious little to go on. He had appeared from nowhere and disappeared into the night, having carried out a seemingly random attack.

AUGUST 24, 1961

Wounded girl lives after A6 shooting

The hunt for the hitchhike killer of the A6 switched to Ilford, Essex, last night. The car that the killer hijacked late on Tuesday night after shooting dead the driver and seriously wounding a girl passenger was found outside Redbridge Underground Station, near Ilford. From Redbridge the Underground runs to Epping in one direction and through London in the other.

·DEADMAN'S HILL·

The hi-jacking was at Deadman's Hill, near Clophill, Bedfordshire - about 50 miles away. The killer shot down 34-year-old Michael Gregsten - a married man with two children - and 22-year-old Valerie Storie after forcing them to drive 40 miles at gunpoint from the Old Station Inn, Taplow, Buckinghamshire. A quarter of a mile past Clophill he told Gregsten to drive off the main highway into a side-road used as a lay-by. He ordered Gregsten out of the car and pumped five, .38 bullets into him.

Then he forced Miss Storie into the back seat and attempted to assault her. Terrified, she pleaded with him. The gunman ordered her back into the front seat and said: "Tell me how to drive this car. "When she had explained he fired the remaining bullet in his revolver into her chest and pushed her out of the car. He then calmly reloaded, fired another shot at Miss Storie, and drove off with a crash of gears. The couple were found early yesterday.

Last night Miss Storie was still too ill to give a full account of what happened. The wanted man is described as aged about 30, 5ft. 6in., medium build, with deep-set brown eyes, dark hair, and pale-faced; believed to be wearing a dark lounge suit. He speaks with a Cockney accent.

> The Enfield .38 revolver that killed Michael Gregsten and maimed Valerie Storie was discovered under the seat of a London bus.

ABOVE: Thirty-six-year-old Michael Gregsten. He and his colleague Valerie Storie were having an affair.

LEFT: Mine detectors were used by the men of the Royal Engineers who were called in to search the scrubland on Deadman's Hill to find the murder weapon.

'Be quiet, will you, I am finking'

A breakthrough came on 11 September, when two spent cartridges that had come from the murder weapon were found in a basement room at the Vienna Hotel, Maida Vale. The room's most recent occupant had been a Mr J Ryan, who gave a Kingsbury address. Police quickly learned that Jim Ryan was an alias used by James Hanratty. Another name in the frame was Peter Alphon, who had also stayed at the hotel under a false name. Hanratty and Alphon were both petty criminals well known to the police, though the latter was a better match for the identikit picture of the wanted man. Alphon gave himself up after being named in a press conference given by police on 22 September, but was ruled out when Storie failed to pick him out of an identity parade two days later. That left Hanratty as the lone suspect, despite the fact that Storie said the assailant was about her height – just over 5 ft 3 ins. Hanratty was 5ft 8 in.

The hunt was now on for James Hanratty, who had suspiciously gone to ground. Realising he was wanted in connection with the A6 murder, Hanratty called Superintendent Basil Acott on 6 October to protest his innocence. He was tracked down to Blackpool, where he was arrested five days later. Valerie Storie had by now been transferred to Stoke Mandeville hospital, where another identification parade was arranged. Once again, she faltered, failing to pick out Hanratty. A second line-up, in which the men paraded before her were told to speak, yielded a positive result. Storie remembered the assailant's poor elocution, notably when he commanded: 'Be quiet, will you, I am finking'. Those words had been uttered when the gunman shot Gregsten and Storie asked if they could get him to a doctor. Now, they were used to indict Hanratty on a murder charge, since he stood out in the 13-man line-up for being unable to pronounce 'th' correctly.

TOP: Gregsten with one of his sons.

LEFT: The .38 revolver that was used to kill Gregsten and injure Storie was left on a London bus. Ballistic experts matched the bullets from the gun on the bus to the marks on the bullets that killed Gregsten.

BELOW: Police guard Gregsten's Morris Minor.

OPPOSITE TOP RIGHT: Deadman's Hill, near Clop-hill, Bedfordshire, was the scene of the A6 murder. The victim, Michael Gregsten, was in a car with his colleague and lover, Valerie Storie. The two worked together at the Road Research Laboratory in Slough. They were allegedly planning a route for a staff car rally on the day of the murder.

OPPOSITE TOP LEFT: Two pictures of a killer were issued by Scotland Yard. They were built up using the Identikit system. Picture number 1 shows a man with slicked-down hair, thin eyebrows and lips, a sharply chiselled chin, slightly protruding ears and hooded eyes. It was drawn with the help of witnesses whose identities were not revealed. Picture 2 shows a man with dark wavy hair, heavier eye-brows, a thicker nose, fuller lips, and altogether bolder features. It was drawn with the help of Valerie Storie.

OPPOSITE BOTTOM RIGHT: Bernard Daley in the Stevonia café in Blackpool where he served Hanratty with coffee prior to his arrest.

The two minds of a killer

It is just seven days since the A6 gunman murdered Michael Gregsten and shot his friend Valerie Storie through the neck. Seven days in which Scotland Yard's top detectives have been asking themselves: "What kind of man are we hunting?" For this baffling crime does not fit into any known pattern. Was the murderer mad or sane? Was the motive rape, theft, or sadism? Is the man a loner, morbid introvert, likely to be found skulking at home? Or a Teddy Boy-type who loves dicing with danger, and may be haunting the dog tracks in fresh clothes?

Yesterday I went to Harley Street in search of answers to these questions - and found the top psychiatrists equally baffled. One expert on mental health said: "I would say the killer was mad in the legal and medical sense on the night of the murder. My guess is he suffers from paranoid schizophrenia.

Sane

"If so, he is likely to be a closed-in person. He may well be back at his work, apparently normal, but spending most of his leisure at home or in lodgings." Farther along the street I found a consultant in

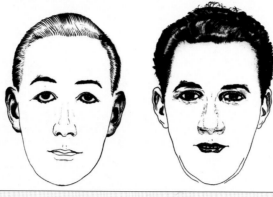

psychiatry at two London hospitals. He said: "I would guess the murderer is sane in the legal sense, but neurotic and unbalanced."

The killer was no ordinary homicidal sex maniac for he first held a gun at his victim's back for 5? hours. He was no ordinary homicidal thief for, offered Gregsten's well-filled wallet, he took only his driving licence, and used the car only to get away from the scene of his crime.

Let us assume for the moment that he is legally sane. Then he must be a stupid man, a braggart, a gambler cruel to the point of sadism. Who but a fool would have left his gun in a bus where it was sure to be found quickly? Who but a braggart would have parked the car near a station with two wheels on the pavement? Who but a gambler would have risked taking his victims to a petrol station?

Mad?

And only a man with a strong cruel streak would have waited 5? hours before killing and assaulting. But even this picture is faulty. A man of this type would surely have pocketed Gregsten's pound notes and given himself away before now by some fresh foolishness. So we are left with the more likely theory - that he is mad. But most madmen kill impulsively, yet he waited hours. Most sex maniacs strangle their victims yet he chose a gun.

The evidence is weighted on the side of the expert who labelled him as a paranoid schizophrenic. What are the chances of his murdering again? According to Harley Street, paranoid schizophrenics seldom kill twice.

But I wouldn't take a bet on that - and neither would Scotland Yard.

Anomalies

The trial opened at Bedford Assizes on 22 January 1962. Hanratty pleaded Not Guilty to the murder of Michael Gregsten, the only charge that was brought. Chief prosecuting counsel Graham Swanwick QC had other witnesses to support Storie's identification of the defendant. John Skillett was on his way to work the morning following the murder when a grey Morris Minor being driven erratically attracted his attention. It skidded and almost collided with him, and when he caught up with the car at a roundabout he wanted to give the driver a piece of his mind. Skillett said he got a clear look at the occupant, whom he identified as Hanratty. A pedestrian named James Trower witnessed the same incident and also identified Hanratty, though a passenger in Skillett's car picked out a different man in two different police line-ups. To cloud the picture further, Hanratty was experienced behind the wheel and therefore hardly likely to have been driving erratically, or, for that matter, to have needed instruction from Storie regarding the controls. Peter Alphon, the man the police eliminated from their enquiries, had not passed his test. This was just one of the anomalies that would lead to accusations that the police tailored the evidence to suit their case.

Another arose when Superintendent Acott took the stand. He testified that during a telephone call he received from Hanratty on 7 October 1961, the latter said he had been in Liverpool when the A6 murder was committed but couldn't name the people who could vouch for him as they were members of the criminal fraternity and didn't want the police brought to their door. Acott said he pressed for the names of the three men, but Hanratty

refused to comply, saying he would take a chance on getting out of the bind without providing that information. Defence counsel Michael Sherrard seized upon this, saying that Hanratty had spoken only of 'some friends' who could corroborate his story; there had been no mention of the number of men who could furnish him with an alibi. Sherrard used this to mount a scathing attack on the police's record-keeping. He accused Acott of being selective with the evidence. The charge was that once the investigating team assured themselves that Hanratty was their man, they focused only on evidence which supported that view, ignoring any information that pointed in a different direction. Acott called that a 'disgraceful allegation'.

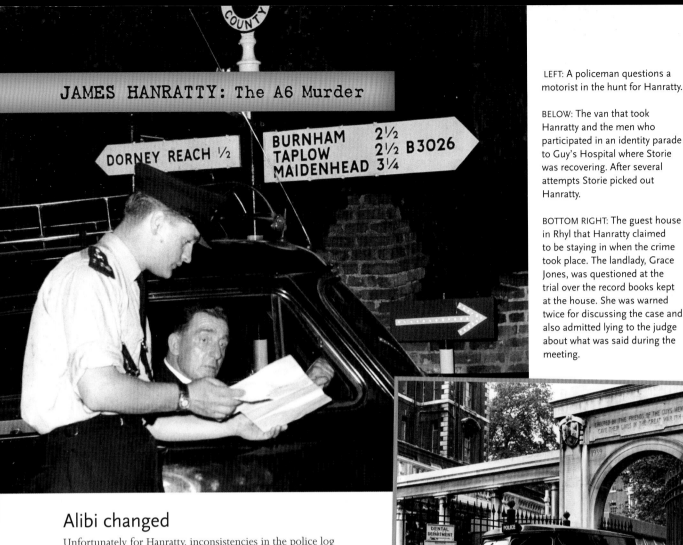

DORNEY REACH ½

BURNHAM 2½
TAPLOW 2½ B3026
MAIDENHEAD 3¼

LEFT: A policeman questions a motorist in the hunt for Hanratty.

BELOW: The van that took Hanratty and the men who participated in an identity parade to Guy's Hospital where Storie was recovering. After several attempts Storie picked out Hanratty.

BOTTOM RIGHT: The guest house in Rhyl that Hanratty claimed to be staying in when the crime took place. The landlady, Grace Jones, was questioned at the trial over the record books kept at the house. She was warned twice for discussing the case and also admitted lying to the judge about what was said during the meeting.

Alibi changed

Unfortunately for Hanratty, inconsistencies in the police log became a mere side show as the defendant then changed his alibi completely. After the case for the prosecution was wound up, Sherrard confidently predicted: 'We shall call evidence to snuff out even the whisper of suspicion'. Now he had to convince a jury that had just learned that the defendant's first alibi was total fabrication.

Hanratty went into the witness box to explain the dramatic volte-face regarding his whereabouts at the critical time. He testified that he was staying at a boarding house in Rhyl at the time of the murder, though he couldn't recall the exact location of the establishment or anyone there who might vouch for him. It was the flimsiness of that alibi that persuaded him to invent the story he recounted to the police. Hanratty said he spent the night of 21 August at the Vienna Hotel, travelling to Liverpool by train the following day. The purpose of the trip was to sell on some of the proceeds from burglaries he had recently committed. He recalled having a conversation with a woman in a sweet shop over directions, an incident to which a Mrs Olive Dinwoodie would give corroborating testimony. He claimed that he took a bus to Rhyl that evening, hoping to see a friend called Terry Evans. He returned to Liverpool on Thursday 24 August and was back in the capital early the following day.

> He testified that he was staying at a boarding house in Rhyl at the time of the murder, though he couldn't recall the exact location of the establishment or anyone there who might vouch for him.

Sentenced to die

James Hanratty will be escorted from the condemned cell at Bedford Prison today to begin a second fight for his life. "Ginger Jim," 25-year-old convicted killer, will walk 75 paces past cells containing the jail's 178 other prisoners, to a distempered interview room. Across a scrubbed oak table he will confer with members of his legal team who are planning the appeal against his death sentence. Waiting for the report on the prison talks will be Michael Sherrard, 34, the defence counsel who almost collapsed in the stuffy, over-crowded Shire Hall court-room on Saturday night when the 11-man jury pronounced their verdict.

Hanratty - cocky, illiterate petty thief convicted of murdering Michael Gregsten, 36-year-old physicist last August, was whisked away from the court building minutes after stammering out from the dock: "I will appeal." Only a nervous licking of the lips revealed the tension he had undergone during the 21-day trial. Only once had the small-time crook who wanted to be big lost his nerve. In the cells below the court his temper flared. He slammed a door, nearly jamming the hand of a following warder. Then Hanratty was taken to the cell at Bedford Prison, where once Stanley Rouse, the blazing car murderer of the 30s had awaited execution. And there Ginger Jim, who had vowed to be a big criminal when the underworld labelled him "tea leaf" - a petty thief - broke down. He wept.

She just nodded

Forty miles away, at the same time, a nurse tip-toed through a soft-lit public ward at Stoke Mandeville Hospital, Buckinghamshire, and whispered the news of the verdict to 23-year-old Valerie Storie, who was raped and shot on Deadman's Hill. Valerie, now paralysed from the waist down, had fought off sleep that night to hear the result of Hanratty's trial; she just nodded. Then she slept. Soon she will be allowed out from the hospital to start work again at the offices where she met and became fond of Michael Gregsten. For her it will be the start of a new life.

'Perfect gentleman'

The hunt to locate the Rhyl guest house was on. Hanratty's recollection of a green bathroom in the attic led the police to Ingledene, an establishment in Kinmel Street. Landlady Grace Jones said that Hanratty had lodged with her during the week Aug 19-26. During cross-examination the prosecution elicited that Jones kept no records of guests who stayed just for a night or two, and thus could not be sure exactly when Hanratty resided at Ingledene. Swanwick said that Jones's testimony was not only unreliable, but suggested that she might be trying to drum up trade by using the trial as a ghoulish form of advertising.

Of Hanratty's changed story, Swanwick said that one of the hallmarks of a false alibi was when it was belatedly conceived. He accused Hanratty of substituting one set of lies for another. Swanwick also got Mrs Dinwoodie to concede that Hanratty merely looked like the man who had come into the Liverpool sweet shop. Hanratty

countered by saying that the perpetrator of the A6 murder was 'a savage', something that was not part of his make-up. 'I try to live a respectable life, apart from my housebreaking', he insisted. Defence counsel didn't try to downplay his client's misdemeanours, but made sure the jury was aware that none of his previous convictions were for sex crimes or crimes of violence. He wanted to stress that Hanratty was a thief, not a murderer or rapist.

A former girlfriend was called as a character witness, and she testified that he always behaved like a perfect gentleman towards her. Michael Sherrard pressed home the point: even if Hanratty made up his first alibi, it didn't make him a murderer.

Death sentence

The jury was out for almost ten hours before returning a Guilty verdict. Mr Justice Gorman passed a death sentence, which the Appeal Court found no reason to overturn or commute. Home Secretary Rab Butler took the same line, finding no grounds to grant a reprieve. James Hanratty was hanged at Bedford Prison on 4 April 1962. He was 25 years old.

The crusade to clear Hanratty's name began almost immediately. Over a dozen witnesses eventually came forward to place Hanratty in the north-west at the critical time. The Hanratty family argued that the police were less than assiduous in checking the second alibi, and even tried to sue Lord Butler for a breach of public duty in 1970. The suit was thrown out. Three years earlier, in May 1967, Peter Alphon had given a press conference in Paris in which he publicly confessed to being the A6 murderer. The suggestion was that he had been paid by family members of the 'wronged' woman – Gregsten's wife – to give the couple a fright. It was a credible motive, something lacking in the case against Hanratty, and an unexplained £5,000 credit to Alphon's bank account seemed to add weight to the 'hired muscle' theory. Alphon subsequently retracted his statement, though that may have been born of fear that he might have faced criminal charges.

TOP LEFT: The Stevonia café in Blackpool where Hanratty was picked up by the police.

LEFT: The bill for the show at the Queen's Theatre that Hanratty supposedly went to see on the evening of his arrest. Two Blackpool detectives, making routine checks on teenage night haunts, found a man in a café who answered to the description of the A6 man that had been circulated by Scotland Yard.

MARCH 19, 1962

Father of Hanratty wants 250,000 to sign mercy petition

Mr. Hanratty, of Sycamore Grove, Kingsbury, London, NW, has left his window-cleaning business "until my son is reprieved". He is convinced of his innocence. Yesterday he said: "It is amazing the way people have responded. By the end of this week I expect to have at least 150,000 signatures. We have got people assisting all over Britain. "Not only that. Hundreds of people have written to us saying they are convinced of my son's innocence. Yet not one letter has said they think he was guilty."

Hanratty, due to hang on April 4, will be examined at Bedford Jail this week by medical and psychiatric experts, who are compiling a dossier which will be placed before Mr. R. A. Butler, the Home Secretary. Mr. Butler has already been sent a diagnosis from the St. Francis Hospital, Haywards Heath, Sussex, where Hanratty was admitted in 1952. At the hospital an exploratory brain operation was carried out. His brain appeared to be physically normal but, possibly on psychiatric grounds, Hanratty was diagnosed as mentally defective. This evidence, which was sent by the hospital to Brixton Jail two days after his arrest, has been in the possession of the police and his legal advisers.

LEFT: Hanratty is taken from Blackpool police station to Bedford police headquarters.

TOP LEFT: Hanratty was hanged on 4 April, 1962 at Bedford Prison. The crusade to clear his name began almost immediately.

ABOVE AND OPPOSITE BOTTOM: The perceived injustice attracted a huge following. John Lennon and Yoko Ono were among those helping Hanratty's father clear his son's name.

I KILLED GREGSON
ON THE A6.

NOW I HAVE KILLED AGAIN.
ON THE A9

YOU WILL SEE THAT THIS LETTER
IS POSTED IN LEEDS

BY THE TIME YOU GET IT I
WILL BE MILES AWAY.

HANRATTY, THE MAN CONVICTED,
IS INNOCENT

I WILL NOT SEE AN INNOCENT
MAN KILLED HAHA

I KNOW WHAT HIS LIKE, MY BROTHER
WAS HUNG. - HE WAS INNOCENT

I KILLED GREGSON
HANRATTY IS INNOCENT

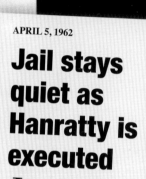

DNA samples

The Hanratty family finally got their wish in 1999, when the case was referred to the Court of Appeal. Hanratty's mother and brother provided DNA samples which were a match for material found on two exhibits: a handkerchief used to wrap the gun and an item of Valerie Storie's underwear. The odds against the DNA coming from anyone other than a member of the Hanratty family were estimated to be 2.5 million to one, and those findings were confirmed when Hanratty's body was exhumed and subjected to a DNA test in 2001.

Lord Chief Justice Lord Woolf said that the scientific analysis 'made what was a strong case even stronger' and ruled that the conviction was safe. Valerie Storie issued a statement saying that the tests proved what she had always maintained: that James Hanratty was the man who shot her and Michael Gregsten on the night of 22 August 1961.

It should have laid the matter to rest, but the Hanratty family were unmoved. They insisted that the evidence was contaminated. The very fact that forensics experts in the early sixties would have had no idea of the techniques that would be developed over the next forty years meant that they took little care when it came to handling exhibits. Geoffrey Bindman, the Hanratty family's legal representative, pointed out that exhibits were regularly transported in the same box, and were freely handled by any number of parties during storage and in court. It was a 'logical impossibility,' he said, that such potentially flawed evidence could be used to ascertain guilt. The DNA traces tying Hanratty to the murder were so microscopic, it was argued, they could easily have been the result of cross-contamination. The scientists, in turn, had their own rebuttal at the ready. If Hanratty's DNA had been transferred to the exhibits at a later date, the killer's DNA should have been on the material tested. No other DNA was found.

Element of doubt

While the scientific debate raged, it still left open the issue of how the police conducted their investigations. In other words, even if Hanratty were the perpetrator, there remained the question of procedural anomalies that left open to question whether he got a fair trial. Michael Mansfield QC, acting on behalf of the Hanratty family, said the police mishandled the case and the evidence that secured the conviction was 'fatally flawed'. Detective Superintendent Acott, who had since died, was singled out for particular criticism.

The balance of probability suggests that James Hanratty was indeed guilty of the crime for which he was hanged in 1962, though procedural irregularities and the possibility of the DNA test being compromised admit an element of doubt which his supporters continue to highlight.

TOP LEFT: An anonymous letter was sent to the editor of the *Yorkshire Evening News* in Leeds stating that Hanratty was innocent. The anonymous writer claimed responsibility for the A6 and the A9 murders.

TOP MIDDLE AND TOP RIGHT: Hanratty's father protested his son's innocence even after his death. Here he is pictured staging a vigil outside the House of Commons and presenting a petition at 10 Downing Street as he pressed for a further enquiry.

APRIL 5, 1962

Jail stays quiet as Hanratty is executed

James Hanratty was hanged at Bedford Prison yesterday, for the A6 murder of physicist Michael Gregsten. There was no trouble inside the prison - no demonstration from the other prisoners. Nearly 200 people were outside the jail gates at 8 p.m., the time Hanratty was due to be executed. Three Oxford students had paraded for eight hours with banners reading: "End Legalised Murder." "No to Hanging," and "Hanging Is No Answer."

No notice was posted on the gates, but at 8.10 a.m. police started to disperse the crowd. Mr. Raymond Miles, 37, of Coombes Close, Bedford, placed a bunch of flowers at the prison entrance. A card with them said: "These flowers are for James Hanratty, who, like Evans and Bentley, has been murdered by our so-called civilised State." Shortly before Hanratty died he wrote to his mother, who is 45 on Friday.

IAN BRADY & MYRA HINDLEY:
Moors Murders

To Ian Brady people were 'maggots', 'cabbages' and 'morons'; their extinction signified nothing. He amassed a library of books on murder, torture and sexual perversion.

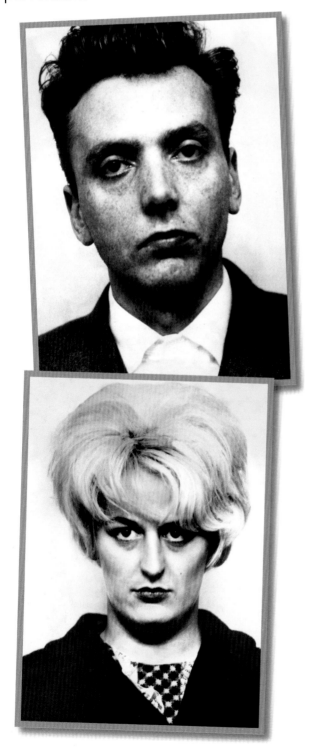

In 1956 American writer Meyer Levin published *Compulsion*, a novel based on the extraordinary tale of two Chicago students convicted for murder in 1924. Nathan Leopold and Richard Loeb were outstanding scholars who chose to pit their superior wits against the police by committing the perfect crime. Intellect, they believed, could not be constrained by morality. They chose a victim at random, a 14-year-old boy, and sent a ransom demand to suggest that it was an abduction in the name of profit. In fact, the boy was already dead, which had been the sole object of the wicked enterprise.

Leopold and Loeb were not as quite as bright as they thought, for they made a catalogue of mistakes that led to their arrest. It was only the brilliant advocacy of the legendary Clarence Darrow that saved them from a capital sentence.

ABOVE LEFT: At age 11 Ian Brady passed the entrance examination for Shawlands Academy, a secondary school with a reputation for academic success, but he soon went off the rails. He was incarcerated several times for various petty crimes and was eventually declared criminally insane in 1985 and sent to Ashworth Psychiatric Hospital, where he remains to this day.

LEFT: Myra Hindley met Brady in 1961 when she joined the secretarial staff at Milward's Merchandise Ltd. They soon became inseparable partners in a sado-masochistic relationship. Hindley spent 36 years behind bars, and remains the longest-serving female prisoner in the annals of the British criminal justice system.

LEFT AND OPPOSITE TOP RIGHT: Police dig in their search for graves on Saddleworth Moor, Yorkshire, in 1965.

BELOW: October 26, 1965: armed with canes for testing the soft peat, 70 policemen start an intensive yard-by-yard probe of a stretch of the moor in the West Riding of Yorkshire. Seen on the left is Arthur Benfield, head of Cheshire County CID.

Obsession

Compulsion struck a chord with one particular reader, one who also espoused Nietzsche's 'superman' philosophy. He, too, became obsessed with committing the perfect crime, using dispensable individuals in pursuit of an intellectual exercise. To Ian Brady people were 'maggots', 'cabbages' and 'morons'; their extinction signified nothing. He amassed a library of books on murder, torture and sexual perversion. A favourite work was *The Life and Times of the Marquis de Sade*, and Brady endorsed beliefs such as: '… murder is a horror, but a horror often necessary, never criminal, and essential to tolerate in a republic'.

Brady might not have been quite an alpha student of the calibre of Leopold and Loeb, but he showed a lot of aptitude in his early years growing up in Glasgow. He was a loner with a chip on his shoulder, having to contend with rejection from both parents. He never knew his father, while his mother, Peggy Stewart, had to farm him out to another family as she was unable to cope. Even her visits dried up when she married Patrick Brady and relocated to Manchester. At eleven Brady passed the entrance examination for Shawlands Academy, a secondary school with a reputation for academic success, but he soon went off the rails.

Sado-masochistic relationship

Brady turned to petty crime, his misdemeanours earning him three court appearances and probation. The authorities thought the best hope of salvation lay in a reconciliation with his natural mother, and at sixteen Brady was ordered to move to Manchester. He took his stepfather's name and got a job as a porter, but failed to turn over a new leaf and his next brush with the law led to his first spell of incarceration. He used his time in prison to study bookkeeping, though he also immersed himself in a lot of unsavoury literature. As well as studying Nietzsche and de Sade, Brady was also fascinated by Nazism. Later, he would call his infamous girlfriend 'Hess', and she would even dye her hair blonde to conform to the 'Aryan' stereotype. Together they would carry out their own unspeakable agenda of imposing their warped superiority on those weaker than themselves.

Brady met Myra Hindley in 1961, when she joined the secretarial staff at Millward's Merchandise Ltd, the Gorton firm where he had worked as a stock clerk for the previous two years. Hindley, too, had a troubled upbringing. Her father had a drink problem and often beat her, a trait she developed when it came to settling differences of opinion with her peers. At the age of four, when her sister Maureen was born, Myra was sent to live with her paternal grandmother Ellen Maybury. She immersed herself in books and established deep friendships, perhaps trying to compensate for perceived rejection. Her capacity for obsessive, all-consuming relationships had a new focus when she started work at Millward's. She wrote in her diary of her attraction for the brooding Ian Brady, and before long they became inseparable partners in a sado-masochistic relationship. At last Brady had a confederate to help him act out his long-harboured dark fantasies.

> Brady was also fascinated by Nazism. Later, he would call his infamous girlfriend 'Hess', and she would even dye her hair blonde to conform to the 'Aryan' stereotype.

First victims

The couple's first victim was 16-year-old Pauline Reade, a neighbour of Hindley's. On 12 July 1963 Pauline was on her way to a dance when she was lured by Hindley to go for a car ride. The advantage of having a woman fronting their depraved schemes quickly became apparent. Hindley drove Pauline out onto Saddleworth Moor, where Brady, who followed by motorbike, raped and killed her. After burying the body, they celebrated by drinking Drambuie.

Brady and Hindley plotted their crimes meticulously, their attention to detail extending to counting the buttons on their clothing before and after to ensure there was no evidence linking them to the scene. That degree of planning paid off in the case of Pauline Reade, and by the following year the local police had two more unsolved child disappearances on their files. 12-year-old John Kilbride disappeared from Ashton-under-Lyne market at around 5.30 pm on Saturday 23 November 1963. Seven months later, Keith Bennett, also aged twelve, disappeared while walking to his grandmother's house. Both boys were raped and strangled.

The evil acts themselves were not enough for Brady and Hindley; they wanted to document their deeds. Photographs of their next victim, and in particular a harrowing 16-minute tape recording of her ordeal, would help to secure a conviction and life sentences for the perpetrators.

Sobbing and begging

Ten-year-old Lesley Ann Downey disappeared on Boxing Day afternoon 1964 when she and a group of friends visited a fairground a few minutes' walk from her Ancoats home. As with the previous three victims, a police search revealed no clues to her whereabouts, or what had befallen her. That day Hindley had driven her septuagenarian grandmother to visit her uncle, a regular practice. The usual arrangement was for Hindley to pick up Ellen Maybury at around 10 pm to take her home but on this occasion she called in to say that the roads, which had a light dusting of snow, were impassable. Eventually it would become clear that Hindley's grandmother could not be allowed to return to 16 Wardle Brook Avenue that evening because Lesley Ann was being held captive there. Pornographic photographs were taken, and the girl was recorded sobbing and begging to be released before she, too, was murdered and buried on the moor. Hindley picked up Ellen Maybury mid-morning the following day.

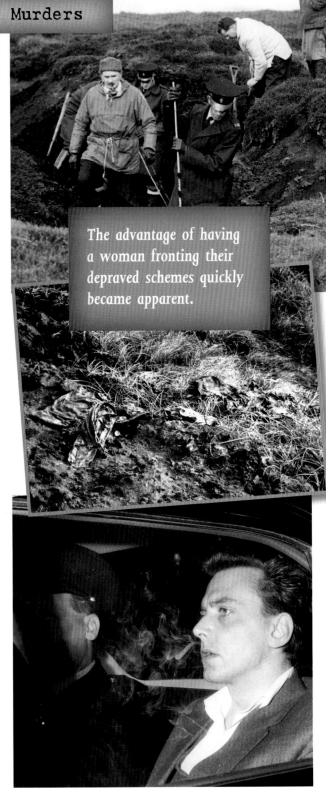

> The advantage of having a woman fronting their depraved schemes quickly became apparent.

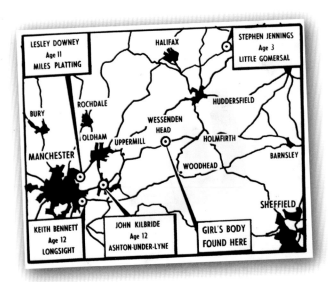

TOP RIGHT: Police hunt for bodies on the Derbyshire Moors in October 1965 after they had extended their search from Saddleworth Moor to the Snake Pass. Using sticks to prod the moorland peat, they attempted to find more of Brady and Hindley's victims.

MIDDLE RIGHT: Clothing was found on the moor two miles from Lesley Ann Downey's grave. Among the clothing were children's socks, a pleated red-and-black striped skirt, a woollen jumper and a nylon stocking.

ABOVE: Brady and Hindley were arrested after they claimed their fifth and final victim, 17-year-old Edward Evans. The murderous pair made the mistake of letting Hindley's brother-in-law into their dark secret. David Smith witnessed the murder of Evans and contacted the police.

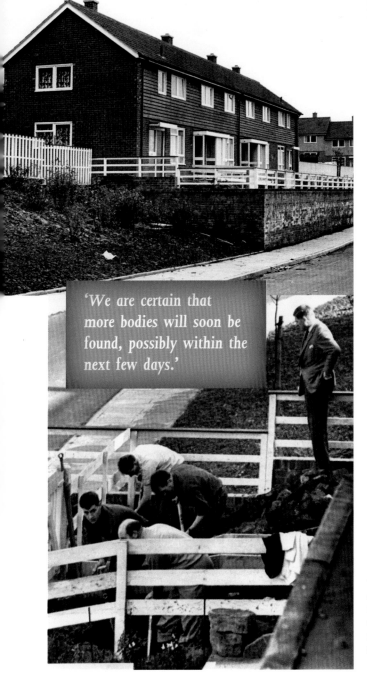

OCTOBER 18 1965

Hunt for more victims on moor

More murder victims are expected to be found buried on the desolate Pennine moors where the body of a ten-year-old girl was discovered on Saturday. A police chief in one of Britain's biggest murder hunts, involving five police forces, said yesterday: "We are certain that more bodies will soon be found, possibly within the next few days. Everything points to this from the information we have so far gathered."

The girl found buried on a Yorkshire moor was identified last night as Lesley Ann Downey, missing since Boxing Day last year when she left her Manchester home to go to a fair. Her body was discovered in a shallow peat grave on Saddleworth Moor, near the main road from Ashton-under-Lyne, Lancashire, and Huddersfield.

Today more than 100 policemen carry on the digging which began on the moors six days ago. They had been told that several bodies were buried in the area.

Eight files

Yesterday police chiefs re-examined their files on eight people - three of them children - who have disappeared from the Manchester area over the past three years. Lesley was one of them.

Last week the murder squad detectives began to tear apart a house in Manchester. Floorboards were ripped up. Dust was collected from crevices and samples, with floorboards, were sent to the Home Office forensic science laboratory at Preston.

Detective Chief, Superintendent Arthur Benfield, head of Cheshire CID, who has taken charge of the combined investigation, last night held a conference at Hyde. A man is said to have boasted of carrying his victims to the moors by car and a man whose information first began the hunt has visited the area with detectives.

Last week's search was in vain. Then a woman was able to narrow the search area on Saturday night. Lesley's body was discovered in thickening mist by a young constable with only a few days' service.

'We are certain that more bodies will soon be found, possibly within the next few days.'

TOP RIGHT: Hindley and Brady with Hindley's sister Maureen. Maureen's husband, David Smith, was witness to the fifth and final murder. He and Maureen phoned the police and ended the 'Moors Murderers' killing spree.

MIDDLE RIGHT: The house on Wardle Brook Avenue.

LEFT AND ABOVE: A police squad digging in the garden of Ian Brady's home.

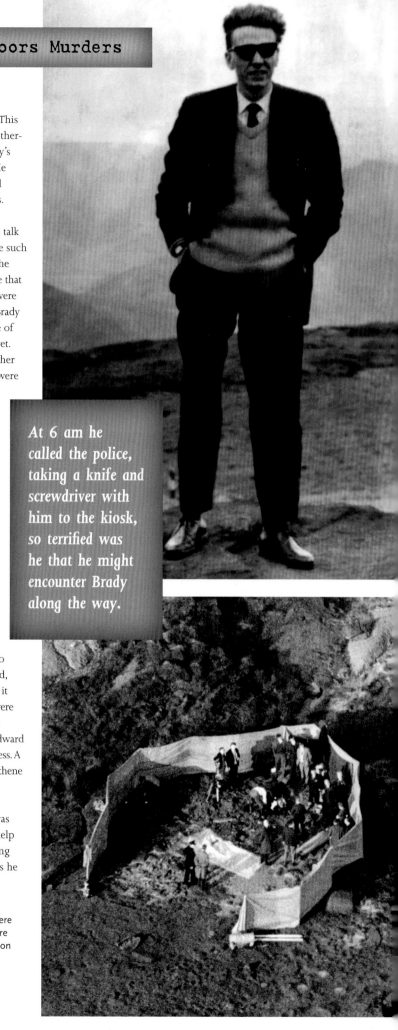

Butcher

The fifth murder proved to be Brady and Hindley's downfall. This time they widened the conspiracy net, drawing Hindley's brother-in-law into the murderous loop. David Smith married Hindley's younger sister Maureen in 1964, when he was just sixteen. He already had a criminal record, and Brady began to groom and school him in the matter of his favourite subjects and authors.

Over the summer months of 1965 Brady launched his machinations to involve Smith in a criminal act. First there was talk of a bank robbery, and Smith was even detailed to stake out one such outlet to observe the daily routine. Target practice sessions on the moors were arranged. Smith initially thought Brady's insistence that they had to be prepared to use firearms was mere bravado, as were his claims to have already committed 'three or four' murders. Brady answered the disbelief by saying he had photographic evidence of the crimes he had committed but wasn't prepared to reveal it yet.

On the evening of 6 October 1965 Hindley paid a call on her sister, and asked Smith to escort her home as the streetlights were not working. Hindley went into the house, telling Smith to wait for the landing light to be flashed on and off before approaching; she wanted to make sure that it was all right by Brady for him to enter. The signal was given and Smith was received by Brady, who invited him in, supposedly to collect some miniature wine bottles they were keeping for him. Brady went through to the living room and seconds later Smith heard screams coming from that direction. He rushed to investigate, in time to see Brady raining hatchet blows down upon the head of a youth.

Smith later said the act was carried out with as little emotion as a butcher carving a dead carcass.

Call to police

Brady used a length of lighting flex to strangle the last gurgling cries of the stricken teenager. When the body was rendered lifeless, he calmly lit a cigarette and exhorted Hindley to get a mop and cleaning materials. It was the 'messiest yet', he said, a comment that would come under the microscope in court, for it contradicted Brady's assertion that references to other murders were a fiction constructed simply to impress Smith. Doctors identified fourteen separate blows to the head of the victim, 17-year-old Edward Evans, a vicious assault which left the room a blood-spattered mess. A terrified Smith helped Brady wrap the body in blankets and polythene sheeting and carry it upstairs into Hindley's bedroom.

It was after 3.00 am when Smith arrived home. He was violently sick, then he unburdened himself to Maureen. He was meant to return to 16 Wardle Brook Avenue later that day to help dispose of the body. Instead, at 6 am he called the police, taking a knife and screwdriver with him to the kiosk, so terrified was he that he might encounter Brady along the way.

> At 6 am he called the police, taking a knife and screwdriver with him to the kiosk, so terrified was he that he might encounter Brady along the way.

TOP: Brady pictured on the moors where he buried his victims. Hindley lured the children on to the moor, asking them to help her find a missing glove. Brady then attacked them, often raping them, and then buried their bodies in the peat.

BOTTOM: Canvas screens were placed around the spot where the second body was found on Saddleworth Moor.

DECEMBER 10, 1965

Brady killed without emotion, says Smith

Ian Brady showed no emotion during and after the murder of Edward Evans, 17-year-old David Smith told the Moorland murders case court at Hyde, Cheshire, yesterday. Brady rained axe blows on to the head and shoulders of his screaming victim without frenzy, Mr. Smith said in reply to Mr. W. L. Mars-Jones, QC. The blows were "almost positioned," he said. And later, while arrangements were being made for the disposal of Evans's body, the behaviour of Myra Hindley, Brady's woman friend, was normal. Neither she nor Brady showed any sign of agitation or worry, he claimed, and she reminisced about another body she said they had disposed of on the moors.

Mr. Smith, whose wife is Hindley's sister, stood for more than seven hours giving evidence yesterday

TOP LEFT: Mrs Crowther, wife of a farmer living near Saddleworth Moor, walks to the spot where she saw a man digging on the moor.

LEFT: Brady pictured arriving at the court where he was first charged with the Moors Murders. Brother-in-law David Smith said he killed with little emotion, as a butcher would do when carving a dead carcass.

ABOVE: A youthful Brady relaxing at home. When a police team descended on 16 Wardle Brook Avenue they found Brady in the process of writing a letter to his employer saying he had hurt his ankle and was unfit for work. That, at least, was true, for Brady had been injured in the previous night's struggle.

119

Evidence uncovered

A police team descended on 16 Wardle Brook Avenue just after eight o'clock. They found Brady in the process of writing a letter to his employer saying he had hurt his ankle and was unfit for work. That, at least, was true, for Brady had been injured in the previous night's struggle. Hindley prevaricated over the whereabouts of the key to her locked bedroom, but when it became clear that the officers were not going to leave without searching the entire house, Brady capitulated. There had been 'a row' the previous night, he said, and the consequences of the altercation were to be found there.

Brady and Hindley both tried to implicate Smith. Brady described how he and Evans had had an argument, which came to blows just as Smith arrived. The latter had joined in the fracas, kicking Evans and beating him with a stick. Brady also said that references to other murders were exactly as Smith surmised: fanciful talk designed to impress him.

Attempts to convince police that this was a one-off incident, a fight that had gone too far and with Smith's hands equally bloodied, were soon shown up for what they were. A left-luggage ticket stub was found, which tied in with Smith's statement that he helped carry two suitcases to Hindley's Mini van on 5 October, the day before Edward Evans's murder. They were recovered from Manchester Central Station on October 15, and the books, photographs and tape recordings contained therein revealed the full horror of what they were dealing with. The contents included pictures of Lesley Ann Downey, which police were able to identify as having been taken in Hindley's bedroom. That prompted police to re-examine their open files on children who had disappeared in the recent past.

The pieces quickly fell into place. A 12-year-old girl who lived two doors from Brady and Hindley led police along the A635 to the spot on the moors where they had taken her for jaunts. She was lucky: her mistreatment extended only to being plied with alcohol.

APRIL 20, 1966

"Cleared the decks for murder"

Ian Brady and Myra Hindley "cleared the decks for murder" the night before killing 17-year-old Edward Evans at their home, the Attorney-General said yesterday. Sir Elwyn Jones, QC, was prosecuting in the "bodies on the moors" murder trial at Chester Assizes. In the dock accused of triple murder were Brady, 28, and Hindley, 23.

Photographs, tape recordings and books were removed from their house, said Sir Elwyn. These were deposited in two suitcases in the left luggage office at Manchester Central Station. The cases contained incrimi-nating material which put police on the trail that eventually led to the discovery of the graves of Lesley Ann Downey, ten, and John Kilbride, 12. By removing this evidence Brady and Hindley were preparing for the Evans murder, Sir Elwyn submitted. He said the three victims lived in or near Manchester. John vanished first and Lesley more than a year later. Evans died about nine and a half months after her disappearance. Extensive police inquiries for John and Lesley went on for months but their fate "remained sealed."

TOP AND LEFT: Brady and Hindley leave Chester Court in a police van after they had been sentenced to life imprisonment, having been found guilty of the charges brought against them.

Just over an hour after being sentenced the couple were driven from Chester Castle to Risley Remand Centre, near Warrington, Lancashire. Women hammered on the windows of the van carrying them as they drove through a crowd of 300 people outside the castle. Two dozen policemen tried to hold the crowd back.

Brady and Hindley were sentenced after the jury had been out for two hours and 22 minutes.

TOP: Police resume digging on Saddleworth Moor, 20 years after Brady and Hindley's conviction. In 1986 Hindley and Brady cooperated in trying to find the graves of Pauline Reade and Keith Bennett.

ABOVE: Brady(right) is pictured on the moors with Detective Chief Inspector Peter Topping during the second visit to Shiny Brook.

APRIL 20, 1966

Out of a detergent box comes an axe

From a carton labelled "Deepio, the complete multi-purpose detergent," the Attorney General took a plastic bag, and from the bag a small hand axe. All eyes were riveted on the familiar-looking firewood chopper as the chief lawyer of the land said with slow emphasis: "This is the weapon which the prosecution says Brady used to launch a murderous attack on Edward Evans."

Ian Brady and Myra Hindley, accused of the "Murders on the Moor," are charged with murdering a girl of ten, a boy of 12, a youth of 17. Today brought the latest act in a drama which opened on the dark Pennines and is now to be played out in this quiet country town.

Myra Hindley, 23, who had a new ash blonde rinse, played cat's cradle with her long fingers. When she made notes she replaced her ballpoint pen precisely on her pad, like the efficient shorthand typist she is. Occasionally, she tugged at the hem of her blue-grey suit, a fashionable three inches above her knees. Brady, on her right, hunched slackly in his chair, frowning and pressing the knuckle of his left forefinger to pursed lips. From time to time the two had whispered conversation, heads bowed.

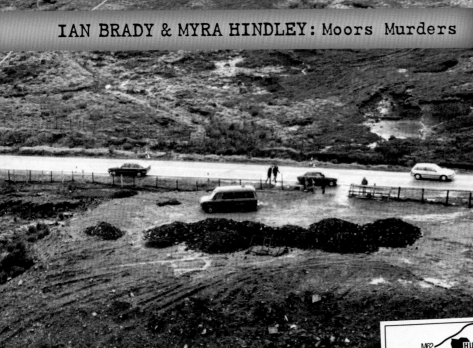

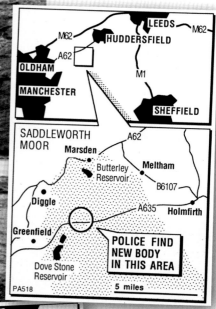

POLICE FIND
NEW BODY
IN THIS AREA

PA518   5 miles

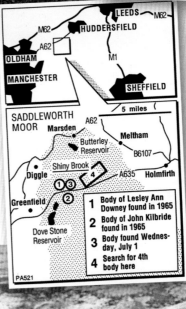

1 Body of Lesley Ann Downey found in 1965
2 Body of John Kilbride found in 1965
3 Body found Wednesday, July 1
4 Search for 4th body here

PA521

Life sentences

On 6 May 1966 at Chester Assizes, Ian Brady and Myra Hindley were convicted of murdering Edward Evans and Lesley Ann Downey. Brady alone was found guilty of the murder of John Kilbride, but Hindley was convicted of harbouring him in full knowledge that he had committed that murder. She was given seven years for the lesser charge, though that was academic. Brady and Hindley remained devoid of emotion throughout the proceedings, which closed a matter of months after the death sentence for capital crimes had been suspended. Presiding judge Mr Justice Fenton Atkinson sent them both down for life. Brady was 28, Hindley 23.

Ian Brady has never sought release. He was declared criminally insane in 1985 and sent to Ashworth Psychiatric Hospital, where his attempts to end his life by going on hunger strike have been thwarted through force feeding. His recent application to be returned to prison has been rejected.

Myra Hindley, by contrast, mounted a long campaign for freedom when she believed she had paid her debt to society. She claimed to have found God, took an Open University degree and turned her back on Brady, whom she said had indoctrinated and intimidated her. Lord Longford took up Hindley's cause and argued that she had been rehabilitated but successive home secretaries refused to sanction her release. The strength of feeling that her name and image provoked was shown to be undimmed in 1997 when artist Marcus Harvey exhibited a portrait made up of children's handprints at the Royal Academy. She died three years later, on 15 November 2002, aged sixty. Myra Hindley had spent thirty-six years behind bars, and remains the longest-serving female prisoner in the annals of the British criminal justice system.

TOP LEFT AND BELOW:
The scene of the renewed hunt for the bodies of Reade and Bennett on Saddleworth Moor.

ABOVE AND LEFT:
Diagrams illustrating the area to be searched in 1986. They also show where the other bodies were found more than 20 years before.

> Myra Hindley mounted a long campaign for freedom when she believed she had paid her debt to society. She claimed to have found God.

Moors killers jailed for life

Ian Brady and Myra Hindley were both jailed for life yesterday. Brady, 28-year-old stock clerk, was convicted of murdering 17-year-old Edward Evans, ten-year old Lesley Ann Downey and 12-year-old John Kilbride. Hindley, a 23-year-old blonde shorthand typist, was found guilty of murdering Evans and Lesley Ann. The jury at Chester Assizes cleared her of killing John Kilbride, but convicted her of harbouring Brady knowing that he had killed the boy.

Just over an hour after being sentenced the couple were driven from Chester Castle to Risley Remand Centre, near Warrington, Lancashire. Women hammered on the windows of the van carrying them as they drove through a crowd of 300 people outside the castle. Two dozen policemen tried to hold the crowd back.

The sentences on Brady and Hindley came after the jury had been out for two hours 22 minutes.

'Guilty, guilty, guilty'

It was 5.10 p.m. when Hindley was led into the glass-enclosed dock by two women prison officers. Seconds later, Brady took his place beside her. They stood as the jury filed into court.

The verdicts on the three charges against Brady were voiced firmly and clearly by the middle-aged foreman: "Guilty, guilty, guilty.

"Brady folded his arms across his chest and stared directly at the judge. When the judge asked Brady whether he had anything to say before sentence was passed, he said: "No, except the revolvers were bought in July 1964."[Earlier the jury had returned to court to ask about the date Hindley bought two revolvers. The judge consulted counsel and told them that one was purchased in the summer of 1963 and the other in the autumn of the same year.]

Hindley was asked if she had anything to say. Almost inaudibly she replied: "No."

Then the judge told Brady: "Ian Brady, these were three calculated, cruel and cold-blooded murders. In your case, I pass the only sentence which the law now allows, and that is three concurrent sentences of life imprisonment." He added curtly: "Put him down."

As the sentence was delivered Hindley took a packet of mints from her pocket and slipped one into her mouth. Brady turned without looking at her and left the dock. Then the judge said: "In your case, Hindley, you have been found guilty of two equally horrible murders and an accessory after the fact of the murder of John Kilbride." On you I pass two concurrent sentences of life imprisonment and, in connection with the harbouring case, a concurrent sentence of seven years' imprisonment."

ABOVE LEFT: Detective Chief Inspector Peter Topping gives a press conference on Saddleworth Moor during the renewed search for the bodies of Brady and Hindley's victims.

ABOVE RIGHT: As the icy mist lifted in November 1986, eight dogs went to work in the continuing search for the bodies of Pauline Reade and Keith Bennett. Sergeant Neville Sharp worked with Jan, a keen-eyed collie.

Daily Mail

WEDNESDAY, NOVEMBER 19, 1986

20p

20 years after the Moors murder trial, police start hunt for two more children's graves

MYRA HINDLEY TALKS AT LAST

By STEPHEN OLDFIELD

MOORS murderess Myra Hindley revealed last night why she is helping police search for two more missing children.

The killer issued a statement from prison saying she would help 'in any way' to solve the mysteries of Pauline Reade and Keith Bennett.

She said she had directed police to the grim moorland where she and her lover Ian Brady buried John Kilbride, 12, and Lesley Anne Downey, ten more than 20 years ago. A major search starts tomorrow.

In her statement dictated to solicitor Michael Fisher, 43-year-old Hindley said: 'I received a letter, the first ever, from the mother of one of the missing children, and this has caused me enormous distress. I have agreed to help the Manchester Police in any way possible, and have today identified from photographs and maps places that I know were of particular interest to Ian Brady, some of which I visited with him.

'In spite of a 22-year passage of time, I have searched my heart and memory and given whatever help I can give to the police. I'm glad at long last to have been continue to do all that I can. I hope that one day people will be able to forgive me for what I have done, and know the truth of what I have and have not done.

'But for now, I want the police to be able to conclude their inquiries so ending public speculation and the private anguish of those directly involved.'

The letter she referred to was sent by Winnie Johnson, the remarried mother of Keith Bennett.

Pauline, 16, and Keith, 12, lived near Hindley and Brady. Both vanished in the mid-sixties when the Moors Murders were committed. But earlier searches of Saddleworth Moor above Oldham, found nothing.

Unlike last time, the police now have dogs trained to detect human remains .... and the co-operation of Hindley. And scientists have told detectives that the moorland peat could have preserved the children's remains.

The area of the search, which will take several weeks, will be close to where the earlier bodies were found.

The new moors follow a police review of the Reade and Bennett files and claims that Hindley was overheard in prison confessing that she and Brady killed another child.

She is also alleged to have said that other bodies are buried on the Moors — and that she knew the location of at least one.

Detective Chief Superintendent Peter Topping, head

Turn to Page 2, Col 6

Hindley: I'll help   Pauline: Vanished July 1963   Keith: Vanished June 1964

INSIDE: Weather 2. Lynda Lee-Potter 7. World Wide 10. Femail 12. Money Mail 25,26. TV 28, 29. Peck 30. Letters 34. Cassie Royale 35. Technology 36 38, 39. Sport 39.44

NOVEMBER 19, 1986

Myra Hindley talks at last

Moors murderess Myra Hindley revealed last night why she is helping police search for two children missing since the Sixties. In a statement from prison, she said she had been moved by an anguished letter from the mother of one youngster. She had seen police and directed them to Pennine moorland in the search for Pauline Reade and Keith Bennett. Police will tomorrow begin hunting for their remains in the windswept area close to where Hindley and her lover Ian Brady buried John Kilbride, 12, and Lesley Anne Downey, ten, more than 20 years ago.

'Enormous distress'

In her statement dictated to solicitor Michael Fisher, 43-year-old Hindley said: 'I received a letter, the first ever, from the mother of one of the missing children, and this has caused me enormous distress. I have agreed to help the Manchester Police in any way possible, and have today identified from photographs and maps, places that I know were of particular interest to Ian Brady, some of which I visited with him.

In spite of a 22-year passage of time, I have searched my heart and memory and given whatever help I can give to the police. I'm glad at long last to have been able to have been given this opportunity and I will continue to do all that I can. I hope that one day people will be able to forgive the wrong I have done, and know the truth of what I have and have not done. But for now, I want the police to be able to conclude their inquiries so ending public speculation and the private anguish of those directly involved.'

The letter she referred to was sent by Winifred Johnson, the remarried mother of Keith Bennett. Mrs Johnson, 53, said last night: 'Never in my wildest dreams did I think Hindley would answer. I wrote asking her to search her conscience and think of me not knowing what had happened to my son. I don't know whether to believe her. I don't know why I should trust her. I'll have to wait and see. It's such a dreadful feeling that I might soon know the truth. I feel numb.'

'I received a letter, the first ever, from the mother of one of the missing children, and this has caused me enormous distress.'

TOP RIGHT AND FAR RIGHT: Detective Chief Superintendent Peter Topping with Mrs Winnie Johnson, the mother of Moors Murder victim, Keith Bennett.

ABOVE RIGHT: A Canberra aircraft flies over Saddleworth Moor taking photographs in an attempt to help police in their search.

RIGHT AND OPPOSITE BELOW: Police work through bad weather as they try to locate the graves of Bennett and Reade in 1986. Massive security operations to protect Hindley and Brady were undertaken when the two assisted police on the moors in the search.

OPPOSITE TOP RIGHT: The house on Wardle Brook Avenue was demolished to deter morbid day-trippers who frequently came to look at the home the killers shared.

Police find body on moors

Police hunting victims of the Moors murderers found a body yesterday. A skeleton, believed to be that of a girl, was unearthed by detectives searching Saddleworth Moor outside Manchester. It was in a shallow peat grave only yards from where 10-year-old Lesley Ann Downey, killed by Ian Brady and Myra Hindley 23 years ago, was found in 1965. Home Office pathologist Geoffrey Garrett was working through the night for clues to the body's identity.

Breakthrough

The scene, Hollin Brown Knoll, was lit by floodlights as police carried on the hunt. A senior detective commented: 'It has been a long, hard inquiry which has been dismissed as a waste of time. We have now made what we believe is a major breakthrough. We think we have found the body of a girl victim of the Moors murderers.'

The police made their grim find seven months after they launched the hunt for the bodies of 16-year-old Pauline Reade and 12-year-old Keith Bennett. The youngsters vanished during Brady and Hindley's reign of terror, and for 20 years detectives suspected the couple.

Then last December Hindley received a letter from Keith's mother, Mrs Winnie Johnson, and broke her silence to admit her involvement in the two disappearances and offer help to the police. She visited the Moors twice to point out possible burial sites.

Trial

The man leading the hunt, Detective Chief Superintendent Peter Topping, confirmed that a body had been removed from Saddleworth Moor in a phone call to Mrs Johnson. He told her: 'We have found a body - but it is not Keith.'

Mrs Johnson said: 'When Mr Topping told me they had found a body my heart stopped. When he told me it was definitely not Keith's he added immediately that the search for my son would continue. I know now that they will find him.'

Myra Hindley's solicitor, Mr Michael Fisher, said she would take the news 'very, very badly.' He went on: 'She is going to react, it is going to be very bad for her. It will be very upsetting and I know she will find it all extremely hard to take.' Mr Fisher said he was going to Cookham Wood prison in Kent, where Hindley is serving her sentence, 'as soon as I possibly can.'

Earlier this year Pauline Reade's father, 61-year-old Mr Amos Reade, said: 'Our family have lived through the sheer hell and torment of not knowing exactly what happened.' When Hindley made her statement about the two missing bodies, Pauline's mother, Mrs Joan Reade, said: 'For God's sake, tell the truth and give me a few peaceful years before it kills me. All I have left now is the hope that one day I will finally know the truth.'

> 'All I have left now is the hope that one day I will finally know the truth.'

MYRA HINDLEY NEAR TO DEATH

Priest gives last rites to gravely ill Moors murderer

By Hugh Muir

MOORS MURDERER Myra Hindley is near to death tonight and has received the last rites in hospital.

Hindley, 45, has suffered a suspected heart attack and a chest infection. The woman who lured trusting children into Ian Brady's clutches and helped him torture, abuse and kill them, is under close guard in a ward seen from all other patients at Bury St Edmunds.

A priest was called to her earlier today. Prison sources say her condition has deteriorated in the past 24 hours. She has

Fire strike hits Tube and now RMT may walk out

By Dick Murray
Transport Editor

TUBE commuters faced a struggle home tonight again after dozens of train drivers refused to work because of the fire strike — although London Underground managers were able to run 80 per cent of services.

There was more bad news, however, for Tube users when the RMT union threatened to call a strike of its own, because management refused to promise not to discipline drivers who would not work during the fire walkout.

Tube workers have claimed the system is unsafe without regular Fire Brigade cover. Yet nine of drivers had refused to work today but Bobby Law, London regional organiser for the largest rail

Evil life of Myra: Pages 8 & 9

Child killer Myra Hindley as she looked at the time of her trial for serial murder

Continued on Page 2

Continued on Page 4

HARRY ROBERTS:
The Braybrook Street Massacre

3 POLICEMEN SHOT DEAD NEAR SCRUBS

Q-car crew murdered

ENGLISH GIRLS IN ROW AT GAMES

The three were planning to rob a rent collector, but a routine police check in Braybrook Street, a stone's throw from the walls of Wormwood Scrubs, led to a shoot-out that left them facing a triple murder charge.

AUGUST 13, 1966

Armed London Police Hunt Killers of Braybrook Street

Armed police joined the hunt last night for gunmen who killed three policemen in a London street. They were issued with .38 revolvers at Shepherd's Bush police station in West London. Other officers with teargas guns were held ready. A police officer said: "More guns will be issued if these men are cornered." Nearly 200 policemen from all parts of London were sent to Shepherd's Bush police station, headquarters of the hunt for the killers. Most were volunteers - men on leave or away on holiday hurried back to help the hunt.

ABOVE: The stark exterior of Wormwood Scrubs Prison towers over Braybrook Street, Shepherd's Bush, where three policemen were mercilessly shot at point-blank range during a routine police check.

ABOVE (INSET): The evening newspapers related the grim events. A child witness had stated to the officers: 'They immediately started firing at the policemen'. Over one hundred police raced to the scene as they hunted for the Standard Vanguard car that had sped away from the area.

LEFT: Police cover the bodies of the dead officers. PC Geoffrey Fox, DS Christopher Head and DC David Wombwell were all in plain clothes and had been in an unmarked Triumph car.

The name of Harry Roberts has reverberated around some football grounds, used in a tasteless chant targeted at the police. The man who inspired the unsavoury refrain was a petty criminal who had no qualms about committing cold-blooded murder if he were backed into a corner, and that is exactly the position in which he found himself on Friday 12 August 1966. Three policemen were shot dead in the incident, the worst death toll for serving officers attending a single incident since the Sidney Street Siege of 1911.

Felonious pursuits

On that August afternoon Harry Roberts had car theft in mind. He and two confederates, John Duddy and John Witney, were cruising the streets of London's Shepherd's Bush area on the lookout for a vehicle that could be used in their felonious pursuits. They were planning to rob a rent collector, but a routine police check in Braybrook Street, a stone's throw from the walls of Wormwood Scrubs, led to a shoot-out that left them facing a triple murder charge.

The gang's blue Standard Vanguard estate was in a sorry condition, and it may well have been the sight of an exhaust tied up with string that first attracted the attention of three plain-clothes policemen on patrol in an unmarked Q car. The officers who thought they were dealing with a possible unroadworthy vehicle were DS Christopher Head, DC David Wombwell and PC Geoffrey Fox. It is quite possible that they then recognised one or more of the occupants, and the prospect of known criminals loitering in the environs of Wormwood Scrubs may have aroused their suspicions still further.

TOP LEFT: Local resident Mrs Ida Collins was one of the first to give a witness statement to the police. Several people had been milling around the road as the events unfolded and fortunately a motorist had taken down the licence-plate number of the getaway car.

RIGHT: The shrouded body of DS Head lies under the Triumph car.

ABOVE: The car is towed away. The windscreen, shattered by the shot that killed PC Fox, is clearly visible.

TOP RIGHT: Stunned local residents, including several children who had witnessed the shooting while playing in the street, watch as police examine the scene.

BELOW: Detectives meticulously search the area around one of the bodies, looking for any possible clues. The entire London police force was on alert and many off-duty officers joined in the hunt for the three men.

Point-blank range

Head and Wombwell approached the car to question the driver, John Witney. Roberts was in the passenger seat, Duddy in the rear. The officers noticed that the car had no valid Road Fund Licence, and Witney explained that he couldn't tax the vehicle until it had passed its MOT test. On request he produced his driving licence and insurance certificate. That merely added to the list of misdemeanours, for the insurance had expired at noon that day, just over three hours earlier. As Witney pleaded for leniency, Roberts became nervous. If the police searched the car, they would find guns and live ammunition, putting the level of offence into a different bracket altogether. DS Head had gone to inspect the back of the Vanguard, and Roberts saw his chance. He produced a Luger and fired at PC Wombwell at point-blank range. The officer was struck in the left eye and killed instantly.

> Roberts and Duddy ran back to the Vanguard, which sped away, leaving some wide-eyed onlookers believing they had witnessed part of a movie production.

DS Head was shot in the back while trying to make it back to the patrol car and fell to the ground just in front of the vehicle. Duddy jumped out to join the fray, running to the nearside of the police car, where he fired at PC Fox through the glass. The .38 automatic was discharged twice more, and it was one of these bullets that inflicted a fatal head wound on the officer. The police car's engine was idling, and as Fox slumped forward, pressure was applied to the accelerator and the vehicle lurched forward and hit the stricken figure of DS Head. Roberts and Duddy ran back to the Vanguard, which sped away, leaving some wide-eyed onlookers believing they had witnessed part of a movie production.

ABOVE AND LEFT: Later that day, after an extensive search, the Vanguard was found in a garage rented by John Witney. The forensic team immediately began an examination of the vehicle before towing it to the forensic laboratory in Holborn for further tests using the most modern techniques available at the time.

TOP: A local resident points to the garage in Vauxhall where the vehicle was found.

OPPOSITE BOTTOM: Frogmen working from a police launch on the River Thames. They were searching for the murder weapon which may have been thrown from Lambeth Bridge.

Drivers of all London's radio-controlled taxis were asked to look out for the gunmen's getaway car - a blue 1955 Standard Vanguard, believed to be a van converted into an estate car. Its number is PGT726. Scotland Yard started a street by street search of garages and yards for the car.

Death came to the three policemen on routine patrol in just four seconds - the time it took to fire a few rounds from one or more revolvers in quiet, sunny Braybrook Street, bordering Wormwood Scrubs Common. The three officers, all wearing plain clothes, stopped their Triumph 2000 Q car - Foxtrot One-One - to make a chance check on the Vanguard parked in Braybrook Street. Two men got out of the gunmen's car. One by one the three policemen, all unarmed, were shot down. They fell within yards of a group of frightened schoolchildren playing on the common, in the shadow of Wormwood Scrubs Jail.

Silent

The Yard, alerted by a 999 call, had radioed to the car believing it to be the nearest to the scene. For a few seconds Braybrook Street, a long crescent lined on one side by council houses was silent. Gunsmoke drifted in the air. The children had run clear. But soon dozens of policemen were on the spot. A senior Scotland Yard officer said: "It was the most callous crime I have known." So callous that PC Wombwell was believed to be holding his hands above his head to prove he was unarmed when he was gunned down.

A man's name scribbled on a pad beside the gear lever of the Q car may help the hunt. It was written by Sergeant Head shortly before the shooting. Police think he may have recognised a suspect in the parked Vanguard and had time to write down his name before he was shot.

TOP: Witney was in police custody by the end of the day and the following Tuesday appeared at West London Court where he was remanded in custody. He had revealed the names of Harry Roberts and John Duddy as his accomplices.

ABOVE AND ABOVE MIDDLE: Witney returned to court a week later where he was once again remanded in custody.

ABOVE LEFT: Police published the name and a detailed description of Harry Roberts, a known petty criminal, and received over 400 phone calls of sightings in the London area and many more from other parts of the country. Sir Joseph Simpson, Metropolitan Police Commissioner, consulted legal experts from the Director of Public Prosecution's office before deciding not to issue his photograph to the general public.

Outrage

The cold-blooded murder of three police officers in broad daylight
shocked the nation. Donations flooded in, the only tangible way
for many to express their outrage and support for the victims'
families. Holiday camp magnate Sir Billy Butlin contributed
£250,000 and the coffers soon swelled to over £1 million. Those
funds were used to launch the Police Dependants' Trust, a body
that continues to this day to support officers who have suffered
debilitating injuries in the line of duty, and the bereaved families
of policemen killed in service.

Witnesses

Metropolitan Police Commissioner Sir Joseph Simpson
appealed to the criminal fraternity for help in tracking
down the killers, convinced that even many underworld
figures would have abhorred the shocking triple
homicide. In the event, information from that quarter
wasn't needed. There were a number of witnesses to the murders,
including several children playing in the street. A passing motorist
took down the registration number of the Vanguard, and before
the day was out John Witney was in custody. He initially said
that he had sold the vehicle that very morning, but when it was
recovered from a garage that he rented in Lambeth, Witney realised
that the game was up and confessed. At least, he confessed to
being in the car with Roberts and Duddy, whom he named, but
vehemently denied firing any shots. Duddy was arrested on
17 August, holed up in a tenement flat in his native city Glasgow.
He, too, admitted to being present in the car but denied doing
any of the shooting. On the flight back to London he changed his
story and admitted to DI Jack Slipper that he had killed PC Fox.
Harry Roberts proved to be a lot more elusive. He evaded capture
for three months, despite one of the biggest manhunts in history.
Roberts used his military training and survival skills to hide out
in Epping Forest, an area
he knew well from his
childhood.

ABOVE LEFT, ABOVE INSET AND
BELOW LEFT: John Duddy was
arrested in Glasgow five days after
the shooting and was immediately
flown back to London by DI Jack
Slipper and DCI George Hensley,
who guided him down the aircraft
steps. He was forced to spend
the flight with his head under
a plastic raincoat in a separate
compartment so his face was
not seen by any of the crew or
other passengers. After landing

he was driven away for further
questioning. During the flight he
had admitted killing PC Fox.

BELOW RIGHT: Children watch the
police activity around the flat in
the Calton area of Glasgow.

TOP RIGHT AND BELOW: Duddy
was taken to West London Court
where he was also remanded in
custody.

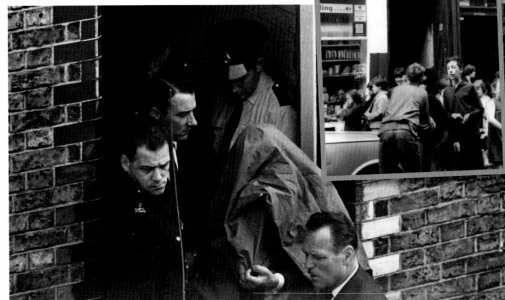

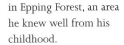

Roberts was still at large when the memorial service for the fallen officers was held at Westminster Abbey.

Parliamentary reaction

Roberts was still at large when the memorial service for the fallen officers was held at Westminster Abbey in early September. Outside there were banners calling for the re-introduction of capital punishment for the murder of police and prison officers, reversing parliament's decision of the previous year. Home Secretary Roy Jenkins said he understood the strength of feeling but explained that it would be wrong to institute a policy change on the strength of a single event, no matter how terrible and tragic that event might be. That autumn, Conservative MP Duncan Sandys sought to introduce a bill allowing the ultimate sanction to be available in certain circumstances. While there was much support for his view, the biggest cheer in the Commons debate followed the comment that most people would be able to sleep more easily if Timothy Evans were still alive. Leave to introduce the bill was voted down by a majority of 122.

The 'Braybrook Street Massacre' also brought forth calls for the police to be armed. Sir Joseph Simpson's response to that kneejerk reaction was to say it would be a sad day in the country's history if officers routinely carried guns. However, the events of 12 August 1966 did lead to the formation of SO19, the police firearms unit, established in December that year.

ABOVE INSET: Donations poured in as the outraged public found a way to express their support for the victims' families. Police officers at Shepherd's Bush station counted the donations which came to over £1,000. This scene was repeated throughout the country and many officers were handed money as they went about their daily tasks.

LEFT: At Scotland Yard, officers were opening letters of sympathy and donations.

TOP MIDDLE: Police search a house near King's Cross. The hunt was now on for Harry Roberts, the final member of the trio suspected of killing DS Head and DC Wombwell. An officer recognised Roberts in Gerrard Street, Soho, and followed him through a maze of streets near King's Cross. Police ringed the area as Roberts leapt on a bus and jumped off by the Sadler's Wells Theatre, Islington. Police swarmed through the theatre while performers were rehearsing.

TOP LEFT: As police continued to search the Islington area, residents from the Spa Green Estate watch as officers secure the roads.

TOP RIGHT: The hunt in Islington extended to a semi-derelict house. Sixty armed officers surrounded this property after a woman had seen a man jumping over a wall at the time of the search.

ABOVE: The West London Air Terminal was also searched. Countless officers joined in to pursue their colleagues' killer.

Roberts finally in custody

The Old Bailey trial began on 14 November 1966. Roberts may not have been in the dock with Duddy and Witney but all three were on the charge sheet. Prosecuting counsel Elwyn Jones QC, the Attorney General, made it clear from the outset that the three men were jointly and severally responsible for the officers' deaths. That statement must have been a blow to Witney, for there was considerable evidence to support his story, namely, that he had taken no part in the shootings. He was to find that as far as the law was concerned, culpability was not restricted to the person who pulled the trigger.

Duddy and Witney pleaded Not Guilty. By 17 November, what would have been the fourth day of the trial, Harry Roberts was in custody, having been tracked down to a barn in Sawbridgeworth, Hertfordshire. It was decided that the three men should be tried together, and to give Roberts's counsel time to prepare a defence a retrial was ordered. That opened 5 December 1966. Witney and Duddy again entered Not Guilty pleas, while Roberts pleaded Guilty to the murder of Wombwell and Head, but Not Guilty in regard of the charge relating to PC Fox. He named Duddy as the man who fired the shot which killed that officer. Lillian Perry, who co-habited with Roberts, provided corroborating testimony. She said Roberts admitted to the murders when he returned home on the evening of 12 August. The following Monday, Perry said she accompanied him to buy camping equipment, after which the two parted, Roberts telling her: 'This is as far as we go together. I am on my own now.'

> The Attorney General, Elwyn Jones QC, made it clear from the outset that the three men were jointly and severally responsible for the officers' deaths.

ABOVE: Police alongside the road as the search for Roberts extended to Epping Forest in Essex.

TOP RIGHT AND MIDDLE RIGHT: Hundreds of officers meticulously search for any evidence in the undergrowth.

LEFT INSET: A pair of shorts and booking form signed 'Roberts' were eventually found in a barn at Standen Manor Farm in Hungerford, Berkshire. Cowman Jock Gordon had disturbed a man who then ran through a hedge and disappeared.

LEFT: An army helicopter joined the 250 officers in the search of the thick woods and farmland just south of Hungerford.

Apportioning responsibility

James Burge QC, acting for Roberts, called no evidence on his client's behalf. Duddy's counsel, James Comyn QC, took the same line, but made it clear that Harry Roberts was the chief instigator, something even Roberts's counsel conceded. Witney was the only one of the defendants to give evidence. He denied knowing that Roberts and Duddy were carrying guns, and insisted that his only experience of firearms had been during his Army training. Witney also said he was terrified of Roberts, who had threatened him with violence after the incident to ensure his silence and co-operation. Witney, a married man with two children, said he was in fear of his own life and that of his family. Duddy, perhaps to redress the balance, called Witney 'the brains of this outfit'.

During the six-day trial there was little dispute regarding the salient facts. The main point at issue was apportioning responsibility for the crimes. The prosecution argued for all three to be treated as one, while the defence sought to establish gradations of culpability. Solicitor General Sir Dingle Foot QC had taken over as chief prosecuting counsel, as the Attorney General was engaged on the inquiry into the Aberfan disaster. In his summing-up, he showed himself to be just as persistent as Elwyn Jones on the subject of joint responsibility. The jury, he said, had three matters to consider: Who carried out the shootings? Did the three share a common purpose in trying to avoid arrest? If Witney was not party to that common purpose, did he assist the other two in their escape, thereby becoming an accessory after the fact?

TOP LEFT: Roberts's picture had been released and this wanted poster offered a reward for information leading to his capture.

THIS PAGE: Harry Roberts was finally found and arrested on November 16, 1966, three months after the shooting and just after the start of the trial at the Old Bailey. Police had been searching Thorley Wood in Hertfordshire when Sergeant Peter Smith, armed with a revolver, searched a barn and noticed a bottle of methylated spirits and found Roberts hiding under a bale of straw. The fugitive gave himself up immediately and offered police no resistance. Half a mile away police also found his previous hideout – a tent thickly camouflaged with bushes and logs. Using techniques he had learnt in jungle survival training he had made storage areas for his kit and had emerged into the local area to buy provisions and newspapers. Roberts had abandoned the tent a few days before to use the barn instead.

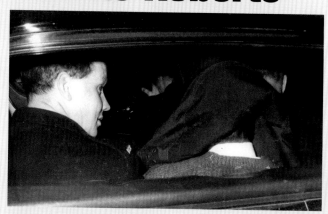

DECEMBER 6, 1966

I Murdered Two, Admits Roberts

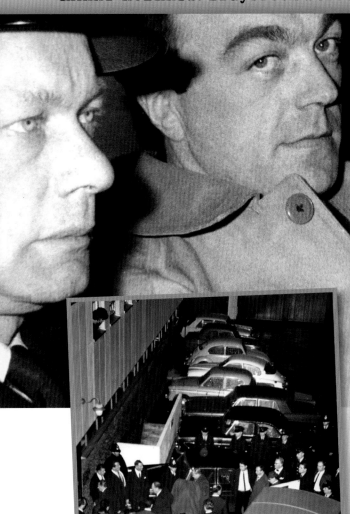

Harry Roberts stood in the dock at the Old Bailey yesterday and admitted killing two of the three policemen shot dead near Wormwood Scrubs Prison in August. Roberts, a 30-year-old carpenter, pleaded guilty as the clerk read out the charges accusing him of murdering Detective Sergeant Christopher Head, 30, and Detective Constable David Wombwell, 26. But he gave a firm "not guilty" to the charge of murdering Police Constable Geoffrey Fox, the driver of the three-man "Q" car.

After a jury of 11 men and one woman had been sworn in Sir Dingle Foot told them: "The Crown say that this was a case of deliberate, cold-blooded murder. The Crown say that the men responsible for these murders, all equally responsible, were the three accused." In the dock with Roberts are John Duddy, 37, a carpenter, and John Witney, 36, also a carpenter. Duddy and Witney have pleaded not guilty and are being tried for the murders of all three policemen. Roberts - because he has pleaded guilty to murdering Sergeant Head and Constable Wombwell - is being tried only for the murder of P.C. Fox.

Sir Dingle said that on August 12 the three accused were in an old Standard Vanguard van belonging to Whitney. All three had loaded pistols and were planning to commit a criminal offence. They were spotted in Braybrook Street by a police Q car containing three police officers -Detective Sergeant Head, Detective Constable Wombwell and P.C. Fox.

> Sir Dingle Foot told them: 'The Crown say that this was a case of deliberate, cold-blooded murder.'

LEFT: The police van that carried Harry Roberts to Shepherd's Bush police station was greeted by a crowd of more than 1,000 who cheered the police and booed the occupant. Many had waited on the streets for over six hours.

ABOVE LEFT: Roberts, with his face covered, is led into Shepherd's Bush police station. He was immediately charged by detectives and received a two-minute visit from his mother Dorothy. He was due to appear in court the following morning. The trial of the three accused had already begun, despite Roberts's absence, but it was then delayed until 5 December to allow his counsel to prepare his defence.

All three men were eventually found guilty, the jury deciding that Witney had equal guilt although he hadn't actually fired a gun.

ABOVE: Roberts, his face covered, is taken to Brixton Prison after a four-minute appearance at the Old Bailey.

TOP LEFT: The following year, while serving his sentence, Roberts made another journey to court handcuffed to two officers, to give evidence at the trial of Christos Costas. Costas was alleged to have sold Roberts the guns used to kill the officers at Braybrook Street. Under the raincoat he wore his prison uniform.

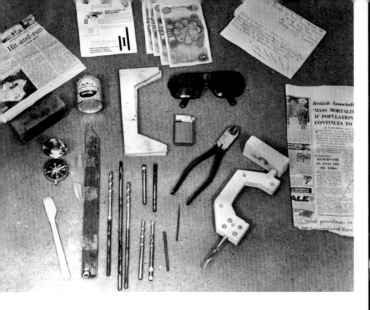

Witney just as guilty

The jury needed just thirty minutes to decide that Witney was just as guilty as the self-confessed murderers. After sentencing the three men to life imprisonment, with a recommendation that they serve a minimum of 30 years behind bars, Mr Justice Glyn-Jones added that the heinous nature of the crimes meant that in this case the life tariff might well be literal in its implementation.

John Duddy served fifteen years, which in his case was indeed a life sentence; he died in Parkhurst jail in February 1981, aged 52. John Witney spent 25 years behind bars, when it was decided he had paid his debt to society. He was released in 1991 and enjoyed eight years of freedom before his death, aged 69.

Harry Roberts is still in jail, now in his fifth decade of incarceration. His case has been reviewed by the Parole Board on a number of occasions since the recommended 30-year term expired in 1996. Roberts has done himself few favours with those empowered to grant his release, for his prison record includes escape attempts, contraband smuggling and abuse of home-leave privileges. Now a septuagenarian, Roberts is currently serving time at Littlehey, the low-security Category C prison in Cambridgeshire. With each passing year, the likelihood increases that the prime mover in the Braybrook Street Massacre will end his days behind bars.

DECEMBER 13, 1966

30 Years for Roberts and Gang

Harry Roberts and his two accomplices were jailed for a recommended minimum of 30 years at the Old Bailey yesterday for the murder of three London policemen. Mr. Justice Glyn Jones passed the statutory sentence of life imprisonment on the three men. Then he said: "Unless any Home Secretary in the future should be mindful of considering your release on licence, I have to make a recommendation you should not be released until 30 years have gone by."

Roberts, 30, John Duddy, 37, and John Witney, 36, stood impassive in the dock of No. 1 Court as the jury of 11 men and one woman found them all equally guilty of the three murders. The judge said: "You have been justly convicted of what is perhaps the most heinous crime that has been committed for a generation or more. I think it likely that no Home Secretary in the future regarding the enormity of your crime will ever think fit to show mercy by releasing you on licence. This is one of those cases in which a sentence of imprisonment for life may well be treated in the meaning of exactly what it says."

> I think it likely that no Home Secretary in the future regarding the enormity of your crime will ever think fit to show mercy by releasing you.

TOP LEFT: During his time in jail Roberts has made several escape attempts. In 1973, he used this escape kit to try to gain his freedom from Parkhurst prison. Roberts's last attempted escape from prison was in 1976 but since then he has tried to become a model prisoner in the hope of gaining parole, but without success. Duddy died in prison and Witney was released in 1991, although he died eight years later.

TOP RIGHT: A police officer displays a card and donation sent after the shootings.

LEFT AND FAR LEFT: Twenty-five years after the shooting wreaths were laid at the memorial in Braybrook Street which marks the place where the three officers fell. Actors Roger Moore (right) and Michael Caine (left) attended the ceremony.

RUTH ELLIS:
The last woman to be hanged in Britain

Ellis emptied a revolver into Blakely. One bullet ricocheted off a wall and injured a passer-by, but the others found their target.

Ruth Ellis had a short and deeply troubled life. Abused by a succession of men, the insecure, unstable mother of two young children finally cracked over the Easter weekend of 1955, shooting dead her lover in a fit of jealous rage.

Betrayal

Ruth Neilson was born 9 October 1926 and brought up in Rhyl, North Wales. Her elder sister Muriel claimed that both she and Ruth were abused by their musician father, which, in the latter's case, would set the pattern for unhappy, dysfunctional relationships with men. Although she was an attractive woman – she would spend some time working as a photographic model – Ruth craved affection and attention, usually from the wrong type. She was needy and dependent, but the men in her life rarely offered dependability.

The Neilson family relocated to London during the war. Ruth had left school and was eking out a living in shops and factories when the next emotional blow struck. She fell for a French-Canadian soldier, Andre Clare, by whom she became pregnant. There was talk of marriage, but Clare omitted to inform her about his existing wife and family back in Canada. A son, Andrew, born in 1945, was the product of a union that ended in betrayal and abandonment.

Ruth drifted into Soho's sleazy club scene, which no doubt paid a lot better than the low-level clerical jobs she was used to. It may not have been part of the job description for her to sleep with the men who patronised the Court Club in Duke Street, though taking hostess work a stage further was an easy way to supplement her income.

LEFT: Ruth Ellis was the last woman to be hanged in Britain after she was found guilty of murdering racing driver David Blakely. Ellis was reported in the media to have been 'utterly indifferent, disdainful in regard to her chances of survival'.

Stormy, obsessive relationship

In 1950 she married divorced dentist George Ellis, one of the club's regulars. He was seventeen years her senior and a chronic alcoholic. Ruth suffered many drink-fuelled assaults before she managed to escape, now with a second child, Georgina, to look after. She drifted back to what she knew: the club scene and hostess work. Former employer Morris Conley installed her as manager of the Little Club in Brompton Road, Knightsbridge, and it was here that she made the acquaintance of David Blakely. Superficially, Blakely was a good catch: ex-public schoolboy, good looking, well off, a playboy whose chief passion revolved around the glamorous world of motor racing. But scratch not very far beneath the surface and a less appealing picture was revealed. He was a philandering rogue capable of the most boorish behaviour when intoxicated – which was often – and not above resorting to using his fists on a woman.

Ellis and Blakely had a stormy, obsessive relationship, punctuated by violent rows and passionate reconciliations. Businessman Desmond Cussen seemed to offer salvation, and some hope of a better life. He was besotted with Ruth, but although she revelled in the adoring attention and had a brief sexual relationship with him, it was not a love match. Ruth was repeatedly drawn back to the bad penny, sharing a bed with Blakely even when she was living under Cussen's roof

Fired until the bullets ran out

By the spring of 1955, Blakely had had enough and wanted to sever all ties with Ellis. On 9 April, Good Friday, he sought sanctuary at the home of friends, the Findlaters, with whom he planned to spend the holiday weekend. Ellis became increasingly distraught and frustrated at her thwarted attempts to contact her lover. Convinced that he was having an affair with the Findlaters' nanny, she went round to the house and damaged his car, calming down only after the police were called. For Ellis it was merely a tactical withdrawal.

That Sunday the Findlaters hosted a party, and when Blakely and a friend, Clive Gunnell, slipped out for more supplies of beer and cigarettes, the spurned woman struck. As the two men came out of the Magdala public house in South Hill Park, Hampstead, Ellis emptied a revolver into Blakely. One bullet ricocheted off a wall and injured a passer-by, but the others found their target. Even when he was lying prostrate on the ground, with Gunnell crouching over to attend him, Ellis kept firing until the bullets ran out, then calmly asked for the police to be called. She was still holding the weapon when an off-duty officer arrested her. There was no doubt about the perpetrator, but had the crime been committed in cold blood? Ellis admitted her guilt on the night of her arrest, adding: 'I am confused.' Unfortunately for her, the ability of the defence to cite a disturbed state of mind during the commission of murder was far more constrained than it is today. Experts interviewed her and she was also given an ECG examination. They found no evidence of mental illness.

ABOVE RIGHT: Ruth Ellis with David Blakely, whom she shot outside a pub in Hampstead on Easter Sunday, 1955.

JUNE 22, 1955

Ruth Ellis jealousy appeal?

Mrs. Ruth Ellis turned to a nurse attendant in the dock at the Old Bailey yesterday and smiled as the jury announced their verdict: guilty of murder. That smile was the first sign of emotion the 28-year-old platinum blonde had given during her trial for shooting her lover, David Moffatt Blakely, 25-year-old racing motorist, in a Hampstead street on Easter Sunday. Mr. Justice Havers donned the black cap and spoke the death sentence. Before she walked calm and unassisted from the dock, Mrs. Ellis heard him say: "The jury have convicted you of murder. In my view it was the only verdict possible."

Permission was given for her father, Mr. Neilson, to see her in the cells before she was taken to Holloway Jail. Mr. Neilson and Mrs. Ellis's mother are caretakers of a block of Hampstead service flats.

Mrs. Ellis's legal advisers were last night considering the possibility of an appeal on a new point of law - that of provocation brought on by jealousy. It was the only defence offered by her lawyers, who asked for a verdict of manslaughter. The appeal, on the grounds that a woman thwarted in love is more irresponsible than a man, could be taken to the House of Lords. It is the first time that such a point of law has been offered in a murder trial.

BELOW: The newspaper headline the day of Ruth Ellis's execution. Despite pleas from family and friends Ellis had refused to talk about the events leading up to the shooting. The day before the execution she changed her mind and claimed that another man had given her the gun, loaded it and driven her to the scene of the crime.

137

Not guilty plea

Ellis pleaded Not Guilty when she appeared at the Old Bailey, though by the time the jury retired, she had sealed her own fate. Defence counsel Melford Stevenson had wanted to focus on the provocation angle, telling the court that Ellis was 'driven to a frenzy which for the time being unseated her understanding'. He called a psychologist, who testified that women faced with infidelity tended to show impaired judgment to a greater extent than men in the same situation. She loved and hated Blakely at the same time; her mind was in a state of turmoil, a problem she resorted to the gun to solve. Stevenson hoped to persuade the jury that Ellis was of unsound mind when the crime was committed, and that manslaughter was, therefore, the appropriate charge.

The presiding judge, Sir Cecil Havers, was having none of that. He gave the jury no leeway in the matter by issuing the following ruling: '…where the question arises whether what would otherwise be murder may be reduced to manslaughter on the grounds of provocation, if there is no sufficient material, even upon a view of the evidence most favourable to the accused, that a reasonable person could be driven by transport of passion and loss of control to use violence and a continuance of violence, it is the duty of the judge, as a matter of law, to direct the jury that the evidence does not support a verdict of manslaughter. I have been constrained to rule in this case that there is not sufficient material… to reduce this killing from murder to manslaughter on the grounds of provocation.'

Havers said that if he had ruled in error, it would be rectified on appeal, but for now the jury was unable to return a manslaughter verdict.

'I intended to kill him'

Stevenson's hands were tied. He was undone by his own client who, in answer to a question from prosecutor Christmas Humphreys regarding intent, replied: 'It is obvious that when I shot him I intended to kill him'. Ellis had been caught with a smoking gun, admitted intent and, with manslaughter ruled out, Stevenson knew that the game was up. He declined to make further comment to the jury, for he decided he could make no worthwhile closing argument without contravening the judge's ruling. Humphreys chose not to make any closing remarks either to maintain equilibrium, though that was hardly too gracious an act since the outcome could only be in his favour.

The jury retired with the judge's solemn words ringing in their ears. 'I am bound to tell you this, that even if you accept every word of Mrs Ellis's evidence, there does not seem to be anything in it which establishes any sort of defence to the charge of murder.' It took just twenty minutes to return a Guilty verdict.

'A life for a life'

Ellis showed little inclination to appeal, calmly accepting the axiomatic wisdom of 'a life for a life'. It was left to others to take up the cudgels on her behalf and petition for a reprieve. In some ways that was strange, since it appeared to be a watertight case with no obvious reason why she shouldn't follow the fifteen other women who had gone to the gallows since the turn of the century. The dissenting voices were up against it, for a pro-capital punishment Conservative Party had just been returned to office. The pleas for clemency fell upon the deaf ears of Home Secretary Gwilym Lloyd-George. Crowds gathered outside Holloway Prison, some chanting the names of Evans and Bentley before police restored order. They couldn't save Ruth Ellis, who was hanged on 13 July 1955. She was 28.

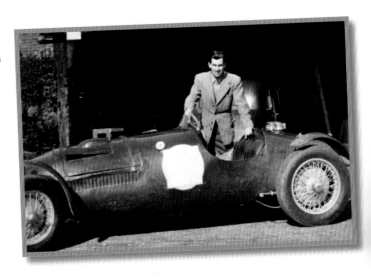

ABOVE: Ruth Ellis took on modelling work to make ends meet. Through this she became a nightclub hostess, which paid significantly more than the various waitress, factory and clerical jobs she had had since leaving school.

RIGHT: David Blakely, a handsome former public school boy, was involved in glamorous world of motor racing, but he also had a darker side.

OPPOSITE PAGE: Ruth Ellis was hanged on 13 July 1955 at Holloway Prison. In 2003 Ellis's family members tried to have the conviction reduced to manslaughter on the grounds of severe provocation but their claims were rejected by the Court of Appeal.

Abolition of capital punishment

The Ellis case was an important staging post on the road towards the abolition of capital punishment, though there were many struggles ahead for those wanted the ultimate sanction removed from the statute book. A year after Ellis's execution, the abolitionists went down by 143 votes in Parliament. Change was on the way, however, and in 1957 the concept of diminished responsibility officially became part of a defence counsel's armoury. Before then, provocation leading to retaliation 'in hot blood' was acceptable as a form of mitigation, but that didn't apply in the case of Ruth Ellis, hence the judge's ruling. The case was instrumental in widening the parameters in which the perpetrator's state of mind could be taken into account, though it came too late to help Ellis herself.

'Battered woman syndrome'

In 2003 members of the Ellis family tried to get the conviction reduced to manslaughter on grounds of severe provocation. Michael Mansfield QC argued that she had been subjected to numerous assaults, including one blow which caused her to miscarry ten days before the shooting. Ellis was already taking anti-depressants, and now had the loss of a child to contend with. Ellis, it was said, was suffering from 'battered woman syndrome' and should not have been found guilty of a capital offence. The Court of Appeal rejected those claims, stating that Ellis had been convicted in accordance with the law as it stood at the time.

There was a second contentious issue, glossed over during the original trial. Where had Ruth acquired the Smith & Wesson revolver she used on Blakely? On the eve of her execution, she told solicitor Victor Mishcon – who would later be ennobled and act as legal advisor to Princess Diana – that Desmond Cussen had given her the weapon and taught her how to use it. Cussen even drove her to the Magdala pub, Ruth having told him that she intended to kill Blakely. Cussen had an obvious motive for wanting

JULY 14, 1955

'She died a brave woman'

In Holloway Prison last night the staff were saying that Ruth Ellis was the bravest woman ever to go to the gallows in Britain. For the 28-year-old mother who, eight hours before her execution, had broken down and pleaded for life, died calmly.

The emotion was all outside the prison walls. By 9 a.m. – the time of the execution – a crowd thousands strong surged behind a massive police cordon. By then Ruth Ellis had resigned herself to death. She was tranquil.

On her execution eve she had read a little from her Bible. Just before midnight she had said goodnight to the wardresses with her and composed herself for sleep – the deep sleep of exhaustion.

Refused breakfast

At 8.15 a.m. yesterday, while the crowd wept, prayed, and peered at the prison gates, she was roused by a gentle touch on the shoulder. Quietly she told the wardresses that she did not want breakfast, but she accepted a drink - a small glass of brandy.

At one minute to nine, while a street musician outside the walls played Bach's "Be Thou With Me When I Die," the prison governor, Dr. Charity Taylor, and the hangman entered her cell. With them were two men warders taken from duty at the prison gates, a wardress, the prison medical officer, and the chaplain. Of the women Ruth Ellis was the most composed.

In the silence outside the walls a radio somewhere intoned the chimes of Big Ben. A man threw the torn-up shreds of a newspaper in the air and shouted: "Another murder."

Blakely, his love rival, out of the way, and discussions took place over the possibility of charging Cussen as an accessory. In the end, those plans were dropped, for with Ellis dead, the case would have been impossible to try. Cussen's alleged involvement didn't help Ruth's cause, either, for it merely highlighted the calculating premeditation that justified a guilty verdict.

Ruth Ellis's body rested in the confines of Holloway Prison for sixteen years, her remains reinterred at St Mary's Church, Amersham when the prison was completely remodelled in 1971. There was no doubt that she was guilty of the crime for which she was tried; whether she received justice is a different matter.

BRINKS-MAT:
The Biggest Robbery Ever Staged in Britain

The gang who got away with £26 million in the Great Gold Robbery defeated some of the most advanced electronic gadgetry in the world with stark unsophisticated torture.

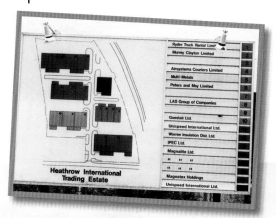

£26 million haul

In the 1980s, the warehouses of the Heathrow International Trading Estate were used as short-term holding bays for precious metals and gemstones on their way into and out of the country via the nearby airport. Over the years the multi-million-pound freight had become a magnet for criminals, so much so that the warehouse complex was dubbed 'Thief Row Airport'. In April 1983 thieves made off with £6 million from a Security Express depot, but that record haul was dwarfed seven months later when an armed gang raided the Brinks-Mat warehouse and got away with £26 million, the biggest robbery ever staged in Britain.

Six masked gunmen struck at around 6.40 am on Saturday 26 November 1983. The timing was crucial, for the valuables were guarded purely by electronic means until the day shift came on duty at 6.30 am. The thieves' plan required the co-operation of security staff, and they showed they were prepared to go to extreme lengths to ensure swift compliance.

6800 gold bars

The guards were handcuffed and blindfolded, their legs bound with tape. Two had their clothing cut away and petrol poured onto their bare skin, with the threat of being set alight if they didn't tell the gang what they wanted to know. The men targeted were the crew supervisor and the 'key man', who controlled all the doors and the alarm system. Each knew half of the combination to the vault, information that was soon surrendered. Only then did the gang realise that they had struck gold, quite literally. They had expected a three-million-pound cash haul; what they got instead was 6800 gold bars worth £22 million, a consignment bound for Hong Kong later that day. It was in the warehouse for one night only; the raiders had been fortuitous indeed. The bullion weighed three tons, and even with the aid of forklift trucks it took two hours to load the booty. They had to commandeer another vehicle, for their van was not up to the task, but were clean away by the time one of the security staff managed to free himself and raise the alarm.

NOVEMBER 28, 1983

Electronic secrets

When the electronic secrets had been surrendered, the gang went to work with military precision knowing that no alarms would be sounded. The gang, all armed with pistols and wearing balaclavas, had to race to pack their haul into a lorry and leave before a genuine collection van due later in the morning turned up.

Using the security firm's own fork lift trucks they began removing 76 blue-grey cardboard boxes from the strongroom. Each measured 10in. by 7in. by 4in. and weighed one hundredweight. In all they contained 6,800 gold bars, each numbered and impressed with a refiner's stamp.

The genuine security staff sighted only three of the robbers. But they say they heard voices and movements indicating there were six in all. The raid was over within an hour. The gang drove off - after closing the warehouse doors behind them and threatening the staff with death if anyone tried to raise the alarm. But by 8.30 a shocked guard managed to press an alarm button.

Inside information

This was 'no mean robbery team', said Commander Frank Cater, head of Scotland Yard's Flying Squad. It was undoubtedly a well-planned heist, but almost immediately police suspected that the gang had inside information. Employees were screened and one of the staff on duty when the heist took place was found to have connections with someone well known to Scotland Yard. The guard was Anthony Black, whose sister's partner was Brian Robinson, a notorious underworld figure known as 'The Colonel' for his organisational ability. Robinson was soon splashing large amounts of cash around, suggesting that the police were on the right lines.

Black cracked under questioning and confessed to his part in the heist. He supplied information regarding daily routine, photographs of the interior layout and a key to the warehouse door for duplication purposes. He also gave the signal that started the raid. Black turned Queen's Evidence when he was tried in February 1984, and was given a lenient six-year jail sentence in return for his co-operation.

Information supplied by Black led to three more arrests. Brian Robinson was tried at the Old Bailey in October 1984 along with Michael McAvoy and Anthony White. All denied the charges. Robinson and McAvoy were convicted and jailed for 25 years; White was acquitted due to lack of evidence.

OPPOSITE PAGE: The anonymous warehouse where the gang struck.

OPPOSITE PAGE INSET TOP: The estate plan which had no Brinks-Mat name next to Unit 7: Brinks-Mat understandably did not wish to advertise its presence on the industrial estate.

OPPOSITE PAGE INSET MIDDLE: The gang tortured security guards until they gave up the security codes for the vaults inside. They poured petrol over one man and threatened to set his clothes alight, they stabbed another in the hand and pistol-whipped a third.

OPPOSITE PAGE INSET BOTTOM: The phone book that showed exactly where to locate Brinks-Mat. The gang had an insider, Anthony Black, whose sister's partner, Brian Robinson, was a notorious underworld figure.

ABOVE: Police on the hunt for the bullion worth £22 million raid the home of jeweller John Palmer. Palmer was away on holiday when the police moved in on those suspected of handling the Brinks-Mat gold. He was one of 20 wanted men named later that year by Scotland Yard. When he eventually returned to England he faced trial for handling Brinks-Mat gold. Despite a hidden gold smelter at his home, the Old Bailey jury accepted his assertion that he did not know he was smelting Brinks-Mat ingots, and acquitted him. His business partner Garth Chappell, who was at the heart of the operation to disguise and pass the bullion back on to the legitimate gold market, was jailed for 10 years. Palmer was later forced to pay a substantial sum to loss adjusters acting for Brinks-Mat.

Following the money trail

By now police had tracked down five men wanted in connection with both the Brinks-Mat raid, and the Security Express robbery seven months earlier. They were living the high life on the Costa del Sol, but the police were thwarted by the absence of extradition arrangements between Britain and Spain, which had ceased in 1978.

The money trail proved a more fruitful line of inquiry. A series of suspicious transactions at a Bristol bank led police to Hollywood Cottage, West Kingsdown, Kent, the 26-acre estate of 38-year-old Kenneth Noye. Police suspected that the gold was being taken from here to a Bristol-based company and put the property under surveillance. They were right. Noye had been brought in for his knowledge of the precious metals market, and in particular his experience of smelting. It was his job to melt down the bullion and recast it into untraceable units that could be disposed of without attracting attention.

Policeman killed

On 26 January 1985 DC John Fordham and DC Neil Murphy entered the grounds of Noye's property in advance of the execution of a search warrant. Noye was alerted by the barking of his Rottweilers and confronted the men with a knife. Murphy escaped and went to call assistance, but Fordham was attacked, suffering fatal stab wounds. Noye was cleared of murder, his counsel convincing the jury that he had acted in self-defence, a panic reprisal attack against an intruder. Fordham had been wearing a camouflage jacket and balaclava, and Noye insisted he hadn't identified himself as a police officer.

That verdict went in Noye's favour but he was still facing separate charges of laundering the stolen gold. He wasn't so fortunate in his next court appearance, fined £700,000 and given a 14-year jail term for handling the Brinks-Mat bullion. Two years after his release in 1994, Noye took another life. His victim was 21-year-old Stephen Cameron, stabbed in an apparent road rage incident, though it was later suggested that the altercation was over a drug deal. Noye's self-defence plea cut no ice this time; he was convicted of murder and given a life term.

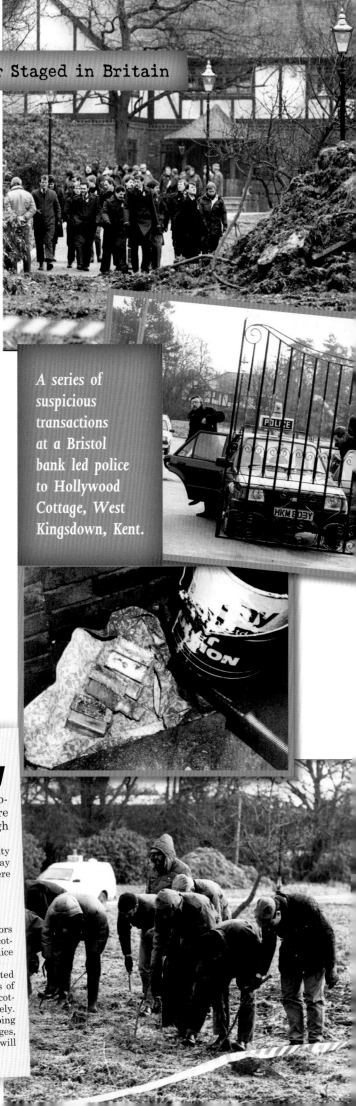

A series of suspicious transactions at a Bristol bank led police to Hollywood Cottage, West Kingsdown, Kent.

DECEMBER 4, 1984

'Protect us' appeal by jury

Frightened jurors in the £26 million gold and diamond robbery case have appealed to police for protection. They are to be guarded day and night by armed officers even though the case has ended.

The jurors were among those who on Sunday found two men guilty of taking part in the robbery at Heathrow Airport a year ago. Yesterday the two, builder Michael McAvoy and motor trader Brian Robinson, were each jailed for 25 years at the Old Bailey.

Armed officers

Last night armed officers were on guard at the homes of worried jurors who had made their unprecedented plea for continued protection to Scotland Yard. The entire jury, including seven women, were under police guard throughout the four-week trial on the orders of the judge.

After the case, several told police they were afraid to go unprotected because of the insight the trial had given them into the operations of members of the bullion gang who had not been brought to justice. Scotland Yard agreed to extend the protection for worried jurors indefinitely. They will be guarded wherever they go. Armed officers will go shopping with housewives. They will attend Christmas parties with their charges, and be close to their homes during the night. The jurors' phones will continue to be monitored.

A quarter of a century on from the biggest heist in British history, many unanswered questions remain. It is believed that up to 15 people were involved in the Brinks-Mat robbery, which means that only a fraction of the perpetrators have been brought to book. Some may never be brought to justice, for several of those suspected of having played a part in the crime have met violent ends.

Perhaps even more intriguing is the whereabouts of the £26 million haul. Apart from the recovery of a dozen bars in the wake of Kenneth Noye's arrest, none of the bullion has been recovered. It is thought that anyone in possession of gold jewellery bought in Britain in the past 25 years is probably wearing part of the proceeds of the Brinks-Mat robbery.

> While it was the daring of the gang that allowed the raid to succeed, it was the expertise of the fences that allowed the loot to slip out of Britain so smoothly.

JULY 24, 1986

Luxury

Two separate gangs were employed; one to carry out the £26 million raid and take the gold to the three 'drop-off' points and one gang who were highly professional 'fences.'

Three members of the first gang are serving long sentences, while detectives would still like to question ex-East End publican Clifford Saxe, Ronnie Knight, the former husband of Carry On actress Barbara Windsor, and three others all living in luxury on the Spanish Costa del Sol beyond the reach of the Yard.

But while it was the daring of that gang that allowed the raid to succeed, it was the expertise of the fences that allowed the loot to slip out of Britain so smoothly. And the Old Bailey was told, it was to Kenneth Noye that the 'contract' fell for disposing of the three tons of gold.

He devised a brilliant plan. The gold was melted down at secret addresses. The size of the bars was changed and copper coins added to change their quality. Small parcels of the re-moulded gold were released on to the legitimate market by providing bogus documents to give it an 'honest background.' This part of the operation had an added lucrative twist - VAT was collected but never passed to Customs.

Ironically, it was this greed that put detectives on the trial of Noye. Police set up a watch on the bullion chain which began at Noye's £1 million home where the gold was collected in small parcels of 11 bars at a time.

Bankers

In one of the most extraordinary twists in the whole story, it was the bankers Johnson Matthey, who bought back most of the gold - it had been the bank which had originally owned the bullion stored at the Heathrow depot.

OPPOSITE PAGE AND TOP LEFT: Police at Kenneth Noye's £1-million home. Noyes was tried for the murder of Detective Constable Fordham but convinced the jury that it was self-defence. Eleven gold bars were found hidden beside Noye's garage (opposite middle). Despite being found not guilty of murder he was convicted of laundering the stolen gold. He was fined £700,000 and sentenced to 14 years in jail.

TOP RIGHT: A police helicopter lands near West Kingsdown after filming the area surrounding Noye's home.

LEFT: Apart from the discovery of a dozen bars following Noye's arrest, none of the bullion has been recovered from the Brinks-Mat raid.

DENNIS NILSEN:
One of Britain's Most Macabre Mass Murderers

A routine plumbing call-out to a property in Muswell Hill in early February 1983 set in motion a train of events that would unmask one of Britain's most macabre mass murderers.

Cranley Gardens

A blockage in the waste system brought a drain-clearing operative to 23 Cranley Gardens in the north London suburb. He was taken aback when he lifted the manhole outside the property and saw the cause of the obstruction: lumps of flesh. He reported his macabre findings, but by the time the police came to investigate the following day, most of the organic material had disappeared. Most, but not all. There were enough traces to confirm that these were no animal remains; it was human flesh.

OPPOSITE BOTTOM: Former policeman Dennis Andrew Nilsen is handcuffed to two officers after appearing in court accused of the murder of 20-year-old Stephen Sinclair of no fixed address. After a two-minute hearing he was remanded in custody by Highgate magistrates.

OPPOSITE ABOVE: In another of his many court appearances Nilsen was charged with four more murders at an address in Melrose Avenue, Cricklewood, where he had lived prior to his move to 23 Cranley Gardens in the north London suburb of Muswell Hill.

LEFT: In 1961 Nilsen left school and enlisted in the British Army where he served for 11 years before leaving in 1972 to briefly join the police force. From the mid 1970s, Nilsen worked as a civil servant in a local Job Centre.

BELOW: Nilsen had moved to the attic flat at 23 Cranley Gardens in 1981. It proved far more difficult to dispose of his victims' remains in this confined setting and he had to improvise and find creative methods of disposal.

BOTTOM: Nilsen was born at 47 Academy Road in Fraserburgh, Scotland, on 23 November 1945. He was the only child of his Scottish mother, Betty, and Norwegian father Olav Magnus Moksheim, who had adopted the surname Nilsen.

Grim discovery

The occupants of the ground-floor flat told DCI Peter Jay that there had been some strange comings and goings over the previous 24 hours involving the tenant who lived above them. His name was Dennis Nilsen, a 37-year-old civil servant who worked for the employment service. Jay challenged Nilsen when he arrived home, and the latter initially expressed surprise at the grim discovery. The pungent smell of decaying flesh in the top-floor flat told a different story, and the detective invited Nilsen to come clean and reveal the whereabouts of the rest of the body. Without hesitation Nilsen directed him to two plastic sacks inside the wardrobe. How many bodies were there, Jay enquired, one or two? Maybe 15 or 16 came the chillingly frank reply. Some of those had met their end in that house, most at his previous address, in Melrose Avenue, Cricklewood. The police thus found themselves in the strange situation of having cracked the case wide open almost before the inquiry had got under way. Even more bizarrely, they had solved a string of murders that weren't part of any current homicide investigation. Their task now was to piece together the evidence and try to put names to all the victims. Nilsen co-operated fully, giving chapter and verse on a killing spree stretching back over five years.

Fascination with death

Dennis Andrew Nilsen was born 23 November 1945, growing up in Fraserburgh on the east coast of Scotland. His father, Olav, was a Norwegian immigrant who married local girl Betty Whyte in 1942. It wasn't a happy union, and Nilsen had long spells living with his maternal grandparents. They were strict Presbyterians who had little time for fun and frippery, yet Nilsen adored them. His first taste of death came in 1951, with the passing of his beloved grandfather. Nilsen viewed the body, more fascinated than shocked at being in the presence of a cadaver. It was a fascination that would remain with him into adulthood.

Nilsen was a something of a loner, his social development not helped by his confused feelings regarding his sexuality. He became further withdrawn when his mother remarried and had four more children by a man who had little time for his stepson. Soldiering provided an escape route. Nilsen became an army cadet in 1961 and went on to serve in the Catering Corps, rising to the rank of corporal by the time he returned to civilian life a decade later. His time in the military furnished him with the butchery skills that he would later use to render his victims into manageable pieces.

CRANLEY GARDENS N.10

FEBRUARY 11, 1983

Plumbing problems

The grisly investigation started when new tenants of a flat in the house at Cranley Gardens had plumbing problems and called in the Dyno-Rod firm. Plumber Mike Cattran came round - and discovered human remains in a drain. He called the police.

Forensic experts established that the remains were of three young men. Soon after their investigations began detectives took away a black and white mongrel dog. Then they went to the second house, in Melrose Avenue, Cricklewood, where a search was started last night under floodlights for, it is feared, 13 more victims.

The police had been told of several specific spots in the garden where they should dig and today will cover every inch of the ground and the house. They will be using sensors which respond to changes in earth temperature where remains are buried. The police face a huge problem of identification. There are unlikely to be fingerprints and it is thought that each victim's possessions and clothing were meticulously removed and disposed of.

DENNIS NILSEN

Dark obsessions

There were brief spells as a probationary policeman with the Metropolitan force and as a security guard, after which Nilsen settled down to a life in the civil service as a Job Centre worker. His conscientiousness gained him promotion, and he also became an active trade unionist. Privately, however, his life was in turmoil. There were still dark obsessions with death, and when his first long-standing relationship broke down in 1977, Nilsen found a way to ensure that he would not face the desolation of rejection again. It was easy to pick up drifters and runaways in London, lost souls who would not be missed. To some he offered money, to others friendship, while there were those who were simply grateful for a roof over their head and a bed for the night. A private party usually followed, convivial at first with booze flowing freely. His victims were often undernourished and not in the rudest health, and when they were further incapacitated by their alcohol intake, Nilsen struck. Strangulation was the method he favoured, using his collection of neckties as ligatures. In his statement to the police Nilsen used his modus operandi to estimate how many lives he had claimed. 'I started with about 15 ties. I have only got one left.'

Ex-PC charged with murder

Scotland Yard detectives last night charged an ex-policeman with murder. He is 37-year-old Dennis Nilsen, now a Civil Servant. He will appear at Highgate court in North London this morning. Nilsen is charged with murdering Stephen Neil Sinclair, 20, of no fixed address, on or about February 1, 1983, at 23 Cranley Gardens, Muswell Hill, North London.

Resigned

Scottish-born Nilsen's home is a flat in Cranley Gardens. He is unmarried. He served as a probationary London police constable from December 1972 to December 1973 in 'Q' District, which is centred at Wembley. He joined the Metropolitan force immediately after leaving the Army, where he was in the Catering Corps.

After resigning voluntarily from the Metropolitan Police he worked as a security officer for a private firm and lately has been working with the Manpower Services Commission in the Kentish Town area of North London.

His father, Norwegian-born Olav Nilsen, served as a police sergeant in Bergen. He is now dead. Dennis Nilsen's mother, 62-year-old Elizabeth, is remarried to Mr Adam Scott, of Baird Road, Strichen, near Fraserburgh. She said: 'This has come as a great shock. I have not seen my son for about ten years. I have had phone calls and a letter now and again but very seldom. There are good connections between us, although he has not been here for ten years. I understood he was doing very well in his job.'

Stephen Sinclair grew up in the hamlet of St Martin's near the Scottish town of Perth. He was the foster child of retired traffic examiner Neil Sinclair and his wife Elizabeth, a needlework teacher. Mr Sinclair said yesterday: 'He left us several years ago and went to live in Perth. He stayed there for a while before moving south. We lost contact with him and he was never in touch again.'

> Nilsen found a way to ensure that he would not face the desolation of rejection again. It was easy to pick up drifters and runaways in London.

TOP RIGHT: Nilsen served as a probationary London police constable in Wembley from December 1972 to December 1973. He had joined the Metropolitan force immediately after leaving the Army, where he served in the Catering Corps.

TOP LEFT: When he lived at 195 Melrose Avenue, Nilsen had access to a large garden which made it far easier to dispose of human remains.

ABOVE RIGHT: A plastic make-shift tent erected in the back garden of the house at Melrose Avenue.

LEFT: When the police searched the house and gardens at Melrose Avenue, they were looking for the remains of 13 bodies. They used sensor equipment in order to try to establish where the corpses of the victims might be buried.

OPPOSITE PAGE: Army cadets were used to help with the grisly search at Melrose Gardens. The garden had provided Nilsen with a graveyard for burying parts of his numerous victims. He had also resorted to burning some body parts on bonfires, adding rubber tyres to mask the smell.

Fierce resistance

One victim, ex-Guardsman John Howlett, presented a tougher proposition. He put up fierce resistance until Nilsen finished him off by drowning him in the bath. Those who succumbed to the necktie treatment were also bathed, and Nilsen would often share a bed with the corpse before disposing of the body. In some cases the viscera were bagged up and left on waste ground, to be devoured by scavenging animals. Another method was to boil down the remains in a large cooking pot, while some body parts were burnt, tyres thrown onto the bonfire to mask the smell of putrefaction. He also took to flushing some of the soft tissue down the lavatory, the disposal technique that precipitated his downfall.

Some men had lucky escapes. Douglas Stewart passed out in an alcoholic haze, waking to find his legs lashed to the chair and Nilsen attacking him. He managed to escape and reported the incident to the police, but found that domestic tiffs between gay lovers were not a high priority for the local constabulary. Paul Nobbs woke up feeling unwell after spending a drunken night with Nilsen in November 1981. A hospital visit confirmed that someone had tried to strangle him.

Dispensing life and death

Nilsen revelled in the power he exerted over his victims. During the Old Bailey trial there would be references to his acting as a 'quasi-God', dispensing life or death as the mood took him. 23-year-old Malcolm Barlow found himself on the wrong end of that judgement call when chance put him in Dennis Nilsen's path in September 1981. He collapsed outside 195 Melrose Avenue, and was grateful when Nilsen came to his rescue and called an ambulance. Barlow returned the next day to thank the Good Samaritan and was invited in for a meal, which turned out to be his last. On 26 January 1983, Nilsen picked up 20-year-old Stephen Sinclair, a Scot who had had a troubled life, much of it spent in institutions of one kind or another. Nilsen saw his death as an act of mercy, putting an end to a lifetime of misery and suffering. 'Nothing can touch you now,' he recalled uttering as he dispatched his final victim.

'Nothing can touch you now,' he recalled uttering as he dispatched his final victim.

147

Nilsen's state of mind

Only half of Nilsen's victims had been named by the time he went to trial on 24 October 1983. He thus faced six murder charges and two counts of attempted murder. A seventh victim, Graham Allen, had just been identified through dental records but that discovery came too late for inclusion on the indictment.

Most of the trial was spent trying to ascertain Nilsen's state of mind when he committed the crimes, and thus the level of responsibility he had to bear. He pleaded not guilty on grounds of diminished responsibility, defence counsel Ivan Lawrence QC arguing that manslaughter was the appropriate charge. Douglas Stewart and Paul Nobbs described their brushes with death, as did Carl Stotter, whose story came to light too late to appear on the charge sheet. Stotter recalled the night in May 1982 when he woke to find Nilsen at his throat. He passed out, and in a semi-conscious state became aware of being carried to the bathroom. Fortunately for Stotter, Nilsen had a change of heart on that occasion.

The defence produced two expert witnesses to pronounce on Nilsen's mental health. Dr Patrick Gallwey said Nilsen had paranoid and schizoid tendencies, which the defence hoped would satisfy the conditions for a plea of diminished responsibility as laid out in the 1957 Homicide Act. Dr James MacKeith testified that Nilsen had a personality disorder, which manifested itself as a craving for attention and desire for an enduring relationship. If the men he met during the one-night-stands showed apathy towards him, he took it as a rejection, a personal affront.

Nilsen covered the same ground in his statement to the police, which was read out in court. 'In the normal course of my life I feel I have normal powers of mental rationality and morality. When under pressure of work and extreme pain of social loneliness and utter misery I am drawn, compulsively, to means of temporary escape from reality.'

'Overwhelming desire to kill'

For the prosecution, Dr Paul Bowden agreed that Nilsen exhibited abnormal behaviour in his 'overwhelming desire to kill', but didn't concur with his fellow professionals that it was indicative of a severe personality disorder. In his opinion the defendant was cognisant of, and responsible for, the actions he had taken. Much of the evidence given by the expert witnesses was too

abstruse for the lay person to follow. In his summation Mr Justice Croom-Johnson simplified matters, pointing out that mental abnormality was not a pre-requisite for evil intent. After 12 hours' deliberation the jury returned guilty verdicts with a 10-2 majority. Dennis Nilsen was given a life sentence, with a recommendation that he serve at least 25 years. He completed the minimum term in 2008, and although successive home secretaries had indicated that a whole-life tariff was applicable in this case, that ruling was being challenged in the European Court of Human Rights.

'It amazes me I have no tears for my victims'

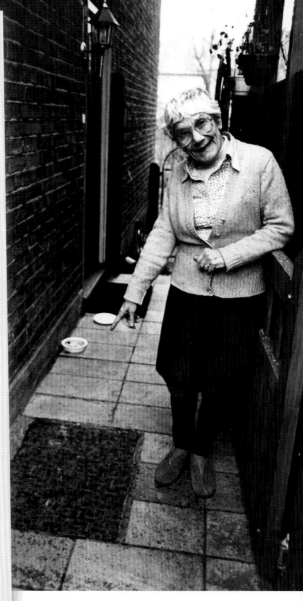

An astonishing insight into the mind of mass killer Dennis Nilsen was given to the Old Bailey yesterday. In a series of letters alleged to have been written from prison to the man who arrested him, he described his anguish, torment and the motivation which led him to kill.

At the start of the trial yesterday Mr Allan Green, prosecuting, said there was no dispute that Nilsen killed each of the men named in the murder charges. The only issue was whether he was guilty of murder or the lesser charge of manslaughter. Yesterday he sat with his hands clasped in the dock as Detective Chief Inspector Peter Jay read extracts from Nilsen's letters.

In the first, the author admits: 'There is no disputing I am a violent killer under certain circumstances. It amazes me I have no tears for these victims. I have no tears for myself, or those bereaved by my action. Am I a weak person, constantly under pressure, who just cannot cope with it, who escapes to revenge against society through the haze of a bottle of spirits? Or maybe it was because I was just born an evil man?'

Unbearable pressures

Another letter states: 'I am tragically a private person, not given to public tears. The enormity of the act has left me in permanent shock. The trouble was that, as my activities increased, so did the unbearable pressures which could only be escaped from by taking the best routes to oblivion via the bottle. I think I have sufficient principle and morality to know where the buck must come to rest. The evil was short-lived and cannot live for long inside. I have slain my own dragon as surely as the Press will slay me.'

Nilsen's letters expand on the part alcohol played in his life as a means of 'escaping from reality.' One letter says: 'This is achieved by taking increasing draughts of alcohol and plugging into stereo music which mentally removes me to a high plane of ecstasy, joy and tears. That is a totally emotional experience. I relive experiences from childhood to the present - taking out the bad bits.'

Headless

Two of the records which helped him into the state of 'true emotional experience' were Rick Wakeman's Criminal Record and the eight-minute long Oh, Superman, by Laurie Anderson. He said the latter helped him evoke an hypnotic trance. He once played it ten times in succession until the Bacardi ran out.

Nilsen also allegedly listed those that he remembered to have escaped alive from his flat. He recalled turning away a friend who had come to visit him from Exeter because: 'I would obviously not admit him when I had a headless, naked body lying on the floor of my front room.'

Cross-examined, Mr Jay said he had never come across a case when someone was 'so immediately willing to co-operate'. Nilsen had voluntarily given samples of blood, hair, and clothing, and even up until last week he had been offering to go over police photographs of missing people to see if he could identify them. Mr Jay agreed that Nilsen had always seemed matter-of-fact about the bodies.

The detective found it very difficult to associate him with the horrifying catalogue of events. The trial continues.

OPPOSITE: Sieves were used to sift through the debris in the back garden at Melrose Avenue.

LEFT: The white tent covers an area where the search had uncovered fragments of human skulls. Nilsen had willingly accompanied police to the house at 195 Melrose Avenue and pointed out where he had buried some of the bodies.

OPPOSITE BOTTOM RIGHT: Policemen outside 23 Cranley Gardens. Nilsen found it increasingly difficult to dispose of the corpses and neighbours had begun to complain about the smell. He had stored body parts under the floorboards and in various cupboards and chests.

ABOVE: Mrs Peggy MacPherson points to the blocked drain which precipitated the arrest of the mass murderer. Nilsen had used a variety of methods to dispose of the bodies, including chopping the entrails into small pieces and flushing them down the toilet.

DENNIS NILSEN

OCTOBER 27, 1983

'It could have been thousands of bodies'

Dennis Nilsen told police he might have killed thousands of victims if he had not been caught, the Old Bailey heard yesterday. The former trainee policeman was said to have told officers: 'If I was arrested at the age of 65 then there may have been thousands of bodies behind me.'

Detective Superintendent Geoffrey Chambers, who conducted nine interviews with Nilsen, said the killer always believed he would be caught. He said that in his statement Nilsen said: 'I knew it would happen again. I was resigned to the fact that it would happen again and I would get caught eventually but I would do the best I could to dispose of the evidence.'

Shopping bags

Mr Chambers revealed details of how Nilsen got rid of the bodies of his young victims. He said that when Nilsen was living at Melrose Avenue, Cricklewood, he would cut the bodies up on the kitchen floor. The organs were buried in shopping bags in the garden while the remains were put under the floorboards with deodorant tablets. Nilsen sprayed the air twice daily with an air freshener and insecticide.

Before leaving the flat in 1981 he built a giant bonfire in the back garden, on which he burnt the stored bodies. Afterwards he crushed the ashes with a garden roller in case any pieces of bone were still visible and buried them in a corner of the garden.

Mr Chambers said that when Nilsen moved to Cranley Gardens, Muswell Hill, he used a different method of disposal. After strangling and drowning his victims Nilsen dissected the bodies with a kitchen knife and stored some of the flesh in the wardrobe of his bedroom.

The jury of eight men and four women were shown saucepans that Nilsen allegedly used to boil parts of the bodies before flushing them down the lavatory. Other pieces of flesh he would cut into strips – some the size of a fist – and also flushed away, said Mr Chambers.

Nilsen's last boast: There may be more

Britain's most macabre mass murderer, Dennis Nilsen, was given a life sentence of at least 25 years yesterday. And it was revealed that the man who admitted claiming 15 victims is to be re-interviewed by Scotland Yard after boasting: 'I may have killed a lot more.'

The statement was made by Nilsen as he sat in his cell below the famous No. 1 Court at the Old Bailey while waiting for the jury to return their verdicts on his crimes. He had recalled the 15 killings because the victims' bodies had been at his home, he said. But there could easily have been 'many more' because sometimes he had gone to other men's rooms for drinking sessions and it was possible that he had killed on those occasions. Detectives will now reopen the dossiers on unsolved murders of young men going back ten years.

Anxious to help

Last night his solicitor, Mr Ralph Haeems, said: 'He is anxious to help. He is willing for police to show him pictures of any young men in unsolved murder or suspicious death cases that might fit the pattern - and if he remembers being with them, he will say so.'

There was complete silence in the court yesterday when the jury of eight men and four women gave their verdicts after 12 hours 36 minutes of discussion. As the foreman announced that they had found him guilty by a majority of 10-2 on six charges of murder, Nilsen, 37, who was once a trainee policeman, bowed his head and stared at the wooden floor of the dock. He was also convicted by a majority of 10-2 on one charge of attempted murder. On the other, the jury's guilty verdict was unanimous.

Nilsen had described himself as 'the murderer of the century.' But in court he had maintained that his crimes were not murder, but manslaughter by reason of diminished responsibility.

Crowds

Nilsen, flanked in the dock by four burly prison officers, stood with his hands clasped tightly behind his back as Mr Justice Croom-Johnson told him: 'It may well be that even if the verdicts had been manslaughter, it would have been impossible for me to pass any other sentence than life imprisonment.'

With one final glance round the court, and still carrying the notes he had made throughout the ten-day trial, Nilsen - wearing the same cream shirt, blue tie, grey herringbone jacket and black trousers he wore each day - was led down to the cells.

Exhibits

A grisly array of the exhibits in the case went on display immediately after the end of the case. Photographers were shown the copper pot in which Nilsen boiled the heads of some of his victims. Police also displayed two knives that Nilsen had used to cut up the bodies. He had learned butchery techniques in the Army Catering Corps. With the knives was a sharpener and a wooden board on which Nilsen placed the remains before beginning the dissections. The display was in a disused Old Bailey court annexe opposite the Central

Criminal Court mainbuilding

For Chief Supt. Geoffrey Chambers and Det. Chief Insp. Peter Jay it was the final duty after weeks of painstaking work preparing the case against Nilsen — work which had led to their being congratulated by the judge.

OPPOSITE TOP RIGHT: Estate Agent Leon Roberts stands in the attic flat at 23 Cranley Gardens as it goes on sale in November 1983. The house had become known as the 'House of Horror'.

OPPOSITE TOP LEFT: The former home of the serial killer was open for viewing. After Nilsen's conviction in 1983, his former homes were sold cheaply to investors who renovated them and put them back on the market.

OPPOSITE BOTTOM LEFT: Dennis Nilsen leaves Highgate Magistrates' Court. He had been charged with six counts of murder and two charges of attempted murder.

RIGHT: The trial began at the Old Bailey on October 24, 1983. The charges were read and Nilsen pleaded 'Not Guilty' to each one. The jury was shown key exhibits found in the flat of the accused after his arrest. Among the prosecution witnesses were several of Nilsen's potential victims – those who had managed to escape from his clutches.

ABOVE RIGHT: Nilsen's solicitor, Ralph Haeems, decided to go for a defence of 'diminished responsibility', citing a personality disorder in Nilsen, thus asking for a charge of manslaughter.

RIGHT: Dennis Nilsen returns to court in June 1984 with a visible scar on his left cheek. The court heard how he had been attacked with a razor by a fellow prisoner.

THE WESTS: The House of Horror

In August 1992 police turned up at the Gloucester home of Frederick and Rose West to investigate an allegation of child abuse. As a result of those enquiries, five children were removed from 25 Cromwell Street and taken into care, and West found himself facing a rape charge. He was saved by the fact that the abused daughter couldn't go through the further ordeal of having to relive the horrific events in court and give evidence against her father.

It seemed that West would not have to answer for his incestuous predilections, but a chance remark to a social worker changed all that, and the picture that emerged was much darker than the authorities imagined. It was noted that another daughter, Heather, was a conspicuous absentee from recent family photographs and home movies. The West children revealed the 'family joke', that their missing sister was buried under the patio at 25 Cromwell Street. It took police eighteen months to gather enough evidence to obtain a search warrant, and when they began digging, in February 1994, the 'House of Horrors' gave up its gruesome secrets.

TOP: The 'house of horror' – 25 Cromwell Street, Gloucester. Police attention was drawn to the house after allegations of child abuse.

ABOVE: Missing poster for Catherine (Rena) Costello, Fred West's first wife. She and her daughter Charmaine were killed by Fred and Rosemary in 1971. Over 20 years later her relatives were still searching for her.

Perversion was the norm

Frederick West was born 29 September 1941 in the Herefordshire village of Much Marcle. His family had been agricultural labourers for generations, and Fred spent his childhood summers in the fields, helping with the harvest. He was driving a tractor by the age of nine, and the heavy farming workload took its toll on his education, for he was virtually illiterate when he left school at fourteen.

Physical and sexual abuse was rife in the West household. Fred's mother Daisy took his virginity, while the patriarch, Walter, regularly abused his daughters; perversion was the norm in their tied cottage. Fred took his cue from his easygoing father, who encouraged him to seize whatever opportunities came his way. Fred would interpret carpe diem as a green light for sating his lust, particularly after sustaining a serious head injury in a motorcycle accident at the age of sixteen. The family reported that Fred underwent a personality change, becoming an habitual liar and petty thief. His going off the rails reached a wider public two years later, when he was charged with impregnating his 13-year-old sister. The case was dropped when the girl refused to testify. Perhaps this early brush with the law, and the fact that he escaped censure, encouraged him to think he could take his sexual pleasure as he pleased with impunity.

ABOVE AND LEFT: Police search the 'house of horror'. Among the nine bodies that were exhumed was that of Fred and Rosemary's daughter, Heather, who vanished when she was 16. It was a 'family joke' that if the other children did not behave, they would end up under the patio like Heather.

MARCH 2, 1994

Specialist search teams

Heather West disappeared in 1987. Detectives are understood to have gone to her family house in Cromwell Street last week following tip-offs from a number of teenagers. Specialist search teams have been working in the 40ft by 15ft garden since Friday. A lane behind the houses has been closed to the public. Police used a small mechanical excavator to help remove the concrete paving stones forming a patio which covered a large part of the ill-kept garden. The excavator was also used to dig trenches in a grid, removing the top soil. To begin with, officers dug through the rain-sodden search with spades and used large sieves to search for clues. But their work halted temporarily with the discovery of the remains.

Home Office pathologist Bernard Knight, from Cardiff University, then began directing what Det Supt Bennett described as an 'archaeological-type' dig, painstakingly cataloguing and mapping the bones before removing them for forensic examination and identification.

The search of the garden is expected to last for several more days.

Diet of voyeurism

West was working as a lorry driver in 1962 when he picked up and befriended Scottish runaway Rena Costello. She was pregnant and trying to escape the clutches of the Asian pimp who was the baby's father. Fred and Rena married after a whirlwind romance and moved to Glasgow, where Charmaine was born the following March. Rena worked as a stripper and a prostitute, which merely excited a husband who had been raised on a diet of voyeurism. While Rena was selling sexual services, Fred got a job driving an ice-cream van, which afforded him numerous opportunities for extra-marital encounters. One such dalliance, with a girl called Ann McFall, became something more serious. Fred would call her the love of his life, yet she would be his first victim.

Rena gave birth to Fred's child, Anne Marie on 6 July 1964. The new arrival couldn't paper over the cracks of a volatile relationship, and a year later Fred returned to Much Marcle, taking both children with him. Ann McFall tracked him down there, becoming his childminder and mistress. She, too, became pregnant, but shortly before she was due to give birth, Ann was murdered and dismembered, her body buried in Fingerpost Field, a remote spot around fifteen miles from Gloucester. In a police interview some twenty-seven years later, West would cast the blame for Ann's death on Rena. The two women knew each other, and Rena did pay sporadic visits to Gloucester for short-term reconciliations, but this was not a crime committed by an enraged, jealous wife who had found herself supplanted in her husband's affections. Ann McFall undoubtedly perished at Fred's hands – hands that had become even more skilled in butchery through his current employment in an abattoir. Some believe Ann sealed her fate when she demanded that Fred marry her, others that she was killed when a violent sex game went too far. What is certain is that he now had blood on his hands, and once again he had got away with committing a crime.

Second Victim

West's second victim was probably Mary Bastholm, a 15-year-old waitress who disappeared in January 1968 while waiting at a bus stop. West patronised the café where Mary worked, and made off-the-record hints suggesting she numbered among his early victims. Her body has never been found. When West was finally brought to book, the police concentrated on building a case around the murders to which he had confessed. The case of Mary Bastholm thus remains unresolved, despite the strong indications pointing straight towards Fred West.

'Moved to London'

With Ann McFall dead and Rena back in Scotland, Fred needed practical help in looking after Charmaine and Anne Marie, who were being shunted in and out of care on a regular basis. He found it in the shape of 15-year-old Rose Letts, yet another casual pick-up while he was out on the road. She may have been twelve years his junior, but Rose was attracted to older men and the two hit it off immediately. She, too, had been brought up in a violent, abusive family; she, too, had been a slow learner at school; and she, too, had a strong sexual appetite. She moved into Fred's caravan home and was soon prostituting herself for him. Rose also fell pregnant, giving birth to Heather on 17 October 1970. A few weeks later, Fred was given a ten-month jail sentence for theft, leaving his 17-year-old lover to look after their new baby and the two older children. Rose handed out violent beatings, mirroring the parenting regime of her own tyrannical father. Charmaine, the more wilful of the two, came in for particularly severe treatment until sometime in June 1971, when she disappeared. According to her school record, she had 'moved to London', and Rose claimed that Rena took the child away. Charmaine never left Gloucester; her remains would be unearthed at the Midland Street flat where they were then living in May 1994. When the couple were arrested, there would be some difficulty in apportioning culpability. In that respect the events of 1971 were crucial, for the fact that Fred was incarcerated when Charmaine was killed was used as damning, incontrovertible evidence in the case against Rose.

MARCH 2, 1994

The garden of death

Police were last night trying to identify two more bodies found buried behind a Gloucester house. They were under the same patio as the remains of 16-year-old Heather West, discovered at the weekend. Her father, builder Fred West, 52, has been charged with her murder.

The two bodies found yesterday were both of adults or teenagers and had been buried some 5ft deep. The remains had been there so long it was impossible for experts to give an immediate estimate of their age or sex. Police are checking back through missing persons files. Unsolved cases in the area include that of 15-year-old Mary Bastholm, last seen leaving home to visit her boyfriend, and student Lucy Partington, 21.

As the painstaking examination of the garden of death went on yesterday, detectives were also said to have discovered a 'dungeon room' inside the semi-detached Victorian house. A neighbour, whose daughter used to play with the West family, said: 'She told me they had a cellar with a trap door covered by a carpet.'

Wife released on bail

Police are also poised to start digging up the grounds of West's former home in Bishops Cleeve, four miles from Cheltenham. Detectives are trying to trace all twice-married Mr West's children - neighbours have told them he had at least eight. His wife Rosemary, 40, was interviewed by police but released on bail on Sunday, pending further inquiries. She is understood to be staying with relatives.

> Charmaine, the more wilful of the two, came in for particularly severe treatment until sometime in June 1971, when she disappeared.

Commission of murder

The bond between Fred and Rose was now even stronger, for they were united by the commission of murder as well as by their sexual proclivities. And when Rena came looking for her children later that summer, she couldn't be allowed to voice her suspicions. She was murdered – West said he smashed her head against a gate – and buried in the field adjacent to the one that housed the remains of Ann McFall.

Fred and Rose married in January 1972, and in September that year took up residence at 25 Cromwell Street. The family had just been swelled by the arrival of Mae, and again the Wests were in the market for a live-in nanny.

Caroline Owens was hired, but voted with her feet as soon as her employers tried to recruit her into a sex ring. Shortly afterwards, Fred and Rose happened upon Caroline while she was hitchhiking, and although she had been made to feel uncomfortable at the earlier lewd proposal, she also felt a pang of guilt for leaving them in the lurch. She accepted a ride, and was subjected to a 12-hour ordeal which included a sexual assault by both adults. Caroline was one of the lucky survivors, and although she made a statement to the police, she couldn't face court proceedings. The Wests escaped with a £100 fine.

> *Although one victim made a statement to the police, she couldn't face court proceedings. The Wests escaped with a £100 fine.*

OPPOSITE BELOW: Crowds gather outside the Wests' house on Cromwell Street, Gloucester. Among the victims found in the house was Shirley Robinson, who was eight months pregnant with Fred's child when he killed her in 1978.

TOP: Cement is poured into the foundations at the West's house on Cromwell Street. During their search police found a 50ft well below the property that West had covered over when he built an extension on the house.

ABOVE: The home where Fred West was born in Much Marcle, Herefordshire. West claimed that incest was accepted as part of the household and that his father introduced him to bestiality.

Victims silenced

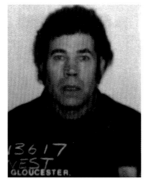

25 Cromwell Street became a revolving door for all manner of waifs and strays, some answering advertisements placed by the Wests. With drink, drugs and sex on tap, the house was a magnet for young runaways, the very people Fred and Rose wanted to attract. Jordan's Brook, a nearby home for adolescent girls with troubled backgrounds also offered rich pickings for their evil intent. The youngsters they drew into their web were invariably looking for a sense of belonging and stability, and Cromwell Street offered just that, initially, at least.

After the narrow escape they had had with Caroline Owens, Fred and Rose were more determined than ever to silence their victims. Between 1973 and 1979 at least nine women met their end at Cromwell Street. Kneecaps and digits were routinely removed; decapitation was also common practice. One of the victims, Shirley Robinson, became pregnant by Fred and bragged that she might become the new Mrs West. She was eight months pregnant when she disappeared in May 1978.

APRIL 11, 1994

Grave is found in hunt for the first Mrs West

House of Horror detectives yesterday found what they believe are the remains of Frederick West's first wife buried in a field. They have spent two weeks searching the isolated Letterbox field for Catherine Costello, whose family have not seen or heard from her since 1969. The discovery, thought to be a small number of bones, was made at the field at Kempley on the Gloucestershire border with Herefordshire after West was taken there and pointed out a spot.

A pathologist will examine the remains today before digging begins again in the hope of making a formal identification. A Gloucester police spokesman said: 'We have got a positive line of inquiry of who we think the remains are, but it is too early to state at this stage.' Catherine's sister Georgina McCann trembled with shock at the door of her West Belfast home yesterday as she said: 'I was expecting this.'

The field at Kempley is a mile from West's childhood home at Much Marcle. Police have excavated more than 150 tons of earth while digging a 6ft wide, 4ft deep trench which by yesterday was more than 150ft long. Landowner Reg Watkins, 38, said: 'Fred West arrived here with a heavy police presence in the back of a riot van. He pointed out the spot to police and they marked it off.' Police used a £50,000 ground-penetrating radar device dubbed the Lawnmower to help in the search. Mr Watkins said: 'They passed a scanner over the place and a policeman told me they thought it had shown up one, maybe two bodies. They seemed to think they could be three feet down or so.'

Charged

Catherine married West in 1962 and they had two children - Anna, who still lives in Gloucester, and Charmaine, who disappeared in 1977. Police think her body may be hidden at 25 Midland Street, Gloucester, which they have yet to search. Builder West, 52, has been charged with the murders of nine women and girls whose bodies were found at his home at 25 Cromwell Street, Gloucester.

Years of abuse

The children also continued to suffer. Anne Marie testified that she was raped by her father at the age of eight, Rose holding her down while Fred penetrated her. She was later forced into prostitution, finally putting an end to the abuse when she left home in 1980, aged fifteen. Her gain was her half-sister Heather's loss. Heather was ten at the time, and the fact that Fred and Rose were her natural parents didn't spare her. She would endure seven years of abuse before she disappeared, probably after protesting too loudly. The violation created a special bond between the children. They knew what was happening was wrong, despite being told that incestuous relationships were normal, if not discussed openly. But they knew no lifestyle other than ill treatment, and also feared that if their parents were jailed for their actions, the family might be broken up.

The police were regular visitors to Cromwell Street in the 1970s, at the Wests' behest. Fred and Rose deflected attention from their own nefarious deeds by informing on their lodgers' drug taking, a ploy that helped them evade justice for twenty years. They were also extremely lucky. The parents of one of their victims, 19-year-old Linda Gough, turned up at the house in search of their missing daughter in 1973. Rose managed to fob them off with a tale that Linda had moved on, although she was wearing some of the dead girl's clothes at the time.

TOP LEFT: Fred West's police mug shot. His daughter Anne Marie testified that she was raped by her father at the age of eight while Rose held her down.

TOP RIGHT: Police use radar equipment in the hunt for bodies in Much Marcle. Rena Costello's and Anna McFall's bodies were found in fields near where West grew up.

ABOVE: The officer leading the enquiry into the Wests and DCI Moore in the yard of the 'house of horrors'.

OPPOSITE BELOW: The coach carrying the jury in the trial of Rosemary West arrives at 25 Cromwell Street.

Police uncover bodies

Rose's involvement was a key factor both in terms of recruiting victims and avoiding detection. Criminologists usually associate sexual sadism with males; women are seen as nurturers and carers, highly unlikely to participate in the violent abuse of any children, let alone their own. Caroline Owens said that she was wary about accepting a lift with Fred West until she saw there was an adult female in the passenger seat. It takes no great leap of the imagination to suppose how the less fortunate young women were also put at their ease by Rose's presence.

By 1992, when police arrived at 25 Cromwell Street to investigate the rape allegation, Fred and Rose West had raised eleven children into what they termed 'our family of love'. Three of them had been fathered by Rose's clients, two were already dead. Once the police got the warrant that enabled them to search the house on 24 February 1994, events moved quickly. They soon found that the 'family joke' was all too real as Heather West's dismembered body was found. When a third femur was dug up, they realised they were dealing with more than a domestic murder case. On 4 March West made a statement admitting to 'a further (approx) nine killings, expressly, Charmaine, Rena, Linda Gough and others to be identified'. The remains of nine women were recovered from the 'House of Horrors' over a period of eleven days. Forensic scientists identified the victims by superimposing photographs onto the skulls. West took officers to the fields where Rena Costello and Ann McFall were buried, and while the excavation work was still ongoing there, Charmaine's body was found at 25 Midland Road.

> They knew no lifestyle other than ill treatment, and also feared that if their parents were jailed for their actions, the family might be broken up.

JUNE 9, 1994

The dig of death

In the past eight weeks, officers have removed nearly 3,000 tons of earth. Using a JCB, a dumper truck, a conveyor belt system and a pump, they have carved out a pit big enough to house an Olympic swimming pool. The site, excavated by a team of 12 is almost 100ft long, more than 60ft wide and up to 8ft deep. Deeper holes have been sunk whenever a ground-penetrating radar indicates underground disturbances or voids. Examinations of the latest remains are expected to take weeks. Further searching will continue but police privately believe the final remains have now been discovered.

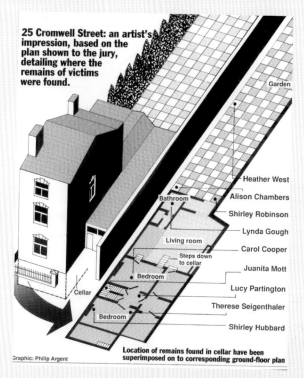

25 Cromwell Street: an artist's impression, based on the plan shown to the jury, detailing where the remains of victims were found.

Garden

Heather West
Alison Chambers
Shirley Robinson
Lynda Gough
Carol Cooper
Juanita Mott
Lucy Partington
Therese Seigenthaler
Shirley Hubbard

Bathroom
Living room
Steps down to cellar
Bedroom
Cellar
Bedroom

Graphic: Philip Argent

Location of remains found in cellar have been superimposed on to corresponding ground-floor plan

The hunt for the body of Anna - who came from Coatbridge in Lanarkshire, and worked briefly as a nanny for alleged mass killers Fred and Rosemary West in the early seventies - was launched in a corner of the field on April 13, when the infant corn crop was barely visible. By the time the search ended on Tuesday evening, the lush green plants were waving more than 2ft high in the sunshine. The dig had begun after the discovery, in adjacent Letter-box Field, of the body of Catherine West, Fred West's first wife.

> When a third femur was dug up, they realised they were dealing with more than a domestic case.

TAYLORS

Complicity

Fred was much more forthcoming than Rose during police interviews, though there were many contradictory statements. For example, before Heather's body was found, he retracted his confession and said she was alive and well, working for a Middle East-based drugs syndicate. He spoke of being haunted by spirits, and offered a warped view of the crimes when he commented: 'Nobody went through hell. Enjoyment turned to disaster, that's what happened...most of it anyway'.

Rose was initially given bail and placed in a safe house, though police were convinced of her complicity from the outset. She was arrested on 23 April 1994, and from that moment, a wedge was driven between the confederates. Rose denied all knowledge of the crimes, laying all the blame at her husband's door. A week later, Fred again retracted his confessions, obliquely indicating that they had been issued as a cover-up: 'From the very first day of this enquiry my main concern has been to protect other person or persons.' When the two came face to face at Gloucester Magistrates' Court on 13 December 1994, the first time they had seen each other in six months, Fred made a gesture of affection only to receive an icy rebuff. He now turned on Rose, telling police that earlier statements had been made to protect his wife.

NOVEMBER 23, 1995

Ten life sentences

Rose West last night began ten life sentences for the 'House of Horrors' killings. Mr Justice Mantell told her: 'If attention is paid to what I say you will never be released. 'West's face stayed as expressionless as it had been through all the evidence of the unimaginable cruelty she inflicted on her daughter Heather, stepdaughter Charmaine and eight other girls and women.

But her lawyers, who said they would appeal, admitted later that she had wept uncontrollably after the first three guilty verdicts were brought in on Tuesday. As the trial ended, a furious row broke over how the Wests were able to go on sexually abusing their own children and torturing and killing other victims for 25 years.

Strands of suspicion

There had been repeated warning signs about Rose West's sexual deviance and violence. Dozens of officials came into contact with the family but missed the clues that should have saved lives. The couple were fined for a violent sex attack on teenager Caroline Owens but no-one closely monitored them. The strands of suspicion were not pulled together even when the West children were treated at hospital on more than 30 occasions for unusual injuries. One was treated for a sexual disease and others suffered from squints and speech impediments - all conditions often associated with child abuse.

Education officials feared that Anna-Marie West was being abused at home but nothing was proved. There were no follow-up checks when her sister Charmaine, then eight, was recorded to have changed schools in 1971. In fact, she had been murdered. Social workers knew girls in their care were visiting 25, Cromwell Street but failed to discover they were being sexually abused there.

Yesterday the jury of four women and seven men ended their 13 hours of deliberations shortly before 1pm, bringing in unanimous verdicts of guilty on the seven charges outstanding overnight.

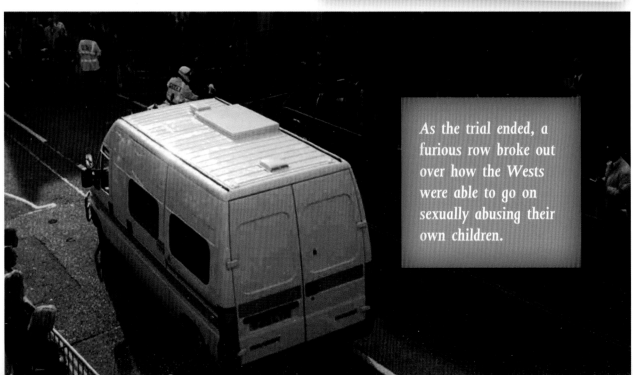

As the trial ended, a furious row broke out over how the Wests were able to go on sexually abusing their own children.

Life imprisonment

Fred West didn't live to answer in court to the twelve murder charges he faced. He took his own life at Winson Green Prison on 1 January 1995, using knotted bed linen as a noose. The trial of Rose West opened at Winchester Crown Court on 3 October that year. She had played no part in the deaths of Ann McFall or Rena Costello, which left her facing ten counts of murder. She pleaded innocent to all charges. Caroline Owens was a key witness, taking the stand twenty-three years after she had been the victim of the Wests' brutal assault. Her evidence, and that of other survivors, including Anne Marie West, was used to establish 'similar fact'. This held that if Rose was the chief aggressor in acts of sexual sadism against them, it was reasonable to suggest that the same situation pertained with the victims who had not survived.

Rose West opted to testify, against the advice of defence counsel. She stated that Fred dominated her, which rang very hollow when set against graphic accounts of her being the instigator of numerous acts of violence and abuse. She tried to present an image of soft-spoken respectability, but that was shot down when tapes of her screaming foul-mouthed vitriol at the police were played in court. After the six-week-long trial, the jury concurred with the prosecution statement, that the ten victims' 'last moments on earth were as objects of the sexual depravity of this woman and her husband'. On 22 November 1995 Rosemary West was convicted on all ten counts of murder and sentenced to life imprisonment.

'House of Horrors'

A year later, the bulldozers moved into Cromwell Street. The 'House of Horrors' was demolished and turned into a pedestrian walkway. The rubble was removed, crushed and incinerated to forestall the possibility of attracting souvenir hunters with a taste for the macabre. That den of iniquity was no more and had yielded all its secrets, but were there others? In the period leading up to Heather West's murder there are several years with no deaths attributed to Fred and Rose. Given their voracious appetite for sexual sadism, their rapacious capacity for torture, it seems unlikely that they allowed years to pass without indulging their depraved tendencies. Thus, the actual number of victims who fell prey to the Wests may never be known.

JANUARY 2, 1995

House of Horrors man kills himself

Fred West hanged himself yesterday with two strips of his prison bed sheets. The man accused of the Gloucester 'House of Horrors' killings was found at 12.55pm in his cell at Winson Green jail, Birmingham. There was loud and sustained cheering among his 800 fellow-inmates as the news swept through the jail.

Final hours

The first detailed account of West's final hours was given exclusively to the Daily Mail. Prisoner WN 3617 spent New Year's Eve playing pool and watching television. New Year's Day began at 6.30am with breakfast of cereal followed by eggs, and he was then allowed into the exercise area. At noon he returned to his cell with his lunch of chicken soup and pork chops and was locked in. During the next hour, West put into action the plan to kill himself on landing D3 of the remand wing, according to prison sources.

At around 1pm, the door was due to be opened so he could wash his crockery and begin his period of 'association' with one other Category A prisoner - a game of pool had been suggested. Before this could happen, however, West jammed the door shut to make sure he would not be found. Next, according to one insider, he tore two strips of green sheet from his bedding and plaited them together for strength. This rope was knotted and threaded through a tiny air vent above the doorway as he stood on a chair. Kicking the chair away, West hanged himself, the weight of his body against the door acting as a barrier to the warders who forced their way in.

ABOVE: Crowds outside the 'house of horror'. Both Wests were convicted of murder and it was recommended they never be released.

OPPOSITE ABOVE: A police photograph of Rose West. A jury of four women and seven men found her guilty after 13 hours of deliberations.

OPPOSITE BELOW: The jury arrives at 25 Cromwell Street. Rose West was tried at Winchester Crown Court and, unlike her husband, did not confess. She was found guilty on 10 counts of murder.

ACKNOWLEDGEMENTS

The photographs in this book are from the archives of the *Daily Mail*.
Particular thanks to Steve Torrington, Alan Pinnock and all the staff.

Thanks also to Alice Hill for her detailed editorial work, Marie Clayton for additional text, Gordon Mills, John Dunne, Mark Brown, Lisa Wright, Alison Gauntlett, Richard Betts, Wendy Toole, Jane Benn, Frances Hill and Melanie Cox.